Making the Grade

How to Score High on ALL Scholastic Tests

PATRICK GRASSICK

ARCO PUBLISHING, INC.
New York

Published by Arco Publishing, Inc.
215 Park Avenue South, New York, N.Y. 10003

Copyright © 1983 by Patrick Grassick

Published simultaneously with Macmillan of Canada,
A Division of Gage Publishing Ltd., Toronto, Canada.
All rights reserved. No part of this book may
be reproduced, by any means, without permission
in writing from the publisher, except by a
reviewer who wishes to quote brief excerpts in
connection with a review in a magazine or
newspaper.

Library of Congress Cataloging in Publication Data

Grassick, Patrick.
    Making the grade.

    Bibliography: p.
    1. Examinations—Study guides.   I. Title.
LB3051.G66696   1983   371.2'64   83-9966
ISBN 0-668-05944-3 (Reference Text)
ISBN 0-668-05818-8 (Paper Edition)

Printed in the United States of America

Table of Contents

Acknowledgements

Several people deserve special mention for their assistance and encouragement. Of my colleagues at University Counselling Services, Bob Hall has been especially supportive. The book was much improved by his valuable comments and suggestions; it is worse for my not having followed his advice more rigorously. Pat Kennedy and Doug Gibson at Macmillan of Canada have been constant in their encouragement. As my editor, Pat has managed to make me appear much more intelligent, lucid, and articulate than is really the case. She and her colleague Eleanor Sinclair have saved me from many errors. Linda Bernbach, my editor at Arco, was extremely helpful in translating the book into an American idiom. Roseanne MacGregor, Paulette Pakosz, Arelene Thomas, and Marnee Manson have shared the onerous task of transcribing my unintelligible scrawls into readable typescript. Their cheerful perseverance in the face of the difficulties I presented deserves more praise than these few inadequate words. Finally, the steadfast support of my wife, Sandi, has to be acknowledged. Her faith in the project and in my capabilities illuminated many a dark hour.

Introduction

Whether we like it or not, exams are a fact of life for most students in high schools, colleges, and universities in North America. Students' performance on exams determines, in large measure, the range of educational opportunities open to them, the type of employment they will find, and, very often, the rate of their career advancement. This being the case, it is truly remarkable how little attention has been given to teaching students how to prepare for and take tests. Rarely does anyone bother to teach these vital skills to students; instead, the assumption is made that students will "just know" how to take exams, just as they are presumed to know how to do a vast number of basic things which, in fact, they do not know how to do.

To be fair, there are some books on the market which can provide limited assistance to students in preparing for tests, but my experience has been that they all fall seriously short of what is required by students who are seriously troubled by problems with tests. Typical of the "college-survival" manuals are *How to Study* (Morgan & Deese, 1969), *Systems for Study* (Raygor & Wark, 1970), *A Guide to College Survival* (Brown & Holtzman, 1972), and *The Whole Earth Textbook* (Pivar, 1978). These four books try to cover everything that a college student needs to know, but, as is typical of books which try to be encyclopedias of student conduct, they devote only a few pages to the critical area of tests. *How to Take Tests* (Millman & Pauk, 1969) has an encouraging title and contains much useful information about standardized achievement and aptitude tests. But, again, the book is seriously deficient, spending only a few pages in a very broad discussion of how to prepare for other kinds of tests. Then there are a whole host of manuals designed for students who have to take one of the standardized admission tests (e.g., the Scholastic Aptitude Test, the Law School Admission Test, the Test of English as a Foreign Language, and so on), but these cover specific rather than general test-taking skills.

In addition, studies suggest that up to fifteen percent of college students are seriously troubled by exam-related anxiety and tension, and that these students turn in test results which are not valid measurements of their actual understanding or competence. How many students never reach college because of incapacitating anxiety is not known, but this number, too, must be substantial.

What is needed, and what this manual attempts to be, is a guidebook which shows students in a comprehensive and detailed way how to organize an effective program of study and review, which shows them how to deal with the commonest examination formats, and which actually helps them to reduce and better manage the effects of worry and anxiety.

There is no magic in this book, no mystical "active ingredient" which can substitute for the work which any student must complete if he or she hopes to do well. None the less, most students will find that the systems and procedures outlined here are helpful in making the most of their efforts.

In the organization of the manual, I have tried to provide students with *strategies*, that is, general rules which apply to many situations, and *tactics* for coping with more specific issues in preparing for and taking exams. Tactics are numbered to indicate the strategy to which they are related. At the end of each chapter, the strategies and tactics are listed, with a master list included in the Summary to facilitate easy reference to the text. To help students learn to apply the procedures, I have tried to include many "how-to" illustrations throughout the text.

The whole point of this manual is to show students how to work smarter, not harder; to show them how they can intelligently prepare for and take tests with minimal personal discomfort and maximum effectiveness.

The procedures outlined in this manual are based on the Exam Skills Workshop, a program I developed at the University of Calgary, beginning in 1975. Over four hundred students have now participated in this workshop, with the vast majority (in the order of 95 percent to 97 percent) indicating that the program has been helpful in assisting them to cope with exam-related problems. In developing the program, I have tried very hard to include ideas and elements that have withstood rigorous experimental and clinical evaluation. Many of the ideas have been tested by participants in the Exam Skills Workshops and by individual students with whom I've worked at University Counselling Services. Other parts of the program were derived from work done at other centers. I believe that the program satisfactorily addresses the most common problems students have with exams and tests, and does so in a way that is economical, straightforward, and clear.

This book is a portable Exam Skills Workshop, intended for students who, for whatever reason, are not able to find appropriate help in other forms. I sincerely hope that it is as useful for students as the real-life program.

A special introduction for adult learners

For many of you the return to school is a profoundly frightening time. Everything that you once knew about studying has long since disappeared into the deep recesses of your subconscious mind, nestled irretrievably beneath memory traces recording how to conjugate the subjunctive and the rules for factoring polynomials.

Not only do you have fears about your study skills, you are also concerned about being thrown into direct competition with people many years younger than you. But the significant difference between you and the younger students, of course, is not age or number of wrinkles. It's that you have many roles and responsibilities to carry—as a spouse or partner, as an employee, as a citizen, and possibly as a parent and/or home-owner—while the kids have it much simpler. It is easy to feel that you're split twelve ways from Sunday—because you are! And this is especially true of adult learners who are engaged in part-time studies, evening studies, or correspondence classes.

What follows in this introduction is some advice and principles culled from the collective experience of people in universities and professional associations who have had the opportunity to work with many adult learners. I hope that it enables you to avoid the many trials and troubles that this group of students can experience with school.

You Must Get Organized

The additional complexities that you face as a student mean that you simply cannot afford the luxury of trying to fit schoolwork into your week "when you can get around to it".

This is particularly true for students in correspondence courses who don't have the built-in routine of a regular class to attend. When there is always something else that urgently requires your attention, you have to be quite deliberate about making sure that you develop and stick to a regular study routine.

How much time you should devote to your courses is a highly individual matter that depends on your own skills, your familiarity with the material, and the difficulty of the course. However, the collective experience of people who work with adult students suggests that you can expect to spend an average of ten to twelve hours a week studying and doing assignments for each course that you are taking.

Okay? Now if you add that to the forty-plus hours you spend on your job and the time that is necessary to maintain your household, you get a picture of what you are up against.

Adult learners very often are not prepared for the intensity and the amount of work required by their courses. Some of the time this is because they simply don't have any familiarity with courses and programs at an advanced level. Or they are basing their judgment on memories (fallible at best) of the idle days of their youth in high school or college, when an eternity yawned between the start of school in September and final exams in June.

It is going to be harder and longer than you think—so it is really a good idea to ease into your program by taking only one or two courses, until you really have a handle on managing school, work, and your family life. Maybe later you will be able to take on more. But do try to avoid biting off more than you can chew.

Get a Place Where You Can Study

The best thing is to be able to go into a room in your home where people will leave you alone and there is nothing around that takes your attention away from your school work. But other arrangements are possible and workable. You can create a kind of portable study—a briefcase or box that has your study in it. When it's time to study, you open up your office on the kitchen or dining-room table and go to it. To make this work, you have to build mental walls, rather than actual physical barriers, that will shut out distractions.

Train the Other People in Your Life To Leave You Alone When You're Working

Obviously this is much easier if you can go into your study and close the door. One person involved in a correspondence program told me that she has issued explicit instructions to her kids not to interrupt unless the house is on fire or unless someone in the family is suffering from a loss of blood. This means no telephone calls, no questions about what to have for dinner tomorrow night, no social chit-chat. Your family has to know that if they take your time away from your studies, it is just going to take you much longer to get your work done. Practically everything can wait...once you make sure that your family and social needs are met.

The critical word here is *balance*. You have to have a balance between your own need to study, your needs for free time and recreation, and the needs of the other people in your household.

When Should You Study?

If you're working full-time, your study time has to come out of evenings and weekends. Obviously. If you have a mate and other family, you pretty well have to wait until after the supper hour. Single parents with small children will find that it is almost impossible to work on school until after the infants are in bed. Until then you want to aim for two things: you want to get the housework done, and you want to have a little bit of *quality* time with your family. This means taking time where the focus is on enjoying each other's company. When your children are older and they have homework as well, you can start some of your work while they are still up, but you will still need time completely by yourself.

How you spread your study out during the week is a highly individual matter, but most people find that it works best if they keep one evening during the week and one whole day on the weekend completely free of schoolwork. Correspondence students may find it helpful to build some continuity by working on two successive evenings. If you are taking classes in the evening, you maintain continuity by studying the day before and the day after your classes.

But whatever you do, avoid all-nighters and other interminably long sessions. The last thing you want to do is to burn yourself out by working too long and too hard at any one time. The parable to keep in mind is "The Hare and the Tortoise"—you simply must do a little bit at a time and maintain a steady, manageable pace.

You can also benefit by learning to use short intervals during the workday on particular study assignments. You can do light reading at lunch or if your work has naturally slack periods. You can carry flash cards with you (see Chapter 4) and work at them when you can't think of anything else to do. Always carry something with you that you can pick up.

All Right, Guys, Take a Break

If you are going to ensure that your brain doesn't turn to rice pudding while you study, you have to build two kinds of breaks into your study routine: the relaxation, or change-of-pace, break and the transition-time break.

The change-of-pace break means doing something different from what you have been doing for the preceding two hours. If you have been sitting still, it means standing up, stretching, and going for a brisk walk. If you have been running around frantically, it means sitting still. And so on.

The transition-time break means allowing yourself time to unwind from one activity and get psyched up for the next activity. It just takes your body and brain time to leave one thing behind and start on the next thing.

Now these breaks do not have to be long. They just have to be there. You have to put them there. Unless you'd rather have your brain turn to mush.

(Oh, yes. One other thing that will turn your

brain to Jell-O is trying to study after you eat a heavy meal. *So*, if you always fall asleep studying during the evening, you can investigate whether you need one of the breaks described above or whether you need to lighten up on the bulk you ingest at supper.)

Writing Essays and Assignments

The first essay an adult student writes on returning to school is usually a pretty anxiety-provoking experience. Typically, the reaction is complete bafflement when you realize that you have absolutely no idea about how to approach the task. Chapter 9 may give you some idea about how to organize yourself to get the essay done, but there are a couple of points I want to make that deserve special mention.

The first thing is that it's helpful if you try to keep a "learning" rather than an "achievement" orientation about your first essays. That is, rather than focussing on the idea that you have to get a good grade, concentrate on learning (in an unemotional way) more about the subject matter and more about how to write essays. Use the professor and other resources to help you learn this before you start, and make sure to get full feedback from the grader after your essay is returned — don't just take your essay away and hide. Use this opportunity to find out how to do it better. It is probably unreasonable to expect that you must get a good grade on your first major essay — unless you have a background in writing academic essays — just as it would be unreasonable for you to expect yourself to be able to schuss down Mount Norquay the first time you put on skis or to ripple off the "Moonlight Sonata" after four weeks of piano lessons. It just doesn't work that way — everything takes time to learn, and there is no way you can avoid making blunders as you learn.

The other thing, of course, is that you should write about something that interests you. An essay is an opportunity for you to learn. If you're fascinated, perplexed, confused, intrigued — interested — by a particular topic, then write about it.

It goes without saying that you're in your course for a good reason. You are interested in the subject and you see taking the course or program as opening up new horizons for you and creating new opportunities. This is the kind of orientation that you should carry forward into working on essays: they present an opportunity for you to build upon your previous knowledge, to look at your experience in a new way, and to integrate your experience with new knowledge at a higher level of understanding.

But you start with what you're interested in, and curious about. For example,

> *A woman I know who was taking her B.ED. part-time had to do a project in a Psychology class where she was supposed to observe a pre-schooler in a kindergarten and to comment on how that child's speech development would be classified theoretically. Most of the class had the opportunity to visit kindergartens during the day and had little difficulty collecting their data. My friend was completely baffled about how she was going to find time to do this until it clicked that she was already spending a great deal of time observing and being fascinated by her own toddler. She approached the professor about using her own child as a subject and was given the okay. The essay became an enjoyable experience that allowed her to deepen her understanding of her child's development.

> *An instructor/tutor who teaches social-science courses to correspondence students (many of whom are in prison) comments that her students are always baffled about what to write about, until she makes the suggestion that they write about their own experience as prisoners from the theoretical standpoint of the discipline they are studying. When they discover that they can use their own experience they suddenly become absorbed in subjects that before had been abstract, and they write fascinating reports on the anthropology, the history, the sociology, the psychology, even the literature of prisons.

You get the picture? Write about something that matters to you — in your own personal life, in the social situations you encounter, or in your work.

Bridging the Gap Between School and Work

One of the most profitable ways in which you can use school in this task of integrating your experience and interests with a body of knowledge is to focus on research and writing activities that can have direct applications at work.

How about:

* An R.N. at a local hospital, who was finishing her B.SC., used essays in her Nursing Research course as an opportunity to assess what could be done to improve the nursing care of critically ill infants in the intensive-care nursery in which she was employed. This resulted in some small but significant changes in the organization of the nursing unit which improved the effectiveness of the nursery staff in giving care to the kiddies in their charge.

* Engineers working on graduate diplomas at the University of Calgary use their classes to work on their employers' problems. The students use these topics both as subjects for major school projects and to devise strategies that will be effective in helping their firms out of their binds. (Naturally, if you are going to do this kind of thing you have to be aware of protecting trade secrets and clients' confidentiality, but this can usually be managed.)

* Then there was the adult student who "had" to take a Psychology course as an elective in his Management program and was uninspired and frustrated until his firm decided to relocate and expand and he was put in charge of planning the move and overseeing the design and layout of the new office. He discovered that there is a small but growing body of knowledge on the psychology of space, and he was able to use this opportunity to collect information for a couple of fine research papers for his course *and* to improve the way he managed the relocation.

* An example suggested by my editor at Macmillan is the case of a person working in the sales branch of a publishing firm who might use his marketing course to write papers on the effectiveness of various strategies for publicizing children's books (which are usually difficult to move in large numbers). Any information would be helpful to his employer, since this is an area loaded with difficulties.

You see how it works? Try to think of how you can use your courses to help you with something that really matters to you.

You and Your Boss

When you approach your employer with your plans for going back to school, you've got two things on your side before you open your mouth. The first is the cultural value that says education is generally a good thing. The second is that most employers are smart enough to figure out that "happy employees are productive employees." That is, if they help you to accomplish your personal goals, the chances are that you will be a better, more useful member of the staff.

Most firms are aware that it costs a lot to lose experienced employees, to hire and retrain new ones, and to lose those employees just when they have learned to do the job. Enlightened firms will try to keep their staff *and* to keep them moderately happy. So reasonable requests will probably get a reasonable reception—particularly if it is obvious to your employer that your taking courses can and will benefit that employer in a pretty direct way.

The general experience of people in adult education is that your employer is likely to be quite co-operative in trying to facilitate your doing well in your course if he or she is paying your fees for the course, or is supporting you in your desire for career advancement either in your firm or in your industry. In these situations you can usually get time off if you need it for a particular purpose connected with school (a couple of days to do some hard work at the library), a chance to hear a speaker at a conference you otherwise wouldn't attend). You may be able to negotiate more flexible hours to make it to class or to work on projects. You may even get permission to use office equipment and personnel to help you put together reports and projects—as long as the office work gets first priority. And so on.

This depends, of course, on employers seeing your course work as something that they benefit from. So it really helps if you make yourself a valuable employee (one the boss wants to keep) and if you demonstrate that school enables you to provide better services to the company.

A Few Last Words

There are a few key words that pretty well summarize the ideas that you have to use to handle school.

One is *balance* —you have to plan for a balance between efforts devoted to work, to school, to family, and to fun.

The second idea is *learning*. If you focus on learning, then achievement will take care of itself. Don't even pretend that you can avoid mistakes; they are an inevitable aspect of learning. Be unemotional about your mistakes. I mean, it hurts to fall off your bicycle when you're learning to ride, but if you walk away from bikes forever, or draw generalizations about the flaws in your personality or intelligence as a result of this "failure", then you stop learning.

The third idea is *responsibility*. You are in the center of your own experience. You are in charge of whether you have an exciting, interesting time at school, or an anxious, harassed, worried, perplexed, overburdened, and dragged-out time. It is your responsibility to arrange your life at school, and nobody else is going to look after it for you. You are the one who is going to have to organize. You are the one who is going to have to take the initiative to negotiate in a spirit of openness and flexibility with your family. You and nobody else.

I trust that you'll find this book useful and encouraging. A lot of what's said here comes out of the experience of adult students like you as they discovered what works well and what merely takes up a lot of time. Mark Twain's comment that "it is easier to stay out than to get out" is particularly appropriate.

For students, it is much easier to stay out of trouble than to get out of it. It is easier to get organized at the start of the term before you're inundated with assignments, tests, and essays. It's much easier to figure out what to do with multiple-choice questions before the test. It is so much more efficient to design a study program two months before the test than the night before —and it saves such a lot of hassle.

All right, this really is enough. I hope that you enjoy reading this and that it helps you extract everything you can out of the experience of school.

Preparing for exams

Chapter 1

The five review strategies

There are only five *strategies* involved in effective exam-preparation. They seem obvious, even simple-minded, but it is surprising how many intelligent and otherwise capable students ignore them in their attempts to study for tests. These five principles lead logically to a variety of *tactics* which can be employed in specific circumstances.

1 Start Preparing for the Exam Early

Many, if not most, students don't start to think about preparing for tests until two or three weeks before one is scheduled—if that early! By then the notes they took at the start of the course have decayed into unintelligibility and they have forgotten so much of what was covered earlier that they must *relearn* instead of simply reviewing. In addition, since so little time is left before the test, students cannot clarify issues they do not understand and otherwise correct deficiencies in their knowledge.

Effective review begins on the first day of classes and continues throughout the term.

1.1 As soon as possible after each lecture, *spend five or ten minutes reviewing and editing your notes*. Do the same after reading and making notes on a section of a textbook.

Many students find that they can easily edit and revise their notes in the breaks between lectures. Others like to spend a half-hour or so in the evening reviewing the entire day's notes, as a way of mentally warming up to study or to work on assignments. See Appendix A for some ideas about how to edit your notes.

2 Review Step by Step

Many students react to their course outlines and their reading lists by boggling at the enormity of the task confronting them. Typically they delay starting to work until an exam is looming over the horizon, by which time the amount of work they have to cover has assumed mountainous proportions. This, of course, is ill-advised. In order to stay out of trouble, you have to develop short- and medium-range plans to organize your work over the school term.

2.1 *Prepare a master calendar*, breaking down the term's work into manageable units and allowing time for cumulative review and cramming. Distribute review times throughout the term.

Your *master calendar* will contain major deadlines and exam dates as well as your review plan. If your instructor has provided you with a course outline and a reading list, your task is relatively simple. Be sure to plan to review everything—not just the material covered in class.

Chapter 2 discusses in more detail how you would go about preparing the master calendar.

3 Practice the Skills You Will Have To Demonstrate on the Exam

Many students think that if they read their textbooks and lecture notes often enough, they are doing a good job of studying. This is nothing more than self-delusion. Others try to memorize their texts and lectures notes, thinking that this will prepare them for exams. Nothing could be further from the truth. Others superstitiously recopy their notes, and then recopy the copies, in the belief that this will enable them to handle the variety of tasks presented on exams. Too late they learn the error of their ways.

These ineffective techniques have a lot in common: they are time-consuming, repetitive, and largely passive activities. For students who regularly indulge in such mind-numbing exercises the slogan to remember is "Don't try harder. Try smarter."

There are times when all of these techniques are appropriate, but they are not appropriate at all times and in all courses. *The specific techniques you employ in studying for a specific course depend upon what it is that you are going to be required to do on the exam*. If you are going to be required to reproduce tracts of your text verbatim, then memorizing the textbook is relevant. If you are going to be required to summarize a particular topic, then summarizing is a relevant study practice. Summarizing, memorizing, and other activities are useful only in preparing for specific tasks. They are worse than useless preparation for other activities. If you're going to have to turn cartwheels, you don't practice handstands.

> 3.1 As soon as possible in the course, *try to clarify the skills and behavior you will be expected to demonstrate during the exam*.

In some courses this will be relatively easy. In a math course, for example, it may be pretty obvious that what you are expected to learn is how to solve a given range of problems using techniques that are the subject of your instruction. Applying this strategy to courses in the social sciences and the humanities (and to theoretical courses in the sciences) is a little more difficult. Chapter 3 is devoted to a further discussion of this issue.

But no matter what types of courses you are taking, it is fair to say that at the end of the course you will be expected to *do* things that you could not do (or do as well) before taking the course. Find out what those things are and practice doing them.

> 3.2 If at all possible, *get hold of copies of past examinations in the course*. Collate questions. List the issues discussed.

Some schools maintain a back-file of old exams to which students can have access, usually in the main undergraduate library. If not, your instructor may be willing to let you see sample problems from his exams. Failing this, see if you can contact students who have taken the course previously and pick their brains about the issues that were important in the course and the kinds of examination questions that were asked.

Don't trap yourself into preparing *only* the answers to past exams. This exercise is meant to be a *guide* to the types of problems posed in the course.

4 Get Feedback on Your Performance Before the Test

Many students appear to operate on the assumption that learning is a kind of mental osmosis: if they just expose themselves to the material enough, then knowledge will just somehow "sink in". In fact, if you treat your work in such a way you will have missed out on perhaps the most important feature of term work — it allows you to test your understanding and to self-correct your performance.

> 4.1 *Whenever you do anything in a course, make sure you get feedback* that would allow you to do that thing better the next time.

If you receive back a graded assignment, make sure you understand and *record* where you went wrong and what kind of answers would have been more appropriate. If the assignment is discussed afterwards in class or if model answers are provided by the instructor, make *notes* of these comments. You can't trust yourself to remember this information for months.

You're supposed to be a learner, so *learn* from your errors. Even if you are doing well in a course, you may want to learn how to be more economical in the amount of work you do or to improve your performance in other ways.

Getting feedback applies to everything that you do as a student. If you read a chapter in a textbook, test your understanding by trying to restate the important ideas in your own words and then check back in the text. If you think that you have solved an age-old problem in your philosophy course, try out your idea on your instructor or another student in the course and invite their comments. If you think you understand a concept in a math course, try out a sample problem to see if you get the same answer as the author of your textbook.

Get it? Thinking that you know something is not the same as *knowing* that you know it. In order to know, you have to try out your understanding in an actual, physical, concrete problem, and pay attention to corrective feedback.

4.2 *Form a study group* which meets regularly to work on assignments, do readings, and prepare for exams.

Studying regularly with the same group of colleagues has many advantages. If you are puzzled about something in a course, a buddy may be able to clarify the issue. If you are writing an assignment, you can ask for comments from the group. If you come up with an idea, you have somebody you can test it out with. In preparing for tests you can take turns asking and answering questions—you can collectively go through old exams and assignments and clear up the problems which any of you have.

This does not mean that you do each other's work. Most schools come down extremely hard, as well they should, on those benighted souls who commit the sin of plagiarism.

A study group has to stay task-oriented. This doesn't mean that mutual support, encouragement, and good times will play no part in the business of the group—precisely the opposite. But it does mean that each of you will have to pull your weight in the group. If one person is doing all the giving and none of the receiving, that person is going to feel gypped.

It is self-defeating to use the study group as an opportunity to score points in a contest of egos, or to indulge in some other infantile interpersonal game. Deal with such interpersonal conflicts in your group and attempt to prevent their recurrence. If somebody persists in such destructive activities, disband the group as amicably as possible and form a new group.

Most successful study groups have a formal rule used in their formation. Study groups usually start with two students who know from previous association that they can work compatibly. One of the two will nominate a third member, who will then be introduced to the other member. After a brief period of mutual assessment the new person may be asked formally to join the group. Nobody gets into the group unless everybody already in the group okays the new member.

5 Safeguard Your Physical and Emotional Well-Being

One of the things that keep university counselling services and health services in business is the astonishing lack of ability to care for themselves that seemingly intelligent people can display.

We see students who conduct experiments in sleep-deprivation during the week of final examinations; people who try to study effectively on a vitamin-free and caffeine-enriched diet; people who try to take their tests even though their grandmother has just died, their new car has been wrecked, and they've developed a case of terminal flu.

We see students who grimly hold on to unsatisfactory relationships with "friends", roommates, or parents, until the additional stress of exams pushes them into a confrontation at the worst possible time.

We see students who try to go through school, month after month, even though they have absolutely no clue about what they are trying to accomplish, what they want out of the place, or where they're heading in the future.

We see students literally working themselves into a physical and emotional breakdown because of some naïve conception that the more hours they work, the better their grades will be (which is true only up to a point).

We see students who are so tyrannized by their own and others' high expectations for their academic performance that they can tolerate no less than perfect grades on any assignment. Their fear of failure (in their eyes, getting any grade lower than a B+) becomes so excessive that they cannot do any school work without an accompanying headache, a bout of insomnia, or an attack of colitis.

Students can conduct such personal campaigns only if they believe three lies:

1. If you ignore a problem, it will go away.
2. Intellectual functioning is independent of anything else that is going on in a person's life.
3. "Holding on", "toughing it out", is a virtuous act, and asking for help is a demonstration of weakness.

These beliefs are quite irrational in that they lead people to persist in difficulties that could easily be rectified if they sought help earlier. Not only is it easier to stay out of trouble than to get out, it's easier to get out early than it is to get out late.

Believe me, I would much rather deal with a confused and drifting student in September, when not much has happened, than in April, after he's blown his finals, his girlfriend has left him because he's been such a drag, his parents are onto his case because he hasn't worked all year, and he's broken out in an inexplicable rash all over his body.

So please, please, please,

> 5.1 *If you encounter difficulties* in your social, personal, or physical life that you cannot handle after making reasonable efforts, *get help* — and the sooner the better.

Any study I have seen that examines the effectiveness of counselling, psychotherapy, or medicine shows unquestionably that the chances for rapid and complete recovery are much increased by prompt and early intervention. Please show as much respect for yourself as you would show for your car if it stopped working properly, or your elbow if it stopped bending.

Throughout this manual we will be referring to these Five Review Strategies repeatedly. If you do nothing else to change the way you prepare for tests, engrave the Five Review Strategies in letters of gold on the wall of your study. Continually refer to them to evaluate and modify the efforts you are making in your studies, and this alone will spur you to more effective performance.

The Five Review Strategies

1   **Start Preparing for the Exam Early** (*p. 2*)

    1.1   As soon as possible after each lecture, *spend five or ten minutes reviewing and editing your notes*. Do the same after reading and making notes on a section of a textbook. (p. 2)

2   **Review Step by Step** (*p. 2*)

    2.1   Prepare a *master calendar*, breaking down the term's work into manageable units and allowing time for cumulative review and cramming. Distribute review times throughout the term. (p. 2)

3   **Practice the Skills You Will Have To Demonstrate on the Exam** (*p. 2*)

    3.1   As soon as possible in the course, *try to clarify the skills and behavior you will be expected to demonstrate during the exam*. (p. 3)

    3.2   If at all possible, *get hold of copies of past examinations in the course*. Collate questions. List the issues discussed. (p. 3)

4   **Get Feedback on Your Performance Before the Test** (*p. 3*)

    4.1   *Whenever you do anything in a course, make sure you get feedback* that would allow you to do that thing better the next time. (p. 3)

    4.2   *Form a study group* which meets regularly to work on assignments, do readings, and prepare for exams. (p. 4)

5   **Safeguard Your Physical and Emotional Well-Being** (*p. 4*)

    5.1   *If you encounter difficulties* in your social, personal, or physical life that you cannot handle after making reasonable efforts, *get help* — and the sooner the better. (p. 5)

Chapter 2

Preparing a schedule for review

There are basically three steps to complete when reviewing for tests:

1. the immediate review you do of lecture notes and material covered in texts;
2. cumulative reviews at regular intervals throughout the course; and
3. cramming sessions just before the exams, to remind yourself of critical, "need-to-know" material.

What? You mean that you actually should cram for tests?

Indeed I do, for all kinds of good reasons which I will get to later. But for now, let's return to the topic of organizing review sessions.

Immediate reviews of notes from lectures and notebooks should become a reflex action as automatic as brushing your teeth in the morning. You will find that with very little practice this review takes only about five minutes, and can easily be squeezed into breaks between classes. These few minutes will pay off handsomely when you have to refer to your notes during the cumulative reviews.

The cumulative reviews, of course, require planning if they are to happen at all, and intelligent cramming requires both careful planning and the previous completion of the cumulative reviews.

So, there's no way to avoid it. If you are going to do the best job you can on exams, you simply have to get involved in scheduling and planning. But before you get all tied in knots about this, let me reassure you that there are ways of planning and scheduling that are relatively painless, and that will actually increase the amount of enjoyable free time you have to squander in whatever

way you, your friends, and the TV guide can devise.

Before You Start

2.2 *Make sure you obtain*, or prepare for yourself, *a course outline and reading list* for every course in which you are enrolled.

These two lists are absolutely essential, but I am steadily amazed by the casual way in which many students treat these valuable pieces of paper. If you are to have any sense of control over what happens to you as a student, you simply must keep in mind what your instructors have planned for you. The course outline and the reading list are the typical ways in which this information is conveyed.

If the dates for quizzes and tests and due dates for assignments are not provided on the course outline, try to establish for yourself at least a tentative notion of what these dates will be. Some schools have formal test weeks integrated into the academic schedule, but be aware that some instructors will slip in tests outside these formal examination periods as a "favor" to students.

If you are not provided with a written course outline and reading list, develop one for yourself. Usually professors will indicate the scope of the course in the first couple of lectures, so try to take decent notes of these descriptions and then, by referring to your texts, try to develop a written statement which links the course descriptions to the texts, giving you some idea of when specific readings will occur. If you have only one textbook in the course, and the prof indicates that you will be covering only the material in this text, then the table of contents of your text becomes your reading list, and all you have to do is to try to get some notion of the pace at which the material will be covered. If all else fails, count the number of pages of material in your text and divide it by the number of weeks in the term to arrive at a number which tells you approximately how much you have to study each week.

Incidentally, in most universities the assumption is made that students will, completely on their own, become familiar with the "recommended readings" as well as with the required text. Even though the prof may never refer to this material in lectures, he is quite within bounds to ask questions on the final exams which presuppose some familiarity with this material. If you don't want to learn this now, you will learn it when you get clobbered with the 30 percent question on the final exam—from the book you never read.

A Scheduling Approach That Really Works

Remember from Chapter 1 that you are going to

> 2.1 *Prepare a master calendar*, breaking down the term's work into manageable units and allowing time for cumulative review and cramming. Distribute review times throughout the term.

To do this you have to start from scratch because there isn't a thing on the market which meets the needs of students. The calendars you get at Christmas from your insurance company are all right if all you have to keep track of is your dentist's appointments, but they're worse than useless if you have to organize work from five or more courses, a part-time job, your social engagements, *and* your dentist's appointments.

Only slightly better are the huge desk-pad calendars which one sees occasionally. They do provide enough space to record the important information, but they have two flaws. In the first place, they usually have all kinds of highly distracting advertising printed around the margins. And secondly, like all month-at-a-time calendars, they hide what's coming up until you turn the page. At the end of each month you get to

have a nasty surprise when you turn the page—"Omigod, I've only got three days to prepare that formal report!"

You need a calendar which allows you sufficient space to organize your work clearly, and you need to be able to see the whole term's work at a glance.

Luckily for you, I am now going to show you how to do this.

Preparing the Master Calendar

On a sheet of standard 8½" × 11" notepaper, prepare a form as shown in Figure 2.1. Each vertical column represents one day in your life as a student, and the horizontal rows represent each class in which you are enrolled, with an extra row to help keep track of personal affairs. If you are involved in a long-term project outside of your regular classes (writing a thesis, say), then provide a row for it as well. Now, either by hand or with a machine-copier, duplicate the form so that you have enough sheets to cover the whole academic year (plus a couple of extras to allow you to make a few mistakes).

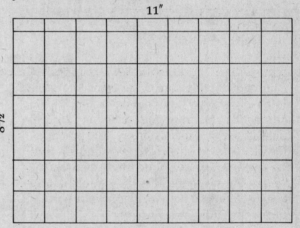

FIGURE 2.1 *The Blank Master Calendar Form*

Next, attach these sheets end to end. Enter days and dates in the space provided, and note the month as indicated in Figures 2.2 and 2.3. At this point you may want to decorate the master calendar with fetching drawings of flowers or abstract motifs, but for crying out loud don't spend more than one evening on this enterprise. You will notice that this calendar is not divided into weeks. This is for the very good reason that your work as a student has nothing to do with

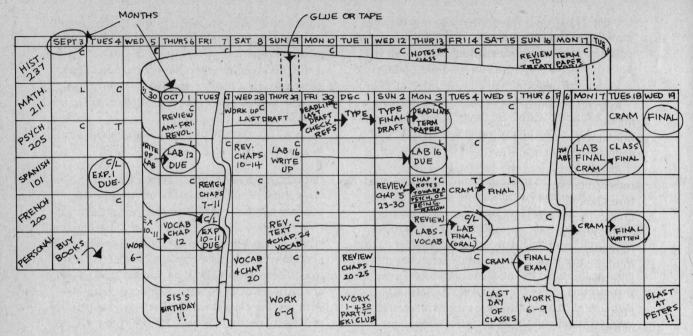

C = class, L = lab, T = tutorial. Very important events are circled. Arrows (→) join related events.

FIGURE 2.2   *The Completed Master Calendar for a Full-Time Student*

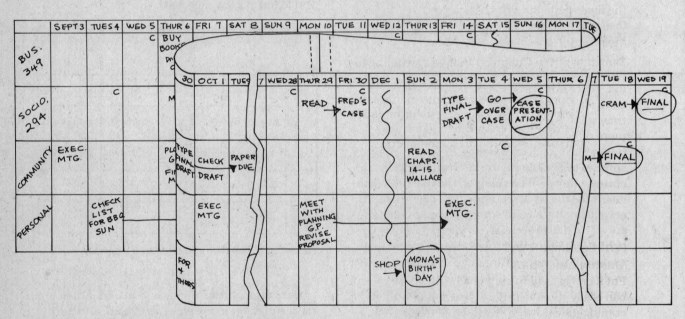

FIGURE 2.3   *The Completed Master Calendar for a Part-Time Student*

the seven-day schedule to which the rest of the industrial work force adheres.

Now you can start to enter the important information and begin to make decisions about how you are going to handle the term. List your classes as shown in the illustration, and note every other important date and deadline of which you are aware. If the date is fixed by custom or university decree (Christmas, last day of classes, etc.), you can note these in colored pen, but otherwise *work in pencil* so that you can correct the master calendar when necessary.

2.3 *Keep your master calendar current*. As you become aware of tests and assignment deadlines, add them to your calendar and indicate the time you will devote to preparation for these events.

Even before these deadlines are established for sure, take your reading lists and course outlines and tentatively schedule times to complete each section of the course.

Assign, again tentatively, times for cumulative review. Plan to review each subject at least three times before mid-terms and three times before finals. (This is not as terrible as it sounds, since each time you look at the materials you actually have to spend less time to master the content.) Allow about three to four hours in each of the cumulative reviews.

When I was an undergraduate, my friends and I figured that it was taking us about thirty hours of review to pass any course in which we enrolled. Of course, we cut things pretty close when we scheduled this thirty hours into the two weeks (and sometimes the two days) before the final exam. But I have just saved your neck by insisting that you spread at least eighteen of these hours throughout the term.

(And listen, the thirty-hour guideline worked for *us* in the specific courses that *we* were taking. There is absolutely no guarantee that it will work for you. You may be dumber or smarter than we were, your courses may be easier or more difficult. So you can start with the thirty-hour guideline, but please exercise some personal responsibility here. You will know after a couple of these sessions whether the guideline needs to be altered to keep you current in your courses.)

What Do You Do After You've Made the Master Calendar?

Put it on the wall in your study place where you can easily use it to remind yourself of what is coming up, and so you can use it in your weekly planning sessions.

The Weekly Planning Session

Because you are not going to carry your master calendar around with you, you need a more convenient way to organize your time on a daily and weekly basis. The best device to use is a date-book (obtainable at any stationer's and in variety stores) with one page for each day and with sufficient space on the page for you to record all the things you have to do.

2.4 *About once a week, plan your activities for the next week*. Plan how you are going to meet requirements for study and review and your other needs. Plan to keep current in all subjects.

In your datebook, list:

—*fixed commitments*, such as classes, times for your part-time job, meals, meetings, appointments;

—*deadlines* for assignments and times of tests; and

—times set aside for cumulative *review* and cramming.

Obviously you can do this before the beginning of each week, as you become aware of these predictable requirements.

Next, list:

—time needed for current studying and working on assignments;

—time for social activities and recreation;

—free time, and time for sleep.

Some items which you will want to list you will not want to assign to a particular time. These tasks will be those where there is no deadline attached, or where there is no obviously better time to do them.

Figure 2.4 shows how one student organized his datebook over a week. Please observe how this very busy student has still managed to squeeze in lots of pleasant and non-work activities.

Note, also, how the student has scheduled studying for French and Spanish.

3.3 *Don't review similar subjects one after the other*.

The reason for this is obvious, if you think about it. Studying similar subjects together will result in your mentally jumbling up information from both courses into one untidy package. If the subjects are not separated in time, you will find it difficult to separate them in memory.

2.5 *On a daily basis, keep track of the goals you have accomplished*, and transfer forward the tasks you still need to do.

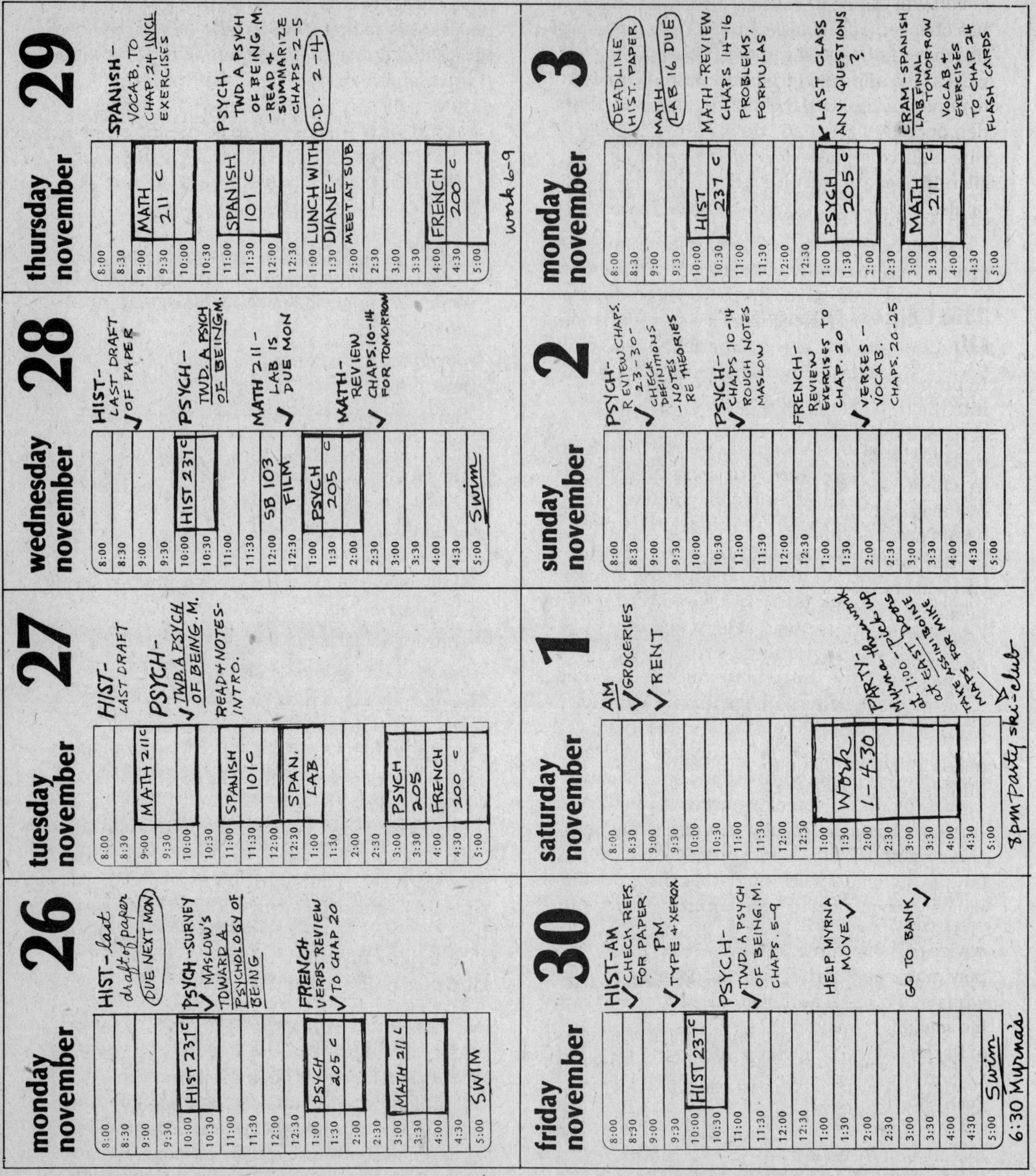

monday november 26

HIST – last draft of paper (DUE NEXT MON)

PSYCH – SURVEY ✓ MASLOW'S TOWARD A PSYCHOLOGY OF BEING

FRENCH verbs review ✓ TO CHAP 20

- 10:00 HIST 231ᶜ
- 1:00 PSYCH 205ᶜ
- 3:00 MATH 211ᴸ
- 5:00 SWIM

6:30 Myrna'

tuesday november 27

HIST – LAST DRAFT

PSYCH ✓ TWD A PSYCH OF BEING. M. READ + NOTES – INTRO.

- 9:00 MATH 211ᶜ
- 11:00 SPANISH 101ᶜ
- 12:30 SPAN. LAB
- 3:00 PSYCH 205ᶜ
- 4:00 FRENCH 200ᶜ

wednesday november 28

HIST – LAST DRAFT ✓ OF PAPER

PSYCH – TWD A PSYCH OF BEING. M.

MATH 211 – LAB IS ✓ DUE MON

MATH – REVIEW ✓ CHAPS. 10–14 FOR TOMORROW

- 10:00 HIST 231ᶜ
- 12:00 SB 103 FILM
- 1:00 PSYCH 205ᶜ
- 5:00 Swim

thursday november 29

SPANISH – VOCAB. TO CHAP. 24, TO INCL. EXERCISES

PSYCH – TWD A PSYCH OF BEING. M. – READ + SUMMARIZE CHAPS. 2–5 (D.D. 2–4)

- 9:00 MATH 211ᶜ
- 11:00 SPANISH 101ᶜ
- 1:00 LUNCH WITH DIANE
- 2:00 MEET AT SUB
- 4:00 FRENCH 200ᶜ

work 6–9

friday november 30

HIST – AM ✓ CHECK REFS. FOR PAPER PM ✓ TYPE + XEROX

PSYCH – ✓ TWD. A PSYCH OF BEING. M. CHAPS. 5–9

HELP MYRNA MOVE ✓

GO TO BANK ✓

- 10:00 HIST 231ᶜ

saturday november 1

AM ✓ GROCERIES ✓ RENT

PARTY! throw party Myrna - Pick up beers at 7:00 at EAST BONE take ASSIN MIKE take for MATS ✓ ski-club

- 1:00 WORK 1 – 4:30

8pm Party ski-club

sunday november 2

PSYCH – ✓ REVIEW CHAPS. 23–30. CHECK DEFINITIONS – NOTES RE THEORIES

PSYCH – ✓ CHAPS 10–14 ROUGH NOTES MASLOW

FRENCH – REVIEW EXERCISES TO CHAP. 20 ✓ VERSES – VOCAB. CHAPS. 20–25

monday november 3

DEADLINE HIST. PAPER

MATH. LAB 16 DUE

MATH – REVIEW CHAPS 14–16 PROBLEMS, FORMULAS

✓ LAST CLASS ANY QUESTIONS ?

CRAM – SPANISH LAB FINAL TOMORROW VOCAB + EXERCISES TO CHAP 24 FLASH CARDS

- 10:00 HIST 237ᶜ
- 1:00 PSYCH 205ᶜ
- 3:00 MATH 211ᶜ

FIGURE 2.4   *The Datebook*

You will notice in Figure 2.4 that the student has checked off the tasks he has completed and has moved other tasks to new times during the week. This approach to scheduling allows him to cope flexibly with the shifting nature of the demands that are made on his time. Transferring unfinished tasks forward has a way of silently nagging you either to get the task done, or else to reassign the priority given to the task.

The Critical Importance of Goofing Off

In preparing your weekly schedule, do not fall into the trap of committing yourself to work activities every moment of the day. Scheduling does not imply a lock-step, hour-by-hour grind, in which every second's activity is determined by the grim tyranny of the daily schedule. The whole point of scheduling is to give *you* control of your time and to increase the chances that you will enjoy what you are doing and get the necessary work done.

Scheduling has to be realistic if it is to work. And one of the things you need to be realistic about is that you *will* take time to goof up, goof around, and goof off. The need for goofing time is a fundamental human need, just like the needs for shelter from the elements and for a minimal amount of food.

> 5.2 *Make sure you allow time for goofing off.*

The high importance of goofing off has been celebrated from time immemorial, as in the advice of Benjamin Franklin: "All work and no play makes Jack a dull boy." And for those of you who need biblical authority in order to live your life sensibly, consider these words from the Book of Ecclesiastes: "Of making many books there is no end, and much study is a weariness of the flesh" (Eccles. 12:12).

I mean this seriously. Free time is *not* a luxury. It is absolutely necessary for proper intellectual functioning. If you are "working" all the time, you are definitely not taking time to mull things over, to freely associate and dissociate material from a variety of different fields, and to integrate information with your personal experience.

The other reason, of course, that free time is a necessity is so that you can take care of the little things that come up to interfere with your plans. If you contract dysentery, or your boyfriend/girlfriend flies in from out of town for a wild weekend, or you are asked to go out for coffee by a classmate, you simply have to have free, unscheduled time to juggle around so that you can still get your work done.

> 2.6 In changing your schedule, *borrow from free time*; don't steal from time you need for work or reviewing purposes.

Planning for flexibility in your schedule, by deliberately leaving some time unassigned, is almost the only way to ensure that you actually will get your work done. If you schedule work for every minute of the day, your entire plan gets thrown into disarray by the slightest unexpected interference.

Sailing Uncharted Waters

What if you don't know how long a particular activity will take, or you don't know how long you should study in a particular subject? This can be a problem if this is your first year at college or if you are taking an unfamiliar subject.

If this is your first year, you can start by recording your fixed commitments and deadlines. Record any social and recreational activities in which you are involved. As a starting-point, arbitrarily assign the same amount of study time to each subject as you spend in classes and labs. Then use the datebook as a log; record how much time it actually takes you to keep current in your courses over a couple of weeks. Thereafter, you should be able to guess pretty well how much time needs to be assigned to studying and working in each subject.

If the problem is only in estimating the time requirements in one new subject, assign times for all the rest of your activities. Then plan to spend at least as much time on the new subject as you devote to your most difficult subject. Again keep track of the actual amount of time you spend on the new subject over a couple of weeks.

If the problem is a new and unfamiliar activity (a special project, your first essay, and so on), follow a similar procedure. Assign time for the activities that you can schedule. The time remaining is composed of free time plus time that you can devote to the new project. It is best to start working well in advance of the deadline, since you have no idea how long you will have to spend on this activity. Keep track of the time that you do spend. The next time you face a similar project, you'll be able to predict fairly accurately the time commitment involved.

But don't diddle around unnecessarily, and do give yourself tentative goals to work towards. You do not have an infinite amount of time to play with, and you do have commitments to your other courses.

How Do I Keep Myself on Schedule?

If you are following the suggestions so far, you have significantly increased the probability that you will give yourself a schedule which allows you to get your work done without too much pain; but there are a couple of things you can do that will further increase the effectiveness of your planning.

In the first place, you have to tell yourself that this is *your* plan. If it doesn't work, you are quite free to change it around until it does—assign more time to a task that proves too difficult for the amount of time you have allotted, reduce the time for easier tasks, change the times assigned to various activities, run a short-term deficit in free time to get an urgent task accomplished, take a one-day holiday when you've caught up, and so on.

> 2.7 *Think small*. Plan study, work, and review sessions for short periods. Give yourself small goals to accomplish.

People are always planning these horrendous study sessions of interminable length in which they plan to complete mountains of work. But every problem, every assignment, every review activity can be broken down into a series of small steps, each one of which brings you closer to the desired larger goal. Nobody says you have to complete all the steps in the same block of time. In fact, this is almost a sure way to induce boredom and burn-out. Work in short, productive

spurts with small goals, and the large goals will take care of themselves.

> 5.3 *Arrange that pleasant events always follow difficult or tedious activities.*

If Statistics give you a pain, but English Lit. is a positive joy, set up your schedule so that you let yourself read part of a novel after you've completed part of your Statistics assignment. Deliberately reward yourself for getting the worst jobs out of the way.

> 5.4 *Allow yourself to be distracted only when you choose to be distracted.*

There is a Zen Buddhist saying that restates this principle:

> If you walk, walk.
> If you sit, sit.
> But don't wobble.

If you want to mess around with a friend, do that. If you want to get your Physics lab written up, do that. But don't try to do both in the same period of time or both activities will suffer. There is absolutely no way you can watch your favorite TV show while you are doing anything more complicated than folding your laundry. You are conning yourself if you even try. If you are addicted to a particular show, fine. Simply arrange to work like crazy towards a small study goal *before* your favorite show starts. First you work and then you play.

If you're addicted to a vice like contract bridge, electronic games, snooker, or drinking coffee you have to learn early how to stop yourself from getting sucked into these activities. (This mostly involves staying away from the environments in which these activities take place. It is much harder to stop these activities once you've started, though it can be done.)

Goofing off *is* necessary and inevitable, but you must decide where and when you goof off—and for how long. Don't let the environment—or other people—make these decisions for you.

The Last Weeks Before the Test

As exams approach, you start to see people behaving in ways that are completely self-defeating. Typically a lot of students will stop attending classes and labs, and many will be engaging in excruciatingly long sessions of review. The rest are so frightened that they avoid the whole question of preparing for the exam by spending their time daydreaming, sleeping, or otherwise messing around.

> 2.8 *Attend the last few lectures before the test.*

The reasons for doing this are obvious. Some professors may review the entire course, giving indications of what is important for the exam. Others may actually tell you some of the questions that are going to be on the test. And still others use this time to deal with students' unresolved difficulties. If you're not there, you don't get the benefits of this.

In particular you want to

> 4.3 *Make special efforts before the test to identify and resolve any difficulties* you have with the course material. Ask questions of the instructor. Check material you are unsure of with your classmates. Use alternative textbooks.

This may seem to be an obvious suggestion, but it is one that is consistently ignored by a large number of students. I suspect that many people do not address this issue because they do not want to appear foolish to their instructors and their peers. In actuality, of course, the only choice they have is *when* they will appear foolish —before the exam or after.

In my experience, very few profs actually will make a big production out of your bringing up your confusion and doubts. Most profs really do want to help students to learn, and they will go out of their way to assist those who take the initiative by coming to see them. But if your prof is an unhelpful sort, find somebody else, or do a thorough search for alternative texts—and don't wait until the last week to do this.

When To Schedule Cramming Sessions

> 2.9 *Schedule major cramming sessions as close to the exam as possible.*

There are lots of dumb ideas floating around about cramming. Some people maintain that you shouldn't cram at all—but these people have not been paying attention to the things that successful students do. There are two good reasons for cramming which have been verified by careful research:

—memory fades with time;

—the more activities there are between the learning of a piece of information and having to recall it, the less you will recall.

So you want to cram as close to the exam as possible to enhance the probability that you will recall all of the material you crammed. But cramming in the way that I use that term is quite a different activity from what most students consider cramming. Intelligent cramming *will* work for you. (More about this later.)

The last thing you want to do is to wait until just before the exam to get organized. You need to know that you've got enough time left before the test to do what is necessary. In addition, you need to know that your cramming isn't going to wreck you emotionally or physically. What's the point of cramming to the point of exhaustion? Any gains you might have made will be wiped out by the sorry state your body is in.

> 5.5 *Avoid cramming at the expense of physical and intellectual efficiency.*

If you cannot function without a solid eight hours of sleep, try to get it, even just before exams. If your brain turns to fluff unless you go jogging in the evening, maintain this healthy habit. And before you consider filling yourself full of chemical stimulants to keep yourself awake to cram for a test, perhaps you should conduct a realistic appraisal of the effects of whatever ingestible you are thinking of consuming. Caffeine, freely available in coffee, tea, and cola drinks (and in rip-off over-the-counter preparations sold in drugstores), can, in moderate dosages, produce increased wakefulness, alertness, and intellectual efficiency. But in higher doses these gains are lost; concentration declines and is replaced by distractibility and irritability. You are the best judge of your tolerance for this chemical. Amphetamines ("speed", "uppers", etc.) are even more of a risk, since it is simply too easy to exceed a desirable dosage. Once you have done it, your time is effectively blown until the effect of the drug wears off.

You get ready for the test in several ways.

5.6 *Structure your study activities so that you can wind down before you go to bed.*

Unless you take fifteen minutes to half an hour to have a little snack, brush your teeth, listen to a record, and otherwise relax and empty your head, you are almost sure to find yourself lying awake, thinking about your schoolwork.

Roommates and study groups will find that it is very useful to agree on a prearranged time when everyone will stop work for a few moments of ritual relaxation and off-topic discussion before knocking off for the night.

5.7 Just before an exam, *make sure you allow time to take care of important physical needs*, like eating, sleeping, exercise, and so on.

5.8 The night before the test, *lay out everything you need for the next day* so that you don't have to rush to get organized in the morning.

5.9 *Make sure you can arrive at the exam on time*, with as little rushing as possible.

Doing these things, just in themselves, will give you an edge that other students who are less organized don't have. In addition, you want to counter any impulses you may feel towards thinking in panicky terms.

5.10 Just before a test, *concentrate on what you know*, not on what you don't know.

In the hour or two just before the test, there is absolutely no way you can learn anything new. Spend this time reviewing to consolidate what you know. Cultivate an air of resignation about the things that you haven't learned—you're not going to learn them now, and the most important thing is to keep cool so that what you do know can come out on the test.

5.11 Just before a test, *do not talk to anybody about* what might be on *the test*.

Again, there is absolutely nothing further you can do. You simply do not need to be exposed to other people's opinions and judgments about what might be on the exam. There's no reason to believe that these people are going to be accurate in any case. And even if their judgments are correct, and you have made big mistakes, it's more important that you stay cool than that you get all sweaty about something that you can't do anything about.

What Do You Do To Cram Effectively?

It works best if you cram in two stages for each test. I call the first session the "major cram", and the second the "minor cram". Cramming only works if you have done a good job of completing cumulative reviews throughout the course.

If this is not the case, and if you are attempting to learn a lot of new material in your cramming session, you will undoubtedly run into problems. All in all, it is just so much simpler to do it right.

When you do a major cram, you have three tasks:

1. to look over and briefly quiz yourself on your review materials to renew your familiarity with this information (preparation of these review materials is discussed in Chapter 3);

2. to identify and restudy areas where you are weak; and

3. to produce a one-page summary of the information you have trouble remembering. This summary, and any troublesome vocabulary items, you will carry forward into the minor cram.

2.10 *For every test, complete a five- or ten-minute minor cram* just before the test begins.

Your task in the few minutes before the exam is first of all to try to keep yourself cool, but also to do a minor cram. A minor cram consists of looking over the one page of notes which summarizes the information you have had trouble remembering, and reviewing the definitions and formulas which have given you trouble. You will *not* try to learn anything new. You will *not* talk to other students about the test.

Back-to-Back Exams

At least once in your life as a student you will face the horror of an examination schedule that gives you back-to-back finals, one test following another with no time in between to study. Most students can cope with the first test, but with each successive test in the series, their performance deteriorates.

But now that you know about the three review stages and the minor cram, you will be offering up prayers of thanksgiving that you bought this book. The minor cram will save your neck in back-to-back tests because these few minutes before the exam starts will allow you to remind yourself of the important information that you have already studied.

The rest of this section of the manual is devoted to considering *what* you should do to profit from review sessions, now that you've gotten them scheduled.

Preparing a Schedule for Review

5   Safeguard Your Physical and Emotional Well-Being

  5.2   *Make sure you allow time for goofing off.* (p. 11)

  5.3   *Arrange that pleasant events always follow difficult or tedious activities.* (p. 12)

  5.4   *Allow yourself to be distracted only when you choose to be distracted.* (p. 12)

  5.5   *Avoid cramming at the expense of physical and intellectual efficiency.* (p. 13)

  5.6   *Structure your study activities so that you can wind down before you go to bed.* (p. 14)

  5.7   Just before an exam, *make sure you allow time to take care of important physical needs*, like eating, sleeping, exercise, and so on. (p. 14)

  5.8   The night before the test, *lay out everything you need for the next day* so that you don't have to rush to get organized in the morning. (p. 14)

  5.9   *Make sure you can arrive at the exam on time*, with as little rushing as possible. (p. 14)

  5.10   Just before a test, *concentrate on what you know*, not on what you don't know. (p. 14)

  5.11   *Just before a test, do not talk to anybody about* what might be on *the test*. (p. 14)

Chapter 3

Figuring out what to practice

Students commonly make critical mistakes before classes even start, mistakes that hamper them all the way through their courses, and that they don't discover until it's too late to do much about them.

Mistake #1: Failing To Remedy Problems Left Over from Previous Courses

One of the commonest assumptions made in universities and colleges is that students will have mastered and retained 100 percent of what they "learned" before.

Actually, many of you will have understood what was happening in previous courses, and some of you will have attained a sufficient grasp of the material to pass a final exam in the subject, but very few will retain more than a nodding acquaintance with this information from one year to the next.

So, a more correct assumption is that you are likely to remember only part of what you studied before. Sometimes this is relatively unimportant, but when you have lost hold of a skill or an idea that is basic to functioning in your present courses, the consequences can be devastating.

> 3.4 *If you have difficulty with basic operations and ideas* that the instructor thinks everyone has mastered, *identify a source of instruction* and specifically *schedule time to remedy your deficiencies*.

If you discover, for example, that you need to know an outline of Soviet history before you can do well in "Current Problems in the Soviet Union", then by all means hunt up a basic text on the subject and spend a weekend quickly reviewing the topic; if you have forgotten the dreadfully dull material you once learned about rhyme schemes and meter in poetry, then find yourself a source of information and relearn the material; and if you are missing an elementary idea in math (dividing by fractions, multiplying negative numbers), or in English usage (using the right pronoun, knowing when to use a semi-colon), find yourself a basic textbook and give yourself lessons. Strike a deal with a friend to assist each other in your areas of weakness. Or, if necessary, purchase the services of a tutor.

Sometimes people fail to develop supposedly simple clerical procedures—things like spelling correctly, writing neatly, and copying accurately.

If you have trouble with *spelling*, make sure you write out flash cards for words that might give you trouble (see Chapter 4). Check to make sure that you have the terms correctly spelled in the first place. Then practice quizzing yourself with the cards, writing out the answers as you quiz yourself. This goes for basic vocabulary as well as technical jargon.

If you make mistakes because of *poor handwriting*, systematically practice writing clearly throughout the year, and occasionally set aside time specifically to practice writing clearly. Some people I know have done this by teaching themselves to write italic script or by learning to print rapidly instead of writing. This applies to math courses as well.

If you make other kinds of clerical errors, it might be an idea for you to skip ahead to Chapter 11 and check out the suggestions for dealing with tests of clerical speed and accuracy.

These techniques might sound kind of rinky-dink. But believe me, if you are throwing away points on these kinds of mistakes, any improvement you make is well worth it. In my case, I am absolutely certain that I raised my math marks by an entire grade-point the semester I decided that I would finally do something about my sloppy calculations.

So let's turn this into a definite tactic:

3.5 *If you usually make a specific kind of error* on tests, *learn how not to make these mistakes*. Practice, practice, practice doing it right.

And approach this relearning objectively. You are not "dumb" because you don't remember a basic idea or have trouble with a supposedly simple procedure. When you're a kid, it is hard to tell what is important and what isn't, and the easiest way to deal with a difficulty is to ignore it. The only difference between you and people who were successful in the subject is that they managed, by a combination of luck, good instruction, and diligence, to forget things that turned out to be trivial.

And there is no need to tie yourself into emotional knots about having to relearn something you took earlier in school. The fact that you got past high school indicates that you have at least average intelligence, and that you can learn things if you just keep your cool. But in your relearning it might help to deliberately *not* use the textbooks you used before, because these textbooks may evoke powerful negative reactions that get in your way. Get different texts with different explanations. Preferably cheap ones.

Mistake #2: Failing To Attend to Language Issues in the Course

Another common mistake that students make is to assume that their instructors are speaking English. This is hardly ever true.

In fact, one approach to doing well in college takes the point of view that the student's job is to find out what language the prof is speaking and learn how to converse in it.

Let me give an example. People commonly fail to notice the difference between the language of English as you and I speak it and the language of *English Criticism*, which differs in many subtle but important respects. For example, consider these terms: romantic, character, plot, structure, conflict, manners, atmosphere, balance, catastrophe, complaint, conceit, crisis, climax, discovery, free, point of view, signature, stock. All of these words mean one thing in English, but they have a narrower and different meaning in Literary Criticism. The same is true in other subjects

as well. The terms multiply, negative, number, sign, group, population have precise and slightly varying differences in common English and in the languages of Mathematics, Sociology, Physical Anthropology, and Statistics.

The point is, of course, that words are used to carry meaning. And if a word is used to convey a special meaning, it is because the distinction is needed in order to understand and explain things in that field (i.e., the new, restricted meaning has practical and important consequences).

Something which can be of great help in this enterprise is to

3.6 *Identify a resource* which you can use to clarify technical vocabulary and in other ways to supplement your text.

There are lots of references available whose express purpose is to unravel these mysterious distinctions. Books such as *A Handbook to Literature* by Thrall, Hibbard, and Holman (Odyssey Press, 1960), or *A Comprehensive Dictionary of Psychological and Psychoanalytic Terms* by English and English (David Mackay Co., 1958), are well worth buying if you intend to pass beyond a mere beginner's understanding of these subjects. Works like David Sells's *International Encyclopedia of the Social Sciences* (Crowell, Collier & Macmillan, 1968) are much beyond the ordinary student's reach and are so broad in scope that there is little point in buying them. But, if you intend to do well in your Social Science courses, you will find out where the library keeps this reference, or one like it, and you will find out how to use it—before you need to.

If you have a lot of vocabulary to understand and remember in a course, and the definitions are quite technical, the best procedure to use is flash cards. These are described later in Chapter 4.

Getting Down to Business

Now that we have taken care of these difficulties we can get down to the matter at hand.

Let's start by recalling the Five General Strategies that apply to preparation for all tests:

1. Start early;
2. Review step by step;
3. Practice the skills you will have to demonstrate on the exam;

4. Get feedback as you study; and
5. Safeguard your physical and emotional welfare.

Of these principles, the first two are motherhood-and-apple-pie ideas. That is, most people know you are supposed to follow them, but very few do. My feeling is that this is because students don't know about the other three principles. How can you start early and prepare in a systematic way if you have no idea *what* to review and how to organize and select the material to study?

Well, of course you can't. So you procrastinate until, with the exam almost upon you, you are frightened into a paroxysm of frantic cramming without any system or order.

There are several things that can be done in order to avoid this difficulty. But before we get into a discussion of these tactics, let me introduce an equation which I find helpful when thinking about learning. It's kind of a rough-and-ready notion, but it does help to clarify your task as a student.

$$\text{Learning} = \text{Understanding} + \text{Retention} + \text{The Ability To Apply the Information}$$

The Learning Equation can help you avoid some of the common pitfalls—such as the trap of assuming that you're in good shape for the final if you keep looking over your notes and texts until the material *looks* familiar.

Alas, recognition is not the same as recall.

So, unless you simultaneously practice *remembering* as well as recognition and understanding, you're due for unpleasant surprises on the test.

Other students focus on the memory element to the exclusion of the other factors. They attempt to memorize everything, even though they don't understand it and can't apply it. This is like learning a song in a foreign language. Unless you learn what the words mean—that is, understand the song—all you have learned is the words to the song.

And finally, of course, many students neglect the third variable in the Learning Equation.

If you want to avoid nasty surprises, you have to systematically ensure that you attend to all three factors in the Learning Equation.

One of the most important things you can do is:

   3.7   *Early in the course, design a global map* which will allow you to see the logical structure of the information in the course. Build your global map throughout the course.

Building a *global map* is possibly the best way to ensure that you do understand the material and that you do learn to apply the information. Let's look at some examples to see how this works.

Remember that the third General Strategy is "practice the skills you will have to demonstrate on the exam." Well, in some courses you can predict the kind of thing you are going to have to do on the test even before you go to one lecture in the course.

Take Psych 399—"Theories of Personality", for instance. Before you even walk into the first class, you know that you will have to do the following on the final:

1. Describe the main points of each theory.
2. Examine the theory critically in terms of internal consistency, applicability, and empirical validity.
3. Compare and contrast alternative theoretical interpretations of observed psychological phenomena. (How would Freud account for a particular thing? How would Adler? Which explanation makes most sense? Is most coherent? Which theory enables a therapist to make an effective intervention?)

So, before you even start the course you can design a global map that looks something like Figure 3.1. Across the top go the names of the theorists whose work you will be examining in the course. Down the side go the categories that are important in outlining the theory, and in assessing the validity and usefulness of the theory. Obviously the trick is in developing a complete and useful list of these categories. For this, you can use the headings employed in your textbook's description of the theories. Pay attention as well to the categories used by your instructor. If he spends time discussing case descriptions or empirical studies, for example, you will want to include these categories in your global map.

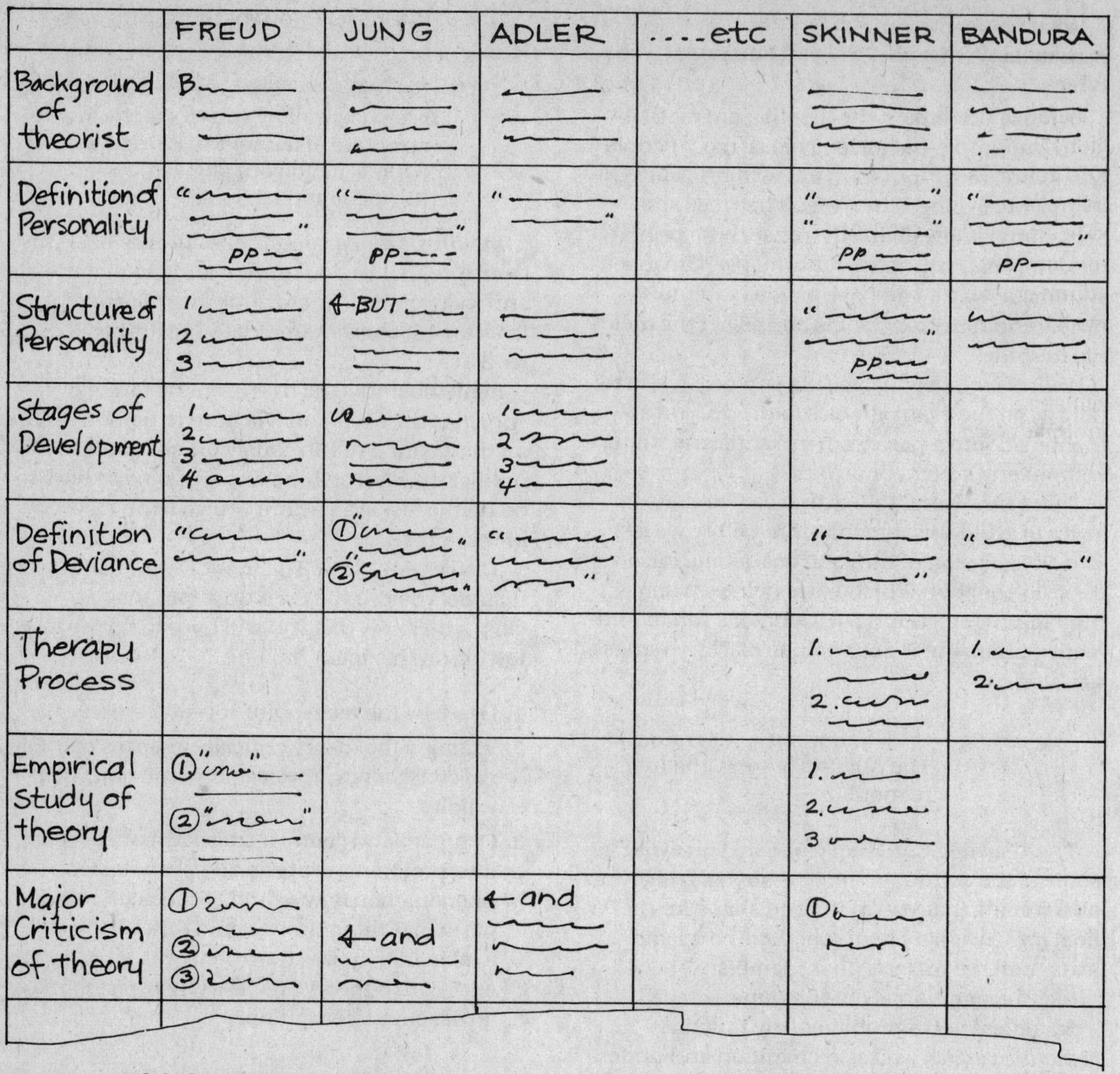

Figure 3.1 is a hand-drawn "Global Map" consisting of a grid.

	FREUD	JUNG	ADLER	....etc	SKINNER	BANDURA
Background of theorist						
Definition of Personality						
Structure of Personality						
Stages of Development						
Definition of Deviance						
Therapy Process						
Empirical Study of theory						
Major Criticism of theory						

FIGURE 3.1   *Global Map for Psychology 399*
(describe/summarize/compare/contrast/criticize)

What you do with the map is to list in point form the important information as you review each theory in the course. When you do this you will notice a couple of things. First, because you allow yourself only a limited amount of space in each cell on the global map, you are forced to understand the material sufficiently well to summarize the important points (there's little danger, then, of wallowing in excessive detail). Secondly, the format of the map is going to force you to highlight comparisons and contrasts between theories as you record information in adjacent blocks. You are not going to be satisfied to make ambiguous statements on the map or to make vague, uncritical comparisons between the theories. Finally, the map will really function like a map; you will carry it around as a picture in your head and will be able to use it as you sort through the information and deal with problems in the course. You see how it works?

What about courses where you have to prepare to demonstrate different sorts of skills? What about History courses, Sciences, Maths?

Figure 3.2 shows how you might lay out a global map for a history course. The map is ruled into columns for the important categories of information with a time line running down the side. Events are shown in the boxes. Trends and tendencies are indicated by a brief, point-form summary. Relationships are demonstrated first of all by the sequence of events, but also by arrows drawn between events in different columns. Completing this map will enable you to think more like a historian: you will understand the sequence of events and can begin to make conclusions about cause-and-effect relationships between events in different spheres.

Figure 3.3 shows a similar map, this one for a course in the history of art in Europe. In such a course you typically have to remember, categorize, and be able to say something intelligent about hundreds and hundreds of art works,

FIGURE.3.2 *Global Map for History*
(outline/describe/trace/show relationships/recall details)

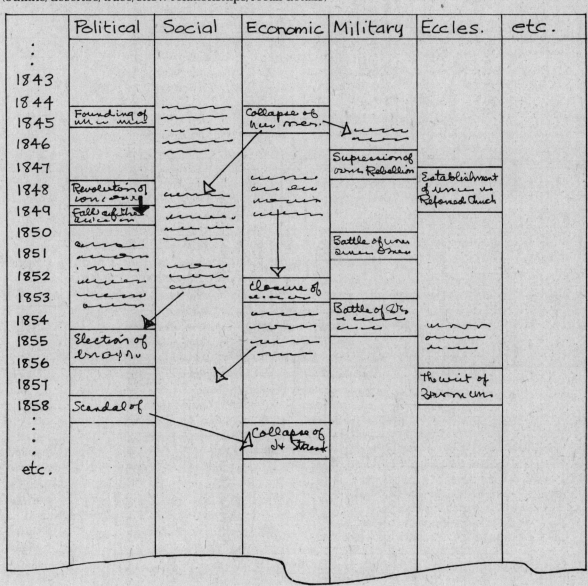

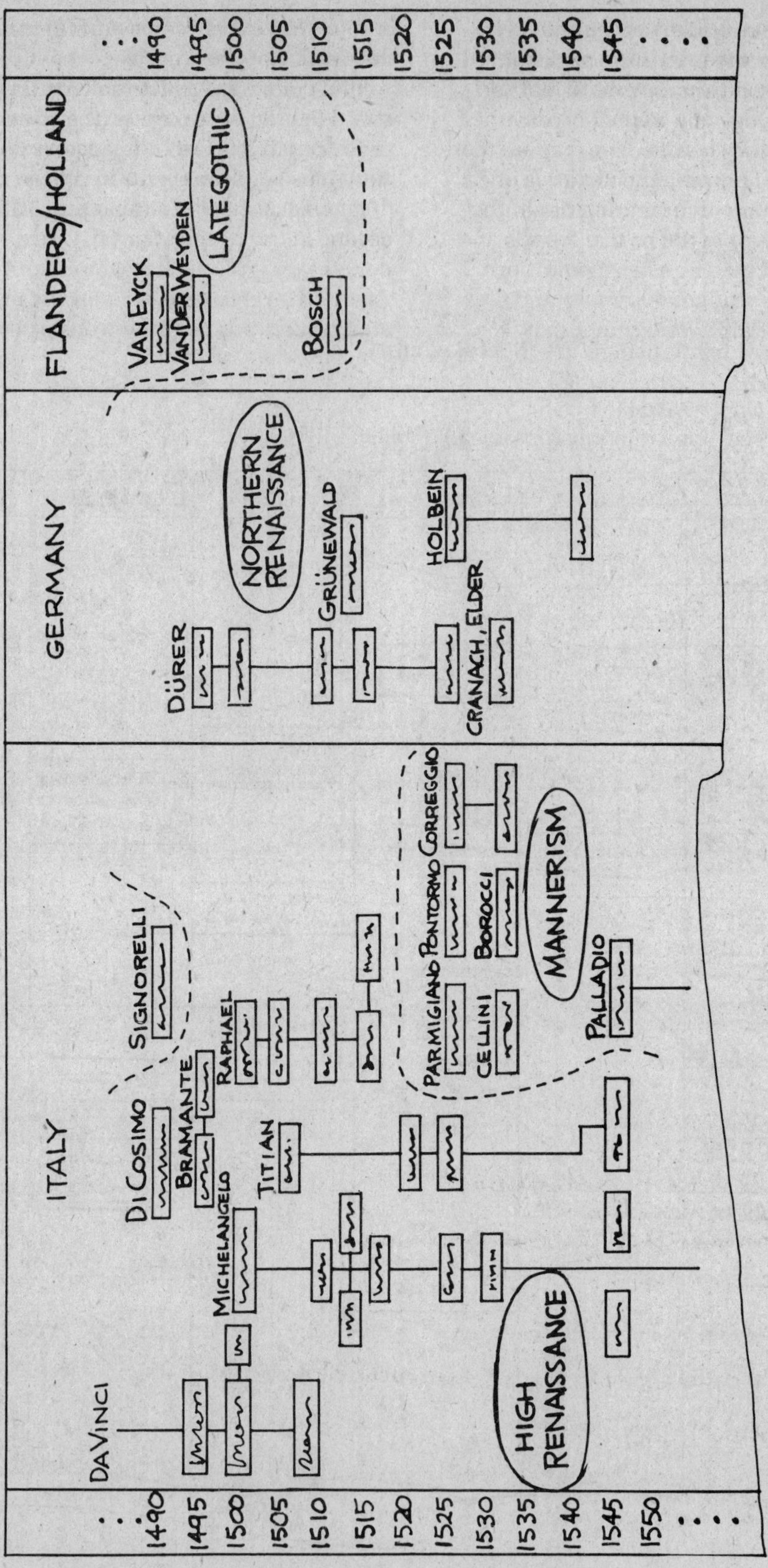

FIGURE 3.3 *Global Map for History of Art in Europe* (identify/describe/show relationships/recall details)

many of which will be studied only briefly. The global map shows one way to make sense out of this mass of detail. Individual works of each artist are listed chronologically. Artists are grouped geographically and are classified into movements or "schools". Mapping the works studied in this way enables you to make judgments about the relationships of artists to each other and to broader movements of the day, and to put the details into perspective.

If I'd done this when I took Art History, I probably wouldn't have flunked the course.

You could map an introductory Biology course using a formal outline of the classification of life forms. Then, as Figure 3.4 shows, verbal and visual description of typical members of

FIGURE 3.4 *Global Map for Biology 101*
(classify/identify/show relationships/describe/diagram)

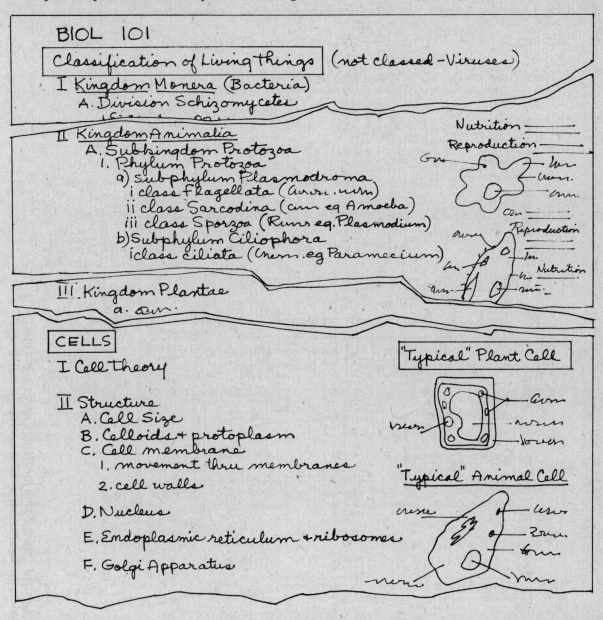

each level in the classification would be the next phase. A formal outline accompanied by *key* diagrams conveys the organization of this endeavor. Once again you are less likely to get bogged down in the social infrastructure of planaria and lose sight of the larger picture when the information is mapped like this.

Math and math-like courses (e.g. logic) tend to be sequential, building-block types of courses, where each process and procedure relies upon the steps that occurred before. The global map consists of important procedures listed in order, from simple to complex, as in Figure 3.5. In addition, the relationship of particular types of prob-

FIGURE 3.5   *Global Map for Algebra II*
(identify/find/problem solve)

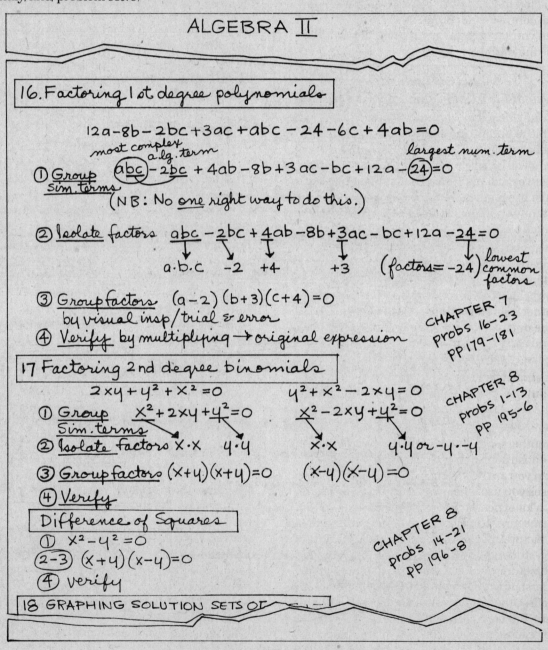

lems to the theoretical matter can be demonstrated.

The structure you choose for the global map depends upon two things:

1. the logical sequence and flow of the material in the course; and

2. the tasks you are expected to accomplish with the information ideas.

Passively recopying your notes onto the global map will not do. You must think, "What will I be expected to do? Trace, describe, evaluate, compare, contrast, find, prove, diagram, solve for...?" Then you set up a global map which facilitates this kind of activity.

Physical Characteristics of a Global Map

1. Your global map should be big. You want to be able to outline the entire course on a single sheet of paper, since this is the only way that you will be able to see the relationships between all the elements on the map. If you just use regulation notepaper, you will be constantly shuffling pieces of paper and losing track of ideas.

2. It should be graphic. Categories should be clearly titled with bold print. Events should stand out clearly. Relationships should be indicated by big fat arrows. Color-coding and other graphic techniques will help you to *see* the organization of the material, and will help you carry the map around with you in your head.

3. It should be clear. While it contains a brief summary of all the important information in the course, you should be able to read it from a yard away.

Another factor you should consider when you are constructing your global map—indeed, when you are reviewing in any way—is what senses you use when you learn best. For example, a lot of people have a highly developed *visual* sense. They can close their eyes and imagine pictures in glorious Technicolor and 3-D. Such students should use lots of color, shading, and pictures in their global maps to help them understand and remember important ideas and details. Other students are not blessed with this talent, but have a tremendous *aural* memory. They can recite, word for word, conversations they took part in years ago and remember incredible details of things that they have heard. It helps aural students to read important things aloud, and to speak to themselves when they are quizzing themselves for tests. Students who are good with their *kinesthetic* senses (body position and movement) should integrate these senses into their studying by focussing on activity—writing things out and doing things rather than merely thinking them. And for people who lack these abilities but who are highly skilled with the written word, the emphasis should be placed on writing out summaries and outlines, rather than on drawing diagrams. There is some evidence that the more senses you use when you are learning, the better able you are to remember and use the information. If possible, use every sense you have—say things to yourself, write things out, form mental images, act them out.

What Do You Do with This Thing? And Why?

Well, in the first place you build it as part of each regular review session, which you so wisely have spaced throughout the course. Building the global map will force you to understand the material in the course, to put it into a perspective which will allow you to perform various kinds of review activities.

These activities will consist chiefly of quizzing yourself and practicing the kinds of things you will have to do on the exam.

4.4 *As you review, quiz yourself on the important information and ideas*, checking on your global map, in your notes, or in the text to confirm your understanding, retention, and ability to apply the material.

For example, during a review for Psych 399—"Theories of Personality", you would ask yourself questions like "How does Jung's conception of the structure of personality differ from Freud's? What are the practical consequences of their difference for psychotherapy?" Then you would briefly answer your own question by trying to outline how you would respond to this question if it were on an exam. After you've either completed your outline or run out of ideas, you refer to the global map to check the validity of your response. Then do whatever is necessary to shape your response into a better one.

Get the picture? This quizzing and checking procedure will ensure that you are attending to all the factors in the famous Learning Equation. You are deliberately attending to understanding the material, attempting to recall it, and trying to apply the information to the solution of various kinds of problems.

Figuring Out What To Practice

3   Practice the Skills You Will Have To Demonstrate on the Exam

   3.4   *If you have difficulty with basic operations and ideas* that the instructor thinks everyone has mastered, *identify a source of instruction* and specifically *schedule time to remedy your deficiencies*. (*p. 17*)

   3.5   *If you usually make a specific kind of error* on tests, *learn how not to make these mistakes*. Practice, practice, practice doing it right. (*p. 18*)

   3.6   *Identify a resource* which you can use to clarify technical vocabulary and in other ways to supplement your text. (*p. 18*)

   3.7   *Early in the course, design a global map* which will allow you to see the logical structure of the information in the course. Build your global map throughout the course. (*p. 19*)

4   Get Feedback on Your Performance Before the Test

   4.4   *As you review, quiz yourself on the important information and ideas*, checking on your global map, in your notes, or in the text to confirm your understanding, retention, and ability to apply the material. (*p. 25*)

Chapter 4

Memorizing stuff

Global approaches are important and valuable and you neglect them at your peril. It is also important that you pay attention to detail, which often will require that you memorize.

The actual amount that you have to memorize varies a great deal from course to course and from field to field. In some areas the mass of detail that absolutely must be memorized is enormous. More typically, though, you have to memorize only a few things: key definitions, spelling of technical terms and names, a few formulas, and so on.

I don't know why students react so hysterically to this. Perhaps it's because they habitually use such ineffective techniques that they can't do it at all well. Also, of course, some people object to memorization on broader philosophical grounds, claiming that memorization is a cognitive activity which is on such a low level that it is not really thinking and is, therefore, beneath the dignity of even an undergraduate. Actually, we all possess vast funds of information which it was only possible for us to acquire by memorization. In any case, memorization does not need to be the burdensome chore that most people think it is. Really, memorization is dead simple if you start early, do it step by step, and use effective techniques.

When most students attempt to memorize things, they do it completely backwards. A common approach is to write the information on a sheet of paper and stare at it for three or four hours, chanting the information over and over.

Tell me, if you were trying to learn to turn cartwheels, would you stare at somebody doing cartwheels for hours and hours? Of course not. You would watch somebody do it a couple of times and then attempt to perform the trick

yourself. When you finally perform a half-decent cartwheel, you practice it and practice it until you can do it automatically without having to think where to put your feet, your hands, and your head, and how fast to make the approach. That is, after seeing a demonstration of the skill, you practice it yourself, all the while learning from corrective feedback.

And this is the whole trick with memorization. Staring at something until you're blue in the face is not going to help you remember something. Trying to remember it and getting feedback on your performance will.

Memorization Made Almost Painless

3.8 *Use flash cards to memorize important details* that must be recalled exactly. Generate flash cards a few at a time and review them frequently.

Buy a bunch of 3″ × 5″ index cards like the ones that are used for recipes. Every day as you review your notes, and every time you study a chapter in a textbook, prepare flash cards for the items that must be memorized. (Don't worry that you will make too many flash cards — it will become obvious fairly quickly which items you do not need to put on cards.)

For *vocabulary* items, write the term to be learned, correctly spelled, on the front of a card. On the back, write the correct definition in your own words, taking care that it is technically precise. You may want to add (1) an example that makes the meaning clear, (2) a reference to a specific author or theory, and (3) a note about terms that you need to distinguish from the one on the face of the card.

For *formulas*, you write the name of the for-

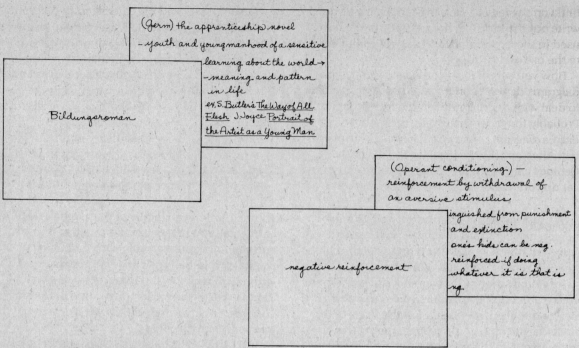

FIGURE 4.1 *Definition Flash Cards*

FIGURE 4.2 *Formula Flash Cards*

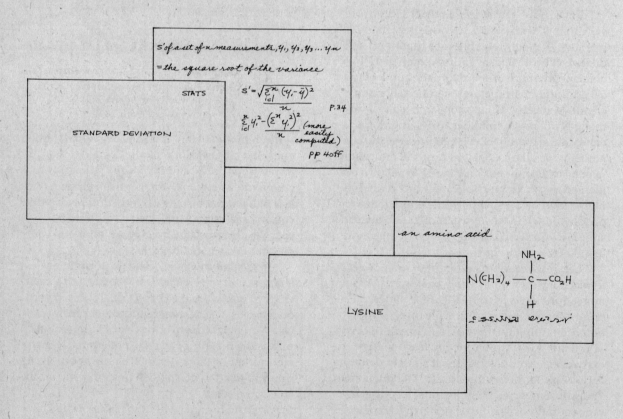

mula on the face of the card. On the back you write out the formula, the meaning of the terms used in the expression, and any rules that apply to the use of the formula.

How you set up flash cards for dealing with diagrams depends on how you are going to have to deal with the diagrams in the test situation. Probably the most straightforward task will be to *draw a diagram* when you have been supplied with the name or the label for the diagram. The Geology card in Figure 4.3 shows how you would set up your cards for practicing this activity.

Different tasks on the exam lead to different modes of preparation. The Psychology example in Figure 4.3 illustrates how you would lay out cards to rehearse for identifying, diagramming, labelling, and describing specific features and structures. Finally, the Art History example focusses on the tasks of identifying and discussing the particular artwork depicted.

The amount of care necessary in producing your diagrams again is a direct function of what you have to do on the exam. In the Geology card, you want to practice the simple line diagram

FIGURE 4.3   *Examples of Flash Cards for Diagrams*

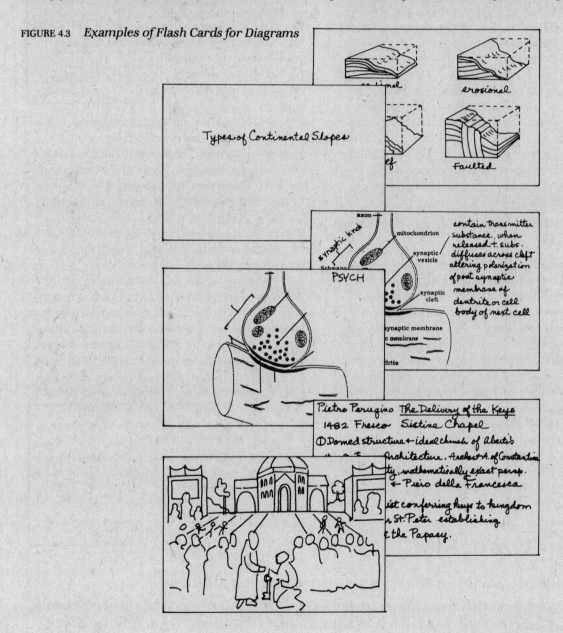

that you will have to produce on the test. In the Psychology example, a fair amount of precision would be necessary in order to make your diagram clear. But in the Art History card, a cartoon-like sketch exaggerating the identifying features is all you need to help you learn to identify a slide of the particular painting.

Sometimes it is well worth your while to photocopy diagrams for your cards—when there are an extremely large number of diagrams to remember, for instance, or when a great deal of precision in the diagram is required. A student in one of my Study Skills classes invented the procedure illustrated by the Psychology card, for dealing with a Paleontology course in which he had to be prepared to instantly identify and label diagrams of several thousands of fossils, many of which were quite similar. Generating a set of flash cards, like the Psychology cards shown, enabled him to do this well enough to raise his mark from a "D+" on the mid-term to an "A" on the final test. Using flash cards may look like a pretty Mickey Mouse procedure, but it is an extremely powerful and effective technique.

How To Use Flash Cards To Rehearse for a Test

Generate a set of cards for each subject in which there are memorizables. Your current set in each subject should consist of from ten to fifteen cards. Carry these cards with you. At least once a day, and several times a week, go through your current cards. Look at the face of the card and, without peeking, give the information on its back —say it out, write it out. When you can't think of anything more, you turn the card over and compare your answer with the correct information given there. Then go on to the next card.

When the top card in your current set comes up again you shuffle the cards. On the test the items are not going to come in any particular order, so you don't learn them in any particular order. After three or four trials, you will undoubtedly have the material memorized for the short term. Put an elastic band around the cards, label them with the name of the subject and a brief description, and throw them in a shoebox. In your regular reviews, and in major crams, bring out all the cards that you have generated to date and go through them in the way described above. Pull out the cards with which you have problems and go through them again, and yet again, until you have the information correct.

You absolutely have to generate the cards a few at a time. If you were taking a course in a foreign language, you would have to learn the meanings of thousands of words. There is simply no way in which you can learn this mass of material except bit by bit, with frequent repetitions.

Spend only a few minutes at a time on memorization, certainly never more than twenty minutes at a crack. Most people find that they can do this during the day in all the little short periods of time they spend waiting for lectures to start, in breaks between classes, while riding the bus, and so on. Other students find that a good time to practice is just before they begin homework or reading in a particular subject as a way of mentally warming yourself up.

For some subjects, it makes sense to go through your cards backwards and forwards (for example, in a language course where you have to translate from English into, say, German, and also from German into English). Or in a course where you have to both label diagrams that are provided on the test and, conversely, provide diagrams for the terms, formulas, or labels given. This clearly depends on your assessment of what it is that you will have to do on the test.

The key to the whole procedure is that you *are* practicing the skill you will have to demonstrate, and you are doing it frequently enough to have the desired effect.

Memorizing Stuff

3 Practice the Skills You Will Have To Demonstrate on the Exam

3.8 *Use flash cards to memorize important details* that must be recalled exactly. Generate flash cards a few at a time and review them frequently. (*p. 27*)

Chapter 5

Reviewing in case-method courses (including English Lit.)

So far we have been talking about what can be called "content" courses, where texts and lectures consist of facts, ideas, data, and descriptions of procedures. In these courses it is the student's job to learn the information (i.e., to understand it, remember it, and be able to apply it). For such courses the approaches discussed so far will work pretty well.

But there is a whole group of courses where such techniques as the *global map* will apply only part of the time, and where you need to develop a different approach:

—in English Literature courses;

—in Management or Business courses that use the case-study approach;

—in Nursing, Social Work, or Clinical Psychology courses where you are expected to integrate theoretical material with practical experiences of various kinds;

—in Law courses which emphasize case material.

In such courses there may be a historical or theoretical structure around which the cases are organized. This material can be put onto a global map. But, not only are you expected to be able to demonstrate mastery of this information, you are also going to be asked to perform various kinds of descriptive and analytical tasks with respect to the case material.

The key to preparation of review materials in case-method courses is to carefully diagnose the skills and behaviors you are going to have to demonstrate on the exam. Let's look at an example to see what this means.

Consider a course in the modern American novel. In such a course one might typically be expected to read twenty or so novels by various authors. In the lectures, the prof will be discussing or commenting on each novel with respect

to how the novel fits into the history of the times —including the intellectual, social, and artistic context in which the author worked. He'll make comments on the form and structure of each novel and on how the author uses language with particular effect. The prof will comment on the themes and ideas in the novel. He'll discuss the development of character, the use of setting and time, the use of metaphor and symbolism, and so on.

Most students "understand" this material as it flows past them in the lectures. That is, they can more or less follow the prof's sentences without getting hopelessly lost. Alas, taking notes and preparing other review material is a different story, so preparing for the test is a big problem.

What the average student will do is to focus almost exclusively on the "content" of the novels, trying to nail down who did what to whom, when, in the novel. This is what the prof means when he talks about "plot summary". Because the student has neglected to examine each work critically and analytically, he will be completely unprepared for a question like:

> "Existential alienation is an important dimension in the novels we have discussed. With respect to any two of the novels on your course outline, show how the authors variously use description of setting to illustrate the existential dilemmas facing the protagonist."

The only way to prepare for such a question is to practice the specific tasks involved. What this means is that you must *complete* the case analysis that the prof has only partially covered in class for each novel under consideration. Let's see how this goes.

You have to read the novel at least once before the related class. (If you must, skim it quickly—

but look at every page at least briefly before the class.) Don't make this a big production; just read the novel the way you would if you were reading it all by yourself for pleasure. If you have any questions or comments, though, it would be a good idea to jot them down in the margin of the book.

Go to class. Pay attention to what the prof says. What words does he use that sound like English but are really in the language of English Criticism? Develop a checklist of these words. What parts of the book does he mention? Why? If he gives examples, what are they examples of? Your notes may be pretty disjointed, but that is okay, because the guts of the course are not in the lectures but in what you do next.

Now, as soon as possible after the class, go back over each novel and read it a second time, locating and marking the passages that the prof talked about and writing in a comment that will tell you why this passage is important. Continue this through the whole novel to identify more examples that illustrate these ideas.

Now go over the novel a third time and mark it up with respect to other kinds of analysis. For example, if your prof talked about the treatment of time in the novel, but didn't say much about myth and symbolism, you go back and take a look at myth and symbolism throughout the novel. In other words, you complete the analysis, or as much of the analysis as you know how to do.

In order to do this you may have to have recourse to a secondary textbook that will tell you the meaning of terms like "symbolism", "characterization", "conflict", "theme", "metaphor", and so on—all the terms you think you understand but don't. It's tremendously helpful to read as widely as you can about the period under consideration. Read other books by the same author and novels written by his contemporaries. Read anything and everything. You may also have to supplement the prof's comments on the particular novel you're studying by looking at a good book-review, or at a biography of the author. Your librarian will be glad to help you to locate this information. And if all else fails, and you're completely boggled by the book, take a look at things like *Coles Notes* or *Monarch Notes*, which briefly summarize many of the important ideas to remember about novels that commonly appear on university reading lists.

Your prof will probably get quite irate if he finds out that you use these references. But don't let that bother you. If you're desperate, you use any method that will aid in your understanding of the novels—short of larceny.

To review for the test, you look over your texts once again to refamiliarize yourself with all the material. And then you practice quizzing yourself to make sure you can remember and apply the information in the way you have to on an exam, following the General Strategies for review.

Let's boil this down to a few tactics.

> 3.9 *In case-study courses, read the cases at least once before the lecture*.
>
> 3.10 *In case-study courses, develop a checklist of headings that the instructor uses to analyze and evaluate the cases*. Add to this list from secondary sources. Check your understanding of these terms.
>
> 3.11 *After the lecture* on a case, *go back and complete the case description and analysis*. Mark your text, locating important examples, and explain what they are examples of, and why they are important.

A similar procedure is followed in a case-method Business course. After you have completed the specific exercise called for in your weekly assignment, and after the prof has discussed the case, go back to the original case discussion and mark it up. Note the information that is of critical importance, recording any decision rules about the use of specific accounting or other procedures. Make sure you know how and when to perform the procedures required. Look at other cases where there might be similarities and try to identify what the similarities and differences are. Further, try to familiarize yourself with other illustrations of the principles discussed. Attempt to read as widely as you can in magazines like *Fortune*, *Business Week*, the *Financial Post*, and others, where you can see more examples of businesses facing decisions and how they respond to these problems.

Nursing and other clinical courses could involve a slightly different approach. The nurses I have talked to had problems integrating information from several different courses in order to prepare for comprehensive licencing exams.

Typically, the students would have taken some theoretical-descriptive course about disease processes, as well as having had a lot of practical experience on hospital wards and in other settings, and, in addition, would have participated in ongoing seminars about such issues in Nursing as "Nursing the Dying Patient", "Helping People Deal with Disability", "Stages in Family Development", and so on. The problem is tying all these bits and pieces together.

In a situation like this, you prepare a global map for the information that can be mapped. For example, for each disease and group of diseases that you have learned about, you prepare a summary with headings like

1. Name of the disease or disorder.
2. Etiology—the causes and origins of the disease.
3. Typical course of the untreated illness; stages in the disease process.
4. Types of medical and other intervention appropriate at various phases (emphasizing the role of the nurse-practitioner)—details concerning specific procedures, likely effects of treatments, usual or common side-effects.
5. Psychological or social problems associated with the disorder.
6. Relationships of this disease with other disorders.
7. Epidemiological or public-health issues related to the disease—preventive measures available, limits to prevention and treatment.
8. Critical issues in the treatment of this disorder (medical-ethical problems, legal issues, theoretical issues).
9. And so on.

This global map enables you to integrate material from descriptive courses as well as from "nursing issues"-type seminars. Now, you use the case material (your experience on the wards and elsewhere) to "flesh out" the bare-bones description outlined on the map. Here is where your study group could help. If you have had experience with a patient with a specific circulatory disorder, you would be able to contribute to the group all the information you have about that real person and help your buddies understand what the disorder is really like. Somebody else, who had nursed a patient suffering from a terminal illness, could help you all to understand the many personal and professional issues that confront both the patient and the nurse in this situation. In other words, you use the case material to get your knowledge out of the abstract and into the real world.

In a case-method Law course, Contract Law, for instance, you would proceed in a similar way. Begin early to prepare a global map to deal with all theoretical-historical information about the development of contract law, including things like the formulation of contracts, offer and acceptance, considerations and formalities, mistakes, representation and unconscionability, termination and frustration of contracts, and so on. Linked to the material on this map would be case summaries which would describe and detail cases which are important from a historical and doctrinal point of view.

Try to locate and read each case before it comes up in class. Summarize the facts in the case—who did what to whom under what circumstances—and record the judgment of the courts in the matter. Try to identify the legal principles involved in this judgment. Then watch what your prof does with each case, and annotate your case summary with any new comments. This is another situation where a study group can be invaluable, since it enables you to divide up the dog-work of locating the cases and preparing the summaries. And, of course, preparation for the exam involves, as always, direct practice in the kinds of behavior you are going to have to demonstrate.

This sounds like a lot of work, right? You bet it is. But it is the only effective way to prepare for tests in these subjects. However, there are two ways in which you can lighten your burden. First of all, you can share responsibilities with the members of your study group. And secondly, you can deliberately give varying amounts of attention to particular parts of the course. For more on this, read on.

Dealing with Incredible Numbers of Cases

In a typical Lit. course you might have a dozen or more novels to read, as well as a thick anthology of peotry containing several hundred poems. In a Nursing program you are going to learn about hundreds and hundreds of diseases and disorders. In a Law course there may be myriads of cases to examine, stretching back centuries in time and taken from several different jurisdictions. All in all, it is a situation in which many students buckle and break under the sheer mass of material.

Let me tell you a little secret that most successful students learn after a couple of years—if they survive. The secret is you don't have to learn everything in order to do well.

I got my B.A. in English and Philosophy, both subjects that typically entail reading enormous amounts of material. Let me assure you that nobody I knew (including students who were at the top of the class) ever read everything that was on their reading lists. And yet we all managed to do moderately or even very well.

In Literature courses, you inevitably find a couple of books you just can't stand. Books that bore you to tears, or books whose authors' political or personal philosophy sends you into an absolute frenzy of rage and disgust. Try as you may, there is just no way you can get through these books. Surprise! It is quite okay to forget about them.

Apart from these one or two dreadful books, there will be a larger number of works that have merely passing interest for you. You can get through them all right, but they don't exactly appeal. These books deserve a cursory acquaintanceship: you should know a little bit about the author and about what he tries to do in the novel, you should have a rough outline of the plot, and you should have pursued the prof's comments on the book as far as annotating the text with his comments.

Then there will be the books that really excite you, the books you will want to know and know well. You'll learn a great deal about the author and about his other work; you'll go back to the books several times to search out new and deeper levels of meaning and significance. You'll know these books inside out.

You can do this deliberately, calmly, and coolly, or you can do it illogically and in the grip of emotions that you can't even identify. But you will do it. I suggest you do it deliberately.

In other words,

> 2.11 In case-method courses, *assign a priority ranking* of 1, 2, or 3 to all the cases on your reading list, *determining the amount of effort you will devote to studying and reviewing each case*.

About 75 percent of the cases should get Priority 1 ranking. These cases will get extensive and detailed analysis and investigation. A further 20 percent will get Priority 2 treatment—a moderately thorough evaluation. And as for the remaining 5 percent—you should know they exist and, in a very broad way, you should know what they are about. Period.

How can you get away with this? Well, in the first place there is no way that you can avoid doing something like this in any case—you won't be able to learn much about the just awful cases, no matter how hard or how long you try. Trying to give Priority 1 treatment to these cases is just going to drive you buggy and rob you of valuable time that you should be investing elsewhere. In the second place, the fact that you have divided your efforts in this way won't hurt you on tests, because there is always an explicit or implicit choice in what questions you answer on the test.

In Literature courses, the choices are usually explicit. The instructions say things like "Do essays on four of the following topics", or "With respect to two of the authors you have studied this year…".

In other courses, the choice may be only implied, but it is there. In the first place, there is no way that the professor can possibly examine you with respect to every case that has been considered—time limitations and other realities pretty well determine that he can only sample your understanding and knowledge. And in any case, no matter what, each student is going to have his own area of weakness. Faced with any exam, you will inevitably do better in some questions than in others. All I am saying is that you should make this a matter where you decide what gets emphasized and what gets downplayed, rather than simply letting it happen.

Of course, the wise student will have done a good job of determining which cases should get Priority 1 ranking. If your professor has a pet theory, or if a particular case has a great deal of historical or theoretical importance, you'd ignore it at your peril. So it isn't just a matter of your personal preference—but don't ignore your personal choices.

Some of my professional colleagues are going to be mightily upset about this proposal. There is nothing, they would say, that gets onto their reading lists that is not of vital and lasting significance. They know, really, in their heart of hearts, that this is rubbish. Teachers know that even they—after years of study and extensive exploration—still have vast gaps in their understanding and knowledge that are the result of deliberate choices they made as undergraduates. They know that really there is no way that they can examine all their students in detail on everything—nor do they even want to try.

So what I am suggesting is that you should do deliberately, consciously, and coolly what you are going to do anyway, which is to make choices about how well you are going to learn about the various cases you study, and to make choices about how much time and effort you are willing to invest in each case. That's all.

Reviewing in Case-Method Courses (including English Lit.)

2   **Review Step by Step**

2.11   In case-method courses *assign a priority ranking* of 1, 2, or 3 to all the cases on your reading list, *determining the amount of effort you will devote to studying and reviewing each case*. (p. 34)

3   **Practice the Skills You Will Have To Demonstrate on the Exam**

3.9   *In case-study courses, read the cases at least once before the lecture*. (p. 32)

3.10   *In case-study courses, develop a checklist of headings that the instructor uses to analyze and evaluate the cases*. Add to this list from secondary sources. Check your understanding of these terms. (*p. 32*)

3.11   *After the lecture* on a case, *go back and complete the case description and analysis*. Mark your text, locating important examples, and explain what they are examples of, and why they are important. (*p. 32*).

Chapter 6

Preparing for standardized exams

Every year in North America millions of students take standardized exams—tests like the Scholastic Aptitute Test, the College Entrance Examination Board achievement tests, the Graduate Record Exam, the Law School Admission Test, the Test of English as a Foreign Language, and so on.

Your performance as a student on standardized tests can make an incredible difference to your later fortunes.

Whether you get into college in the first place, whether you win acceptance at a first-rate or a second-rate school, whether you will be allowed to practice the occupation of your choice—all can depend on your ability to make a good showing on standardized tests.

Not surprisingly, a whole secondary industry has sprung up around the testing establishment itself, offering the test-wary student assistance in the form of manuals and coaching clinics. Some of these resources may actually be helpful.

But the wise student will be cautious about parting with his hard-earned cash to these coaching establishments, unless he is utterly incapable of completing his own personal preparation and review for the test.

Planning Your Personal Review

Lots of people will give you the idea that you can't really prepare for standardized tests. This is absolutely false.

Of course, not everything that you might do to prepare for the test would be productive. It all depends on how you go about staging your review.

As always, the first thing to do is to try to establish, as early as possible, what kinds of skills and behaviors you will be expected to demonstrate on the test. This will be followed by a program of study that is addressed to helping you improve your abilities. The preparation may take a few minutes—or a few months—depending on your own personal assessment of where you stand.

> 3.12 *Long before you have to take a standardized test, try to find out as much as you can about the test*—about the exam format and about the content of the test.

The agency that administers the test will usually provide you with sample questions and a description of the test—but sometimes not until you have actually registered for the test. This may be a little late. Since it is a good idea to start your preparation early, you may want to rummage through a college library to see what information you can discover about the test, and you may want to buy one of the commercially available manuals about the specific test you are going to take. You have two purposes in using these manuals:

1. to familiarize yourself with the examination format and with the types of questions asked, so that you do not have to spend excessive time during the test struggling to understand a complicated procedure;
2. to diagnose where you need to review.

Simply drilling yourself by answering sample question after sample question is going to be largely a waste of time. You want to quickly identify your areas of weakness and then do something to bring your skills up to standard. Having identified a problem area, there is no point going on to answer more questions in that area until you have learned something that'll help you answer better.

What this something is that you have to do will depend on your assessment.

One of my colleagues who took the GRE-Psychology Test (Graduate Record Exam-Psychology Test) claims that he got the scores he did simply because he had the sense to review his introductory psychology course as if he were preparing for a final exam in this subject. He regrets that he didn't review high-school algebra and geometry, because his relatively low score on this section of the test was strictly a result of his not having used this material for a few years. I know of another student who raised her mark on the Miller Analogies Test by close to one hundred points by learning how to reduce tension while taking the test, and by getting some advice about how to attack multiple-choice exams. Another student, who passed his Graduate Management Admission Test with flying colors, told me that he did well only because of the intensive preparation he completed with his study group over the year before the test.

So you see, the amount of time and effort can vary a great deal—from a few hours of picking up a couple of ideas to a year's intensive effort. The kind of preparation you do depends on your assessment of the kind of deficiencies you have. But don't ignore your weaknesses, hoping to get by on your strengths—that is a chancy proposition.

In spite of all the foregoing, there are two areas that all students should systematically review, no matter how smart they are (or think they are): English usage and grammar, and Basic Arithmetic and Mathematics.

Neglect the Basics at Your Peril

Practically every test in print assesses—or attempts to assess—students' competencies in two areas. Even if you've consistently earned good grades in these areas—and sometimes *especially* if you have earned good grades—you need to review Basic English and Math to bring yourself up to snuff.

> 3.13   In preparation for any standardized test, *review Basic English and Basic Math*, even if you feel confident about these areas.

Get yourself a grammar book. (If you're broke, visit the public library.) Systematically go through the text, doing all the exercises and noting and correcting your errors. Learn how to avoid common mistakes in expression and usage. Spend extra time reviewing, and practicing topics which give you difficulty.

Find out what words you misspell and stop doing it. Make a deliberate and sustained effort to learn the meanings and spellings of more words. You can do this in several ways: focus on learning the correct pronunciation of words that are troublesome for you; build your vocabulary by using flash cards to record and study the new words you encounter every day; learn the common Greek and Latin roots for English words and practice discovering them in the words you use; make a habit of using the dictionary to learn more about words; try the vocabulary exercises in the *Reader's Digest* on a regular basis; and so on. Any efforts you make in this direction will pay off handsomely when it comes time to take a standardized test—and in your further studies.

You also need to review Basic Mathematics and Arithmetic. Among the topics you will need to review here are:

—computation with mixed fractions, negative numbers, decimals, percentages;

—interest, compound interest, rates, and discounts;

—roots and exponents;

—computation in algebra, factoring polynomials, ratios and proportions;

—combinations and permutations;

—properties of the straight line, parallel lines, and planes;

—properties of the triangle, circle, rectangle, square, and other polygons;

—methods of reading and using graphs and charts.

Do not assume that you know how to do problems under these headings. Check your understanding by going over your high-school math texts, working a few problems at the end of each chapter and brushing up on the chapters where you have difficulties.

Don't panic about this. You don't have to do high school over. A few problems in each chapter is all you have to do in order to diagnose your weaknesses. But do start early, do it step by step, etc., etc., etc.

If you don't, you'll hate yourself after you take the test.

Preparing for Standardized Tests

3   Practice the Skills You Will Have To Demonstrate on the Exam

3.12   *Long before you have to take a standardized test, try to find out as much as you can about the test* — about the exam format and about the content of the test. (*p. 36*)

3.13   In preparation for any standardized test, *review Basic English and Basic Math*, even if you feel confident about these areas. (*p. 37*).

Taking tests

Chapter 7

The general test-taking strategies

Just as there are common strategies that can be used in preparing for any test, so there are common approaches that should be followed when taking each and every test. These strategies apply to standardized as well as to instructor-made tests, with minor variations. They apply to multiple-choice, problem, short-answer, and essay tests, to oral exams, to take-home tests, to whatever.

And once again it is surprising how common-sensical these ideas are, and how often students let go of these commonsense notions under pressure.

The First Five Minutes

The first five minutes of any test is where most students make it or break it. Students who have their wits about them use this time wisely and appropriately and do specific things that are going to pay off during the whole test. Those who are rattled and disorganized spend the first five minutes making blunders from which they may never recover.

The most important thing to do in the initial period of the exam is to

6   Make Sure You Understand the General Instructions

A lot of students skip over the directions, thinking that they will save time by starting to answer questions immediately. Wrong, wrong, wrong! Half an hour later they discover that they've answered Part A *and* Part B when the instructions clearly said to do Part A *or* Part B. Or they hand in their test, only to find out that they didn't show their rough work, when the examiner clearly said (to those who were listening)

that he wanted to see the calculations and that partial credit would be given for this.

> 6.1   *Underline key words in the instructions* to make sure you focus on and understand these important directions.

Listen carefully to verbal instructions. Read carefully, word by word, any general instructions printed at the top of the exam. How much time do you have for the test? Is there any choice in the questions you answer? How are you to record your answers?

For standardized tests such as the Scholastic Aptitude Test (SAT) you should receive these instructions in the mail before the test. You will have read them carefully. The instructions will be repeated at the beginning of the test. Again, *listen* carefully to make sure you understand.

This is absolutely the only way to ensure that you don't read "and" where it says "or", and that you notice that you are to "Do *ten* of the following fifteen questions."

> 6.2   *If you do not understand the general instructions*, if you have any questions at all about how to proceed, *ask for clarification* before you start the exam.

In standardized tests (the SAT, the CEEB, and so on) there is a period of time before the test begins when the supervisor of the test is to give instructions and to respond to questions asked by the students. Once the test starts, the supervisor *cannot* give any further information about the test. You absolutely have to use the pre-test period to full advantage, so that you don't have to waste valuable time rereading the written instructions.

In other tests, feel quite free to ask for clarification and assistance at any time if you are confused about any aspect of the general instructions or the specific questions. Of course, the sooner you do this the better, but again feel free to ask at any time.

It's quite legitimate to ask for clarification of a term with which you are not familiar; it's fair ball to ask for an explanation of an instruction you do not comprehend; and it's legitimate to ask which of two alternative interpretations of an ambiguous question the instructor wants you to employ. Occasionally, in spite of careful proofreading by those who prepare the test, clerical errors will occur. If you think this has happened, immediately ask for clarification. You will do everybody in the class a favor by checking this out.

The very worst that can happen when you ask for clarification is that the instructor may refuse to answer your question. Usually, though, you will receive the explanation you need.

After you have listened to and read the instructions and you are ready to start on the test, the next thing you do is

7 Survey the Test Before You Start

On standardized tests this is not critical. Take only a few *seconds* to glance through the test to quickly assess the questions. Some of the questions you see will go onto your mental back burner, and you will find that you are more prepared to answer when you get to them. Also, if you get stuck on a question, knowing that there's a question later in the test that you can answer can be useful. But don't take more than a few seconds.

On instructor-made tests it is a different matter. Take a couple of *minutes* to look over the test. Note how many questions there are, and how many *pages* there are (I know of a student who dropped from an A to a B in a course because she missed the last page of questions on the final exam). Are there options or choices in each section of the test? How many points are assigned to each question? to each section? What questions look easier?

If a test is composed of short-answer questions (fill in the blank, multiple-choice, etc.) as well as problems or essay-type questions, take a minute to quickly read over the long questions, but then *do* the short-answer questions first.

The more difficult questions will be simmering away at the back of your mind and you will find that you will almost inevitably come up with ideas to use on these questions.

8 If You Think of Something, Write It Down

At the start of a test, this may mean that you may want to record one or two ideas from your minor cram, so that you don't have to try to remember during the test. While you survey the test you may come up with a couple of ideas about the questions. Write them down! One or two words is all you need to help you remember.

It's better to take the time to do this than to struggle to keep these ideas in mind while you answer the rest of the questions and then lose the ideas. Similarly, later in the test you may think of an answer to a previous question while you're working on something else. When this happens, immediately go back to answer the question if it's a short-answer question. For an essay, jot down a brief note that will help you resurrect the idea later on. If you don't do this, you will have forgotten a lot of these brilliant little flashes by the time you go back to work on the relevant question.

Planning Your Time During the Test

The first few minutes of the test are spent, as I've said, taking in the general instructions, surveying the test, and recording any immediate ideas that you have. The next thing that you should do is

9 Budget Your Time on the Test. Plan How You Are Going To Attack the Test.

On standardized tests this simply means reminding yourself of how many questions you have to answer in the allotted time and making a note of where you should be when a quarter, half, and three-quarters of the time is gone. Always allow some time to review the test before handing it in (see Strategy 14). Keep track of your time and don't spend more time on any one question than it is worth.

On other tests, you should allot time to each

section of the test, based on how many points out of the total is assigned to the section. Again, allow time for review and keep to your schedule. If a question is proving to be more difficult than you originally expected, leave space in your answer booklet and go on to the other parts of the test. If you finish in time, you may be able to come back to complete the answer. But again, don't spend more time on a question than it is worth in terms of marks.

Write down on the test booklet or on a sheet of paper how many minutes you are going to spend on each section and what the time should be when you finish the section. Keep track of the time, and mark off your time budget as you finish each section.

The other thing that you want to do when you are budgeting your time is to make decisions about which questions to answer first.

10 Do the Easier Questions First. Buy Time To Think About More Difficult Questions.

On short-answer or objective tests, don't spend a lot of time hunting through to find the easier questions. Start with the first question and attempt to answer it. If you run into difficulty or can't answer it, go on to the next question. Try that one. If you can answer it, great; if not, on to the next. Make a serious attempt at each question, but don't keep at it if you run into problems.

On tests that require longer answers, it *is* worth your while to take some time to find the question that you know most about. Only after you have answered this question do you go on to the more difficult questions. In the meantime, of course, you will be remembering ideas to use on questions you haven't yet tackled.

Memory works a lot of the time by association. You read something that reminds you of something else, that helps you remember something else, that reminds you of something else, that helps you answer the question you couldn't answer a few minutes ago. Take advantage of these memory chains by allowing them to work while you accumulate points on questions that are easier for you.

Leaving a question alone doesn't mean that you are dumb or that you're doomed on the

exam. It simply means that you need some time to think about the question.

Working Through the Test

Any teacher will tell you that the mistake that most people make on tests is that they don't answer the questions that are asked. They answer another question, and usually a more difficult one. Sometimes this is because of poor preparation for the test, but often it's because the student hasn't read the questions carefully enough.

What can I say? If they ask you to turn a cartwheel, and you show them a handstand, it may be a lovely handstand, but you are not going to get any points.

11 Read Questions Carefully, Underlining Key Terms. Decide What You Are Expected To Do.

Read questions word by word with a pencil in your hand. Underline key terms, and underline the instruction that tells you what you are supposed to do. Table 7.1 lists the commonest key terms. It would be worth your while to go through this list carefully to understand how each term is different from related terms.

Underlining is the only way that you can stop yourself from making occasional—or not so occasional—errors in reading exam questions. This is so important that, even when the instructions are "Do not write in the exam booklet", I tell my students to write in the booklet anyway. Instead of underlining, though (which will get you into trouble with the exam supervisor), just make a very light jot that could be taken for a stray pencil mark. But do it! Do indicate the key terms in each question.

Making Mistakes

Let's face it. No matter how well prepared you are or how well you know your subject, it is almost inevitable that you are going to make mistakes on a test. On an essay test you will write sentences that are awkward or that have mistakes in construction, spelling, or grammar. You'll write paragraphs that are disjointed. There'll be times when you can't think of the

KEY TERMS OF QUANTITY, DURATION, OR DEGREE[1]

All, Always Only Without exception	Necessarily Necessary Never No, None	— any exception makes these statements false
Rarely Seldom, Infrequent(ly) Occasional(ly) Some, Sometimes Few Several About, Around	Almost always Usual(ly), Often, Frequent(ly) Probably Many Most Approximate(ly)	— imply a judgment of frequency or probability

DESCRIPTIVE AND ANALYSIS QUESTIONS

Describe, Review	— give account of the attributes of the subject under discussion (inherent characteristics, qualities)
Discuss	— tell all you know about the subject that is relevant to the questions under consideration
State	— briefly "describe" with minimal elaboration
Analyze	— separate the subject into parts and examine the elements of which it is composed
Enumerate, List, Tabulate	— briefly present the sequence of elements constituting the whole
Develop	— from a given starting-point, evolve a logical pattern leading to a valid conclusion
Trace	— in narrative form, describe the progress, development, or historical events related to a specific topic from some point of origin to a stated conclusion
Outline, Summarize	— give the theme and main points of the subject in concise form
Diagram, Sketch	— outline the principal distinguishing features of an object or process using a clearly labelled diagram

EXPLANATION AND PROOF QUESTIONS

Explain, Interpret	— state the subject in simpler, more explicit terms
Define, Formulate	— classify the subject: specify its unique qualities and characteristics
Prove, Justify, Show that	— demonstrate validity by test, argument, or evidence
Demonstrate	— explain or prove by use of significant examples
Illustrate	— explain fully by means of diagrams, charts, or concrete examples

COMPARISON QUESTIONS

Compare	— investigate and state the likeness or similarities of two or more subjects
Contrast	— look for noticeable differences
Relate	— establish the connection between one or more things

PERSONAL JUDGMENT QUESTIONS

Criticize, Evaluate	— judge or evaluate the subject for its truth, beauty, worth, or significance; and justify your evaluation. "Criticize" doesn't necessarily mean a hostile attack—it is more a matter of comment on literal or implied meaning.
Interpret	— explain and evaluate in terms of your own knowledge
Justify	— ordinarily this implies that you justify a statement on the author's terms. When asked to justify your own statements, defend your position in detail and be convincing.

PROBLEM/SOLUTION QUESTIONS

Find Solve Calculate Determine Derive What is...?	— using the data provided (some of which may be irrelevant) apply mathematical procedures and the principles of formal logical analysis to find a specific quantity in specific units

[1] Adapted from Jason Millman and Walter Pauk, *How To Take Tests*, McGraw-Hill, New York, 1969.

TABLE 7.1 *Key Exam Terms*

right word, or when you misspell common words or skip them in your haste. Sometimes your handwriting may become scrawly and illegible.

In problem tests, you'll make mistakes in transposing data from the problem to your solution, or in simple computation. Sometimes your mistakes will be in "false starts"—starting a solution with one method or approach and realizing part way through that you should be using another approach.

Sometimes the mistakes will involve clerical inaccuracy—circling "c" when you meant to circle "b", filling in the wrong blank on your computer sheet, and so on.

And all these errors can happen in spite of how smart you are and how careful you are in first answering the questions on the test. Time pressure leads to many of them. We all tend to make more mistakes when we are forced to work at top speed.

Obviously, you want to take care that you are not going to make obvious blunders in reading both the general instructions and specific questions, using procedures outlined above. You want to make sure that you are indicating your answers in exactly the way required (e.g., when using a computer answer sheet, that you correctly locate the blanks you need to fill in for each question). But even if you do all of this, you will still have some mistakes to deal with.

Well, what can you do about this?

Two things. First of all, you will have attempted to eliminate possible sources of error by following Tactic 3.5 (p. 18). Second, you should follow a simple and easy-to-do technique on every test or quiz that you take. What you do is to focus, not on avoiding errors, but on answering your test questions in such a way that it is easier for you to spot and correct errors after you have made them.

12   Attack Each Question Systematically

When you review how students respond to tests it becomes obvious that a lot of them attack tests pretty haphazardly. And their test results show it. Some questions they will answer fully and in a well-organized fashion. Some of them they will answer in a pretty hit-and-miss way, with answers that leave a lot to be desired in terms of organization, completeness, and emphasis. Sometimes they will turn in answers that show evidence that they have studied the materials well, that they have assimilated them, and that they can use the information to mount a coherent discussion of the topic. Other answers look as if the student simply hasn't come to grips with the material—even though, when you talk to the student afterwards, he or she demonstrates a good grasp of the material.

When you talk to such students, it becomes clear that they really do proceed in a haphazard way. Sometimes they feel really well organized, and other times they know that they're being completely disorganized about their way of answering.

Well, a haphazard method of attacking questions will cost you points. On a multiple-choice test, if you don't read all the alternatives and consider each one carefully, you are simply going to make the wrong choice a lot of the time. On an essay test, if you don't stop to collect your ideas before you start writing your answer you will miss out some points and/or write an answer that is poorly organized. On problem tests, unless you take time to list the data you are given, formulate a list of unknowns you need to find, diagram the problem if you can, and so on, you are going to waste a lot of time going off in the wrong direction and forgetting valuable pieces of data.

The remaining chapters in this section deal with the strategies and tactics that work for most students in attacking various types of tests. If you have trouble with a particular kind of question, I would encourage you to read the appropriate chapter carefully and try to diagnose where you are making your mistakes. Then try the suggestions offered. Don't wait until the important final to make a change, though, or you will simply be too anxious about the result. Try the suggestions on quizzes and less important tests so that you can remain objective enough about the results to give the suggestions a fair trial.

And even if you usually don't have trouble with a particular form of question, it would still be worth your while to take a look at every chapter. The chapter may help you become more conscious of how you approach the question type so that you can more easily employ the strategies, without having to rediscover them on every test. And you may learn a few things that iron out the wrinkles and help you answer more efficiently.

13 Draft Your Answers So You Can More Easily Find and Correct Mistakes

On a math test, what you do is to leave lots of space to make corrections. Write your solution on the right-hand side of the page. Leave a line between steps. Leave space after you think you have finished your solution and before you go on to the next problem. If calculations give you problems, you want to draft these so that they are easy to correct, so write your calculations neatly and in sequence on scrap paper or on the left-hand page of your exam booklet.

On an essay test the approach to this is basically the same. It involves writing on every second line, leaving a line between paragraphs, and making sure there is additional space at the end of your answer. If you think of additional information, you now have space to include it.

All of this implies that you are going to do something with your test paper after you have answered the questions and before you hand it in. Indeed you are.

14 Review and Correct Your Exam Before Handing It In

You do this for two reasons. First of all you want to systematically check for errors. Since you have left space to make corrections, this will be easier. Secondly, looking over the whole test once again may start off memory chains that help you to answer questions you missed or to improve your answers to other questions.

There's one other thing that you should do, if at all possible, before you leave the test.

15 Write Something Down for Every Question

There are two reasons for doing this. First of all, you may know more than you think you know. Even if you are not confident about your answer,

you may earn partial or even whole credit by putting down an answer you're not sure about. And second, while you are writing you may jog your memory so that you can actually put down something of value. In any case, if you have *something* down you have a chance to earn credit. If you write nothing you have a big fat zero. I'm not saying that you should pad or inflate your answers—the common, impolite expression for this is "b.s."—but put something down, even if you are not confident about the correctness of your answer.

When Do You Get To Go Home?

Not until they throw you out.

Don't leave. Don't go away. Don't turn in your test paper until they make you do it.

If you do leave early, what will almost inevitably happen is that you will think of something you could have said on the test as you wander your dejected way home. It happens all the time; you see this fellow hand in his test while everybody else is still writing, he walks out the door, and seconds later you hear this anguished "Oh no!" echoing from the hallway. The student has just thought of the correct answer to a question he missed. Too bad he's not in a position to use this information.

So...

16 Use All Your Time

Even if you are absolutely certain that you are doomed, that there is simply no way that you can extract a single additional fact from your tortured and fevered brain, do not leave. Stay. Count ceiling tiles. Think about your summer vacation. Do anything. But don't leave. You may just think of something useful.

(The only exception to this rule is, of course, if you become physically sick during a test. If you've been wise, this won't happen very often. But if it does, hand in your test paper and let the supervisor know that you are ill. Practically every school allows for this contingency and has a policy of letting sick students take their tests at another time. So, if you feel yourself getting ill, leave before you throw up. Please. Hanging on until they have to carry you out on a stretcher serves no useful purpose.)

Good Grief!

It suddenly occurs to me that I have so far forgotten to remind you of a very important thing.

> 6.4 Make sure you *write your name clearly on the answer sheet*.

How could I forget? It seems like such an obvious thing to do, after all, but it is fair to say that in any batch of exams ever received by any professor there will be at least one on which the name has been omitted or is written in a script that you'd expect a physician to employ on a prescription. Obviously they can't give you a grade if they don't know who you are.

Okay. Those are the general test-taking strategies that apply to each and every test situation. Now let's go on to look at tactics for handling specific kinds of tests.

The General Test-Taking Strategies

6   Make Sure You Understand the General Instructions (*p. 40*)

   6.1 *Underline key words in the instructions* to make sure you focus on and understand these important directions. (*p. 40*)

   6.2 *If you do not understand the general instructions*, if you have any questions at all about how to proceed, *ask for clarification* before you start the exam. (*p. 40*)

   6.4 Make sure you *write your name clearly on the answer sheet*. (*p. 46*)

7   Survey the Test Before You Start (*p. 41*)

8   If You Think of Something, Write it Down (*p. 41*)

9   Budget Your Time on the Test. Plan How You Are Going To Attack the Test. (*p. 41*)

10   Do the Easier Questions First. Buy Time To Think About More Difficult Questions. (*p. 42*)

11   Read Questions Carefully, Underlining Key Terms. Decide What You Are Expected To Do. (*p. 42*)

12   Attack Each Question Systematically (*p. 44*)

13   Draft Your Answers So You Can More Easily Find and Correct Mistakes (*p. 45*)

14   Review and Correct Your Exam Before Handing It In (*p. 45*)

15   Write Something Down for Every Question (*p. 45*)

16   Use All Your Time (*p. 45*)

Chapter 8

Taking objective tests

Objective tests include true-false, sentence-completion, multiple-choice, and matching questions, as well as combined forms. Unlike essay tests, and to a certain extent problem tests, questions on objective tests are supposed to have only one correct answer. This feature eliminates, it is said, a great deal of the subjective bias which can substantially influence grading in non-objective tests.

This feature of objective tests makes them very easy to score—which appeals to instructors who have to grade these things before they get to go away for summer holidays. In addition, in situations where a great many candidates are taking the test in a number of different settings—as in the standardized college-entrance tests—an objective-test format is the only economical way to evaluate candidates' performances.

Many students and educators object to objective tests on a variety of grounds. For some, the mechanistic, repetitive, and seemingly chance elements in objective tests give offense, particularly in subjects such as philosophy, literature, and history, where intelligent discourse is the hallmark of the scholar. Indeed, there is no objective test which can accurately measure a student's ability to *write* a thoughtful, balanced, and elegant sentence, though there are many that can determine whether or not you can *edit* —i.e., detect errors in others' prose.

Novice test-makers sometimes use objective-test formats unwisely to sample students' memory for little snippets of trivial and inconsequential data, disconnected bits of information drawn more or less at random from the course material. This unfortunate tendency leads many students to adopt a "memorize everything" approach to preparing for objective tests. As has been shown

in previous chapters, this is almost always a fatal mistake. When you attempt to memorize excessive amounts of trivia, without aiming for a wide-ranging comprehension of the whole body of knowledge under examination, you will find yourself unable to respond appropriately and easily to questions that require the use of skills you have not practiced.

In any case, a student who lucks out through school in spite of poor preparation will undoubtedly reach a point when he is called upon to respond to a test prepared by a sophisticated test-maker. Memorizing everything will then almost inevitably be shown to be a grievous error.

So, objective tests present you with a unique set of challenges. Let's look at some principles and procedures that make a positive difference in how you can do on these tests. Most of the discussion will center on multiple-choice questions, but I'm sure you'll find it easy to adapt these ideas to other objective-test formats.

A Rational Approach

Some students go into panic as soon as they hear that they are going to have to take an objective test. And then, because they don't know how to prepare for such a test, they do a poor job of getting ready. Of course, when the test hits the desk in front of them, they are completely rattled and attack the test in a haphazard way, getting completely boggled by the questions. This irrational behavior is the result of not knowing how to predict the kinds of skills and behaviors that the test will call for.

Other students fall prey to another form of

irrational thinking during the test. They look for, and attempt to detect, patterns in their answers that don't really mean anything. On a true-false test you might get a string of answers that look like T, T, F, T, T, F, T, T, _, or a series of answers like a, b, c, a, b, c, _ on a multiple-choice test. A lot of students are going to be mightily tempted to continue the pattern when they answer the next question. What you should do, of course, is to ignore the pattern completely. The answer may indeed follow the pattern established in the previous questions—but there is absolutely no guarantee that it will. Such patterns, if they occur, are either completely accidental or else a deliberate trick by your instructor in an attempt to lead you astray.

So the key is,

> 12.1 *Avoid superstitious or irrational behavior when taking objective tests*. Attack each question separately and logically.

How To Proceed

The first steps in attacking a multiple-choice test —Strategies 6-9—have been adequately covered in Chapter 7. Only one qualifier needs to be added:

> 6.3 *If you are required to answer on a computerized answer form, make sure you know how to do so*. Look at the examples if there are any. Make sure that you know which way the questions are numbered.

This only takes a second but it can save a lot of agony. You're answering merrily along and then you discover that the answer sheet runs like this:

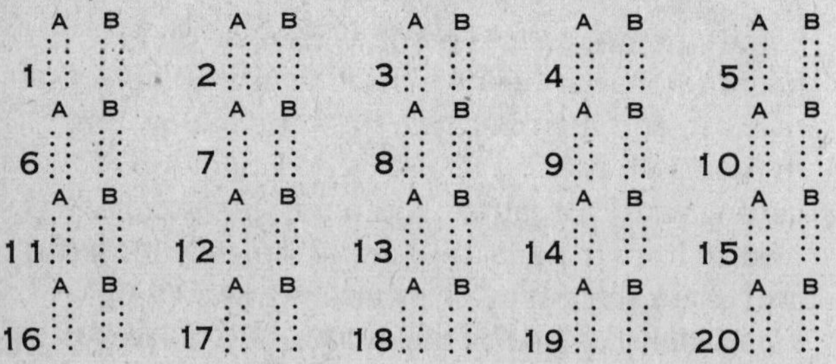

FIGURE 8.1

and not like this:

FIGURE 8.2

This means that you have to attempt to transfer your answers to the correct space, erasing the incorrect answers as you go and keeping track of everything. This can be just an incredible hassle if you've answered a lot of questions. Perhaps you may be able to get a new answer sheet, but often this is not possible. All in all, it's much better not to make the mistake in the first place.

After the first four strategies, which have to do with getting ready to tackle the test, you are now ready to begin responding to the questions.

Strategy 5, you will remember, is, "Do the Easier Questions First, Buy Time To Think About More Difficult Questions."

Well, it's pretty obvious that on a multiple-choice exam, where you may have 50 to 100 questions to answer—or even more—you are *not* going to read through every question before making a decision about where to start. You may spot a question that you can answer off the top of your head when you are surveying the test, but otherwise,

> 10.1 *On an objective test, tackle the questions in the order in which they are given to you*. If you cannot answer a question immediately, leave it and go on to the next question. Be sure to indicate—by leaving a blank on the answer sheet or writing a "?" beside the question—which questions you have not finished.

This will help you find the unanswered questions more easily when you come to review your test, and will help to keep you organized. Again, there is no dishonor in leaving a question alone for a little while so that you can go and answer some easier ones.

As always, you will read each question carefully, underlining key phrases and instructions. Now,

> 12.2 *On a multiple-choice question, try to determine what the correct answer will be before you look at the options.* Then look for this option in the list of alternatives provided.

This is not always possible, depending on the format of the particular question. But when it is possible, do it. It can save you from waffling around and getting confused by the variety of options presented.

But *then*

> 12.3 *Make sure you read each option* in a multiple-choice question *and attempt to eliminate it.*

This is critical. Even if you are absolutely sure that you have selected the correct response, read and check every single alternative. You know how multiple-choice questions are assembled, don't you? Usually there will be one or two options in each question that are just completely out to lunch; but then there will be several options that are quite similar. You have to make sure that you haven't been sucked in to leaping at the first attractive alternative. The only way to do this is to systematically read and attempt to eliminate each alternative in turn—after you have made your first, best guess.

And when I say eliminate, I mean *eliminate*. Do it physically. Cross it off. Put a big black X through the option. Don't try to keep track in your head or you'll get confused. On standardized tests they'll tell you not to make marks in the question booklet. But do it anyway. Be discreet. Make a slight dot or light mark that says to you "I have eliminated this option" but won't mean anything to anybody else. You can erase these marks if you want before handing in the test. But mark on your exam booklet.

At this point, if you do not feel comfortable in selecting an answer from the list of alternatives, follow Tactic 5:1 and go on to the next question. If the answer occurs to you as you work ahead on the test, go back immediately and finish that question rather than risk losing the answer.

The Second Time Around

You've worked through the test once, having attempted every question. Now you review your test to see if a few answers haven't jiggled loose in your subconscious. And if you cannot think of any more answers, then you guess.

What? Guess?

Why sure.

> 15.1 *After you have worked through an objective test once,* and have attempted every question, *make the best guess you can* at the questions you have not yet answered.

Guidelines for Guessing

You don't want to guess blindly, though. On instructor-made tests there are several factors which you should take into consideration when making your guess. *These are guidelines only—a clever instructor will make sure to remove any clues that would help you in guessing.* But, some time, knowing these principles is going to pay off for you, so do pay attention.

> *If one option is much longer (or much shorter) than the others, it is likely to be the correct option.*

e.g. Sickle-cell anemia _____
  a) is associated with beri-beri.
  b) occurs chiefly in blacks and is associated with genetic adaptation to malaria.
  c) is a fatal disease of children.
  d) is caused by malnutrition.

Fat cells _____
  a) act as reservoirs of energy for use when adequate nourishment is not otherwise available to body cells.
  b) are found only beneath skin tissues overlying muscle mass.
  c) are not found in birds.
  d) play an extremely minor role in the maintenance of body temperature.

In the first question, if you selected alternative (b) you would be correct. In the second question you would be tempted to select either alternative (a), the longest option, or (c), the shortest. However, the "not found in birds" option is clearly wrong.

And in any case, in the second question you would be tempted correctly to eliminate alternative (c) because

Options which do not allow for exceptions are usually incorrect.

"Are not found in birds" means *never* found in birds. Not one bird with a little chubbiness concealed beneath its downy breast. All fat installed by the butcher prior to sale.

Ditto for "are found only beneath skin tissues". No fat anywhere else? Ever? No marbled meat? No fatty heart tissue? No fat deposits in veins? No fatty livers among the world's drinkers?

In most objective tests, you can have a fair amount of confidence in selecting options that include words like

sometimes/ some	probably/ likely
occasionally	almost always/ most of the time
normally/ usually	seldom/ infrequently/ not usually
often/ frequently	hardly ever/ rarely

These options are associated with the cautious, balanced, and tentative approaches that scholars prefer. Since hardly anything occurs uniformly without exceptions, and since hardly anything is true in all cases, you would avoid options that include such absolute terms as

all/ always	necessarily
never	only
no/ none/ not	without exception
must	absolutely

Extremes in general should probably be avoided.

When options range in value, reject extreme values and select one of the middle-range alternatives.

e.g. What number is next in this series? 6, 24, 12, 48, 24, 96, _____.
a) 42
b) 124
c) 48
d) 54

If you couldn't figure out the rule that governed the formation of this series after trying everything you knew, you would then consider throwing out the extreme values —(a) and (b). Now can you guess? (The correct answer is (c).)

The reason extreme values are usually rejected has to do with the thinking of novice test-makers. Such people are likely to think that an extremely high or extremely low value is going to attract too much attention, so they'll probably conceal the correct response somewhere in the middle.

(Of course, a test-wise instructor will be wary of falling for this trap and will make sure that sometimes the correct answer *is* one of the extreme values.)

The correct response will agree in gender, number, and person with the question stem, and will otherwise be grammatically consistent with it.

e.g. In *Oliver Twist*, Fagin is a _____
a) pickpocket who recruits Oliver into a gang of boys whom he instructs in his craft.
b) accountant who embezzles Oliver's estate.
c) actor who befriends Oliver and provides him with support.
d) evil member of the gentry who plots to defraud Oliver's family of their inherited lands.

The only option which is grammatically consistent with the stem "Fagin is a..." is alternative (a): pickpocket. All the other alternatives would require the article "an", as in "an accountant", "an actor", "an evil...".

To test this factor, read each of the alternatives in turn under your breath, trying them out to see how they fit with the question stem. Even if you're not testing the grammatical factor, reading the question sub-vocally will often help you sort out and understand the alternatives better. Talking to yourself is a useful strategy to develop —at least for taking tests.

On instructor-made tests, the first and last alternatives are less likely to be correct than one of the options in the middle.

Again, the reasoning here is that beginning test-makers are going to feel that the first and last alternatives stick out too much. They're going to want to "hide" the correct response in the middle of the pack. Of course, it doesn't take long for test-makers to learn that you ought to distribute the correct answers randomly among the alternatives, and the big testing agencies are going to take great pains to ensure that this happens. But if all else fails, and you can't make a choice any other way, then consider selecting an option in the middle, rather than the first or the last.

What About "All of the Above"?

For people who have trouble with multiple-choice tests, no type of question creates more consternation than something like the following:

> As the human grows and ages, the shape of the lower jaw changes. These changes are influenced by _____
> a) accommodations caused by the first and second dentitions.
> b) the development of speech.
> c) the loss of teeth in the aged.
> d) the size and situation of the dental canal.
> e) the destruction of the inferior maxillary nerve.
> f) a, c, and d.
> g) b, d, and e.
> h) all of the above.
> i) none of the above.

Okay, let's try the read-and-eliminate tactic and see what it does for us.

You read the question stem and note key words.

> As the human grows and ages, the shape of the (lower jaw) changes. These changes are (influenced by) _____

Before you look at the options, you might think something like, "Getting your first and second teeth influences the shape of your jaw, and so does losing your teeth when you're old." Now you look to see if those options are presented. They are, so you circle them—or somehow indicate that you think that they are part of the correct answer.

> (a) accommodations caused by the first and second dentitions.
> b) the development of speech.
> (c) the loss of teeth in the aged.
> d) the size and situation of the dental canal.
> e) destruction of the inferior maxillary nerve.
> f) a, c, and d.

g) b, d, and e.
h) all of the above.
i) none of the above.

You have made a guess that "dentition" means "getting your teeth" and the other option is easy to find. Now what about the remaining options? Let's read them and see if there is any reason to eliminate them.

Hm, "development of speech" influencing the shape of the jaw? That doesn't sound right. Probably it's the other way around; the changing shape of the jaw influences the development of speech. Okay, let's eliminate (b). Next, "size and situation of the dental canal", "inferior maxillary nerve"—jeez, who knows?

All right, so now your test should look like this:

> (a) accommodations caused by the first and second dentitions.
> (b) the development of speech.
> (c) the loss of teeth in the aged.
> d) the size and situation of the dental canal.
> e) the destruction of the inferior maxillary nerve.
> f) a, c, and d.
> g) b, d, and e.
> h) all of the above.
> i) none of the above.

What about "all of the above" and "none of the above"? What you do here is to eliminate the complex options that contain simple options that you've already eliminated. Like this:

> (a) accommodations caused by the first and second dentitions.
> (b) the development of speech.
> (c) the loss of teeth in the aged.
> d) the size and situation of the dental canal.
> e) the destruction of the inferior maxillary nerve.
> f) a, c, and d.
> (g) b, d, and e.
> (h) all of the above.
> (i) none of the above.

You can eliminate (g) because you've eliminated (b). You can eliminate (h), again because you've eliminated (b)—that is, "one of the above" has been eliminated so that the correct answer cannot be "all of the above". And similarly you can eliminate (i) because you are sure that (a) and (c) are real factors that influence the shape of the jaw.

Again, it helps if you talk to yourself—if you translate the question and the alternatives into speech that you understand. For example you might say something like

"Which of these factors influence the shape of the jaw? All of the above? That would mean that every single factor influences the shape of the jaw. Now, that's not true because I ruled out (b), so I'll cross that one off. None of the above? Now that would mean that none of the things listed influences the development of the shape of the jaw. And that's not true, because getting teeth and then losing them definitely does change the shape of the jaw."

Okay. You can see that the read-and-eliminate approach has helped us to get rid of almost half the options, including some troublesome compound options. Now what do you do? Presuming that you're still at a loss about the role of the "dental canal" and the "inferior maxillary nerve", you leave the question alone and go on to tackle the other questions. If you think of the answer, of course, you'll come back immediately to mark your answer.

But presuming that you aren't struck by any flashes of inspiration, we're then in a guessing situation.

You're pretty confident that both (a) and (c) are correct. It's fairly clear that what you have to do is pick (f).

In guessing at multiple-choice questions that contain compound answers ("a and b", "all of the above", etc.), select the compound answer that includes the simple options you are most sure about.

In this question we are sure about (a) and (c), so we will select the compound answer that includes these alternatives.

As the human grows and ages, the shape of the (lower jaw) changes. These changes are (influenced by) _____

(a) accommodations caused by the first and second dentitions.
(b) the development of speech.
(c) the loss of teeth in the aged.
(d) the size and situation of the dental canal.
(e) the destruction of the inferior maxillary nerve.
(f) a, c, and d.

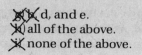

d, and e.
all of the above.
none of the above.

What About Penalties for Guessing?

A common tactic among test-makers is to inject a penalty for guessing into the marking system. On instructor-made tests this is usually a "rights-minus-wrongs" system. This means that if a student earns 75 points for correct answers but has incorrectly answered questions worth 25 points, his final score will be 75 − 25 = 50. There is no penalty for leaving a question blank. On standardized tests prepared by the big firms, the penalty for guessing is usually a deduction of ¼ to ½ point for each incorrect answer.

Well, the penalty for guessing should be taken into account by students writing tests, but don't be completely frightened off by it. The general principle is Strategy 10: Write Something Down for Every Question. Now, if you only write answers to questions when you are absolutely one-hundred-per-cent sure that you have the correct answer, you are not going to earn a lot of points that could very easily come your way.

What you need to do is to carefully gauge the possible impact of the correction-for-guessing on your final score and then proceed accordingly. For example, let's say that on a "rights-minus-wrongs" test you are fairly confident that you've obtained 80 out of a possible 100 marks, but you don't have a clue about the remaining 20 questions. Okay, if you guess incorrectly at the remaining questions, your worst possible score would be 80 − 20 = 60. And your best possible score would be 80 + 20 = 100. Is the risk worth it? What about if you guess at 10 of the remaining questions? Your worst score would be 80 − 10 = 70 and your best possible score would be 80 + 10 = 90. Is it worth it now?

On a standardized test, the risks are even less threatening and the potential gains are enormous. Let's say that on a particular test the penalty for guessing is ¼ of a mark. What this means is that you have to guess incorrectly at four questions before you lose the advantage from getting just one right. Even flipping a coin, the chances are that you will gain marks by guessing. Suppose that you answer 30 out of 100 questions carefully and you are confident that they are correct. You're in deep trouble. Guessing at the remaining 70 marks, your worst score would be $30 - \frac{1}{4}(70) = 12.5$ and your best score would be $30 + 70 = 100$. The worst that can happen is that you'll flunk with 12.5 percent instead of flunking with 30 percent. Clearly the risk is minimal and the chances for gain are great. So guess.

When in Doubt, Try To Think Like the Examiner

In instructor-made tests, it is fairly common to run into poorly worded, vague, or ambiguous questions. What do you do when you run across one?

Where you have the opportunity to appeal to the person who grades the test, you might start by asking for clarification right during the exam. If that doesn't achieve results, you might try writing a short note to the marker explaining your choice and why you made it, and then when the tests are graded you might consider appealing your mark to the instructor. If there is a genuine ambiguity, and if you can make a good case for the reasonableness of your answer, this will sometimes get you at least partial credit.

On a standardized test, like those published by big testing firms, these options aren't open to you. The person supervising your exam can't help you with ambiguous questions, and you have no way of appealing to or discussing the questions with the testing agency.

What you have to do here is to try to think like the examiner—which is sometimes an exercise in lowering your mental horizon. Practice is the key to preparing for this particular activity. Here's where it makes sense for you to spend money on the various "How To Prepare" manuals to give yourself specific practice in learning how test-makers think.

Several commentators and critics of the testing establishment have noted the way that test-makers seem to prefer concrete, obvious relationships of a tangible nature rather than creative, cognitively flexible approaches.

There is little doubt that specific testing establishments employ a systematic approach in the preparation of their questions, and that these systems can be studied to advantage in preparing for standardized tests.[1] Part of the key is to look for the obvious—to think as the man on the street. Test-makers seem to prefer concrete, obvious relationships of a tangible nature. You need to be careful to use *only* the information given to you in the question—you can be *too* clever for your own good! This means cultivating the habit of systematically employing Tactic 12.3: *Make sure you read each option* in a multiple-choice question *and attempt to eliminate it*.

If you detect a half-truth or an ambiguous relationship in a multiple-choice question on a standardized exam, opt for the obvious.

Changing Answers

The question always comes up: Should you change an answer on a multiple-choice test if you think you have made a mistake?

And the reason this happens is that everyone eventually encounters a teacher who suggests that the research evidence says your first guess is more likely to be correct.

This is dangerous and misleading.

I always tell students that it depends on how they themselves perform on tests. Are you the type of student who is rattled at the beginning of a test? Do you start off in a bit of a panic and make a few mistakes before you settle down to think straight? Or do you find that you get more rattled in the last few minutes of the test as you change rush to complete it?

Obviously, whether or not you should change an answer depends on your style of making mistakes—and we all tend to have our own pattern here.

If you know that you make mistakes early in tests, you can feel fairly comfortable about changing answers later on when you have cooled down. But if you tend to panic in the last few minutes, do anything to stop yourself from changing your answer. Sit on your hands. Write yourself a note that warns you to be careful about changing answers. Anything. Obviously you have to know yourself—to study your past

---

[1] James Fallows, "The Tests and the 'Brightest': How Fair Are the College Boards?", *The Atlantic*, February 1980.

test performance and learn where and when you tend to make mistakes.

So, whether or not you fit one of these obvious patterns, the rule is:

14.1   *Change answers on objective tests only when you have a good reason for doing so*.

This may look as if I'm begging the question, but, really, when you ask students about the kinds of mistakes they make, they'll tell you things like "I changed this answer because it looked too simple," and "I guess I change my answers when I'm nervous." Now those are not good reasons for changing an answer. A good reason is one that you can spell out to yourself coolly and logically.

You have to keep your wits about you when you're taking tests. You simply cannot afford to take leaps in the dark and to act in a scatter-brained, haphazard fashion. Even guessing should be governed by careful consideration of the alternatives.

We'll return to some specialized objective tests later in Chapter 11. But now let's take a look at how you can improve your performance on essay tests.

Taking Objective Tests

6   Make Sure You Understand the General Instructions

    6.3   *If you are required to answer on a computerized answer form, make sure you know how to do so.* Look at the examples if there are any. Make sure that you know which way the questions are numbered. (*p. 48*)

10   Do the Easier Questions First. Buy Time To Think About More Difficult Questions.

    10.1   *On an objective test, tackle the questions in the order in which they are given to you.* If you cannot answer a question immediately, leave it and go on to the next question. Be sure to indicate—by leaving a blank on the question sheet or writing a "?" beside the question—which questions you have not finished. (*p. 48*)

12   Attack Each Question Systematically

    12.1   *Avoid superstitious or irrational behavior when taking objective tests.* Attack each question separately and logically. (*p. 48*)

    12.2   *On a multiple-choice question, try to determine what the correct answer will be before you look at the options.* Then look for this option in the list of alternatives provided. (*p. 49*)

    12.3   *Make sure you read each option* in a multiple-choice question *and attempt to eliminate it.* (*p. 49*)

14   Review and Correct Your Exam Before Handing It In

    14.1   *Change answers on objective tests only when you have a good reason for doing so.* (*p. 54*)

15   Write Something Down for Every Question

    15.1   *After you have worked through an objective test once* and have attempted every question, *make the best guess you can* at the questions you have not been able to answer. (*p. 49*)

Chapter 9

Doing well on essay tests

As I suggested in Chapter 3, the biggest problem you are likely to encounter in taking an essay test has to do with how you prepare for the test, and a common failure is not to anticipate and practice the kinds of skills you have to demonstrate on an essay exam. Working with a global map and with the other techniques for rehearsing for an essay test goes a long way toward resolving most students' problems with essays.

But even if you do a terrific job of preparation, it is still possible for you to completely blow the test by behaving inappropriately as you tackle the questions. Here, the commonest mistake has to do with a fundamental misunderstanding (that the schools generally don't do much to clear up) about what the process of writing is actually about.

Most students have the deep-rooted and disastrous illusion that writing an essay consists of three steps: reading the question, thinking of your answer, and writing it down. This is just not true, and if you try to write this way you'll get into all kinds of difficulties.

Writing an essay does not mean taking ideas out of your head and writing them down. You do not work like a computer, where the operator punches in a series of instructions, the computer whirrs, hums, and after a few seconds (ca-choing, ca-choing) the answer appears neatly tabulated on the console. It's nowhere near that simple.

Writing is more like painting or sculpture than it is like computer behavior. Let me explain. If you were Michelangelo and you had just received the commission to paint the ceiling of the Sistine Chapel, how would you proceed? Would you pick a corner and start painting, expanding outwards from this corner until you had covered the ceiling? Would you sit in the middle of the floor and wait until you had a really good idea of everything you were going to paint, and where each element was going to go,

down to the last fold of drapery and wisp of angel's hair? Not likely.

If you tried the first way, you'd end up with a disorderly mess that had no sequence and flow and that didn't complement the architecture of the building. If you tried the second way, you'd be sitting in the middle of the floor to this day trying to work out in your mind's eye what every detail would look like.

And this is exactly what happens to people who try to write essays using either of these approaches. Either they end up with a disorderly mess that needs a lot of reorganization, or they can't start writing at all, because they can't work out in perfect detail what the final, finished, polished essay will look like down to the last jot and tittle. This is called waiting for the Muse, and the Muse never comes unless you give her some encouragement.

Okay, Wise Guy, How Do You Write Essays, If You're So Smart?

There are a lot of little separate tasks you have to complete when you write an essay (any essay, not just an essay test). You have to understand the question or problem well enough to state in your own words what it is you are going to write about. You have to retrieve ideas, information, facts, formulas, details, and memory traces from your remote experience that will be the content of what you write down. You have to have some kind of *plan* that tells you roughly what order things are going to happen in. You have to write your ideas down according to your plan. You have to deal with new ideas and facts that pop into your head as you are writing. And you have to deal with all the multitudinous errors that we all make in writing—the spelling mistakes, the clumsy sentences, the spots where our handwriting turns into Tibetan.

Phew!

And now, isn't it obvious that you can't do all of these things at once?

The First Step Towards a Brilliant Essay

Most of us at one time or other were told that we should always write an outline prior to writing an essay. Usually we draw the conclusion that this is the first step.

Wrong! Wrong! Wrong!

The first step is to understand the question. You begin an essay test by reading the general instructions carefully, word by word, underlining the key terms as you go. Then,

> 8.1 *As you survey the questions on an essay test, jot down any ideas that occur to you beside each question.* Expand this list of points as you work through the test.

How can you outline something if you don't know what that something is? You can't, of course. You have to get an idea of what the general topic is. Then you have to collect the content—all the ideas and information you have to include in expressing your general idea.

So, after you've looked over the whole test, and have collected a couple of points beside each question, you then attack the first question, the easiest one, the one you know most about. You read it carefully, underlining key terms, identifying the instruction that tells you what it is that you have to do in the essay. Take some time to resolve ambiguities in the instructions, maybe even writing a translation of the question in your own words. As you read the question you expand your list of points. At this stage, don't worry about whether your ideas are good ones. Don't worry about whether they are completely relevant. Don't worry about how they fit together. Just write them down so they don't get lost somewhere.

Now your test sheet should look something like this:

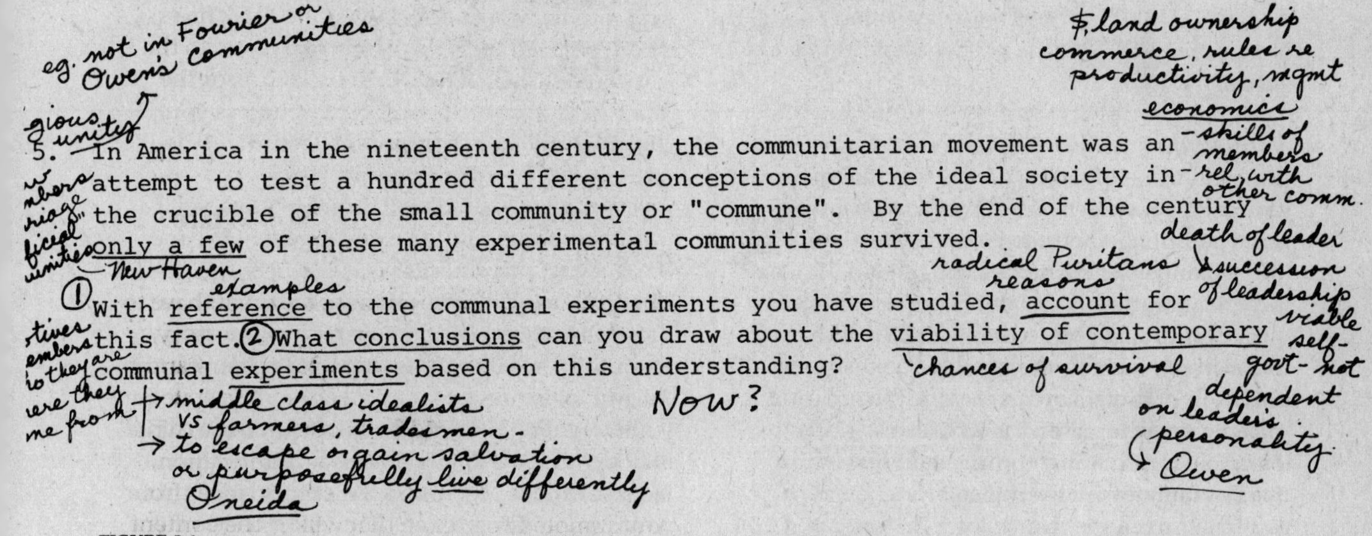

FIGURE 9.1

Instructors commonly present students with options on essay tests. "Write answers to five of the ten questions." "Answer Part A *or* Part B, but not both."

It may be easy for you to decide which options to write about. But

> 8.2 *If you can't decide which option on an essay test to answer, generate a complete list of points for each option* and then decide.

Go on to work on other questions and let these lists grow. Finally it may be obvious which option you have more information about. And if it isn't, if you know equally much (or equally little) about each of the options, flip a coin.

When you think that you have enough information and ideas to write an answer, you can go on to the next step.

Organizing Your Answer

Organizing your answer doesn't mean that you have to write a formal outline (unless the instructions specifically tell you to do so as part of your answer). It simply means that

> 12.4   When you think you have enough information, *organize your essay by stating your main point briefly, and numbering your points and ideas* in the order in which you will use them.

Now you can edit your ideas and throw out the ones that aren't really relevant, the picky details you don't need. Your test paper will now look something like this:

---

eg. not in Fourier or Owen's communities

① *religious unity*

⑤ *new members marriage "artificial" communities*

New Haven

② *motives of members — who they are — where they come from*

examples? See Noyes

③ *economics — skills of members — rel. with other comm*

$, land ownership commerce, rules re productivity, mgmt

④ *death of leader & succession of leadership*

5.   In America in the nineteenth century, the communitarian movement was an attempt to test a hundred different conceptions of the ideal society in the crucible of the small community or "commune". By the end of the century only a few of these many experimental communities survived.

examples

With reference to the communal experiments you have studied, account for this fact. ② What conclusions can you draw about the viability of contemporary communal experiments based on this understanding?

radical Puritans reasons

chances of survival

viable self govt - not dependent on leader's personality, Owen

middle class idealists vs farmers, tradesmen —
→ to escape or gain salvation or purposefully live differently
e.g. Oneida

Ⓐ *Historically*
Ⓑ 1. *Spiritual unity*
2. *Screening of members*
3. *Economic viability*
4. *mech. for govt, dealing with change*
5. *new members*

FIGURE 9.2

How you organize your essay—the essay form that you use—depends on the specific instructions you have been given. You don't want to start painting in one corner and work your way over to the other corner without a plan. Having practiced outlining essays and arguments as part of your test preparation will be of help here.

Basically, though, the principle you should follow in organizing your essay is the old journalistic precept called the KISS rule—Keep It Simple, Stupid. Avoid complicated reasoning. Eschew sententious verbiage.

First you tell the instructor what you are going to do, what point you are going to make, what conclusion you are going to prove. Then you do it. Then you summarize what you have done. Simple, straightforward, to the point.

Isn't There a Draft in Here?

Quite. Just as Michelangelo paused to sketch many of the details of the Sistine Chapel prior to laying brush to the ceiling, so your first attempt at the essay will be a tentative sketch of what you ultimately will hand in for your answer. One hopes it will be a fairly complete and detailed sketch, but a sketch none the less.

So, in accordance with Strategy 13 you will draft your answer. Write on every second line. Leave wide margins. Leave a line between paragraphs and a fair amount of space when you have concluded your answer—just in case you later think of something important that you have to add to the essay.

Remember, this is a sketch. If you can't think of a detail—the spelling of an important word, or a good phrase to express the precise idea that you want—don't panic. Don't stop dead while you engage in a fruitless search for the word you need. Leave space to write in the word and keep writing. If you have to put down a clumsy phrase in order to carry you forward, go ahead, but write a "?" in the margin to help you locate this place later.

As you write the essay, fresh ideas will pop into your head. When this happens, add these points to your outline so they don't get lost. Carry on writing.

Finally you will reach a point where you can't think of anything else to say, when you've covered every point in your outline. Now wrap things up by summarizing what you've said and restating your principal idea to conclude your essay.

Now Go On to Another Question

Before you return to clean up the essay, a brief pause will be helpful. You have been deeply involved in the pursuit of a particular idea and entangled with particular forms of words for some time. In order for you to do a good job of checking your answer you need to draw back for a little while, to take a brief pause that will help you see what you have written with a bit more objectivity.

> 13.1 *After drafting an essay, leave it alone for a little while to work on other parts of the exam.*

If you don't do this you will inevitably miss seeing some mistakes that you could have caught easily if you had allowed yourself to become a bit more distant from what you just wrote.

And Finally

Check grammar, spelling, punctuation, diction. Add examples if they are needed for clarification or to strengthen your argument. Work on cleaning up clumsy or weak sentences. Now is the time to find the "?"s you wrote in the margin and to shape up the awkard phrases in your draft.

Check your handwriting and rewrite or print any illegible sections. Now you know why you double-spaced your draft.

And search for the words you couldn't think of before.

What If You Can't Think of the Word You Want?

It's a little like looking for your car keys as you leave your apartment. Everybody knows they're out in plain sight, so how come they're invisible? The harder you look for them, the more deeply lost they become. Right?

If a word that you want has dropped over the cliff into the unplumbed depths of your remote unconscious, what you have to do is to tease it back up to the surface. It won't come back up if it's bullied.

The specific technique is called brainstorming, and it works like this. You can't think of the precise word you want. What is the word or phrase that you can think of? Write that one down. Now write down the very next word that comes into your head. It won't be the "right" one either, but write it down. Do these two words suggest another word? Write that one down. And keep going.

It's like the word-association game that you see movie psychoanalysts playing with the neurotic starlet. "Now, Miss B., I will say a word and I want you to say the very first thing that pops into your head. All right, here we go." Then he says "black". She says "white". He says "red". She says "blood", and before you know it she is confessing to murdering the butler.

The whole key to brainstorming is not to censor any word or idea but to keep them flowing. If you get stuck and no more words come, there are several steps you can take. You can write the last word on your list over a couple or three times. Usually this will shake something loose. You can go back over your list and write down the opposites for all the words you've written. You can try adding an adjective or an adverb to each of the words.

Usually these brief exercises will be enough to tease the word you want back up into the light of day.

But What If You Can't Think of Anything To Say, Period?

Sometimes what is lost is not just a word or a phrase but a whole answer. You read a question and all you draw is a nice, bright, hollow blank. Even after you've reread the question and allowed it to simmer away as you worked on other questions, you may still come up with nothing. Zero. Zilch. An echoing void.

Nevertheless, you must try to write something down for every question. Make the best effort you can for questions you are unsure about.

There are basically two reasons for doing this:

1. As you write, you may unintentionally start a chain of associations that helps you remember material that is relevant to the question.
2. You may know more than you think you know. While you may be completely *unsure* of how to respond, you may actually know everything that the instructor wants.

Clearly, if you don't answer a question at all, you will get no credit. If you've written something down—even if you think that it isn't much—you stand a chance of earning at least some credit.

You don't have to be obnoxious about this. You don't have to make things up or arrogantly pretend that you know what you're doing. You can merit points in your instructor's eyes by beginning your answer with a statement like "I am quite unsure how to respond to this question. My difficulty starts with the meaning of the term....On the one hand..." and off you go. Now the professor knows you're not trying to snow him and he will probably read your answer honestly intending to see what you do know.

Rushed for Time?

Occasionally we all encounter tests where, even carefully budgeting our time and watching the clock, we simply find it impossible to write full answers for all the questions required.

Either the exam really is too long or we've taken a little more time than we should have to deal with the other questions. What to do with the one or two remaining questions—the ones we know how to answer and want to answer but won't be able to.

> 15.2 *If pressed for time on an essay test, write an expanded outline* rather than trying to complete a full answer.

Just list your ideas in point form. This strategy will probably earn you many more points than trying frantically to rush a full answer that you can't possibly finish.

And Finally...

Don't leave, of course, until they throw you out. Use this time to clean up your essays even more. Then, when you've done that, daydream. Just before the final curtain, glance over your answers one more time to see if another clerical error will pop out.

Doing Well on Essay Tests

6 Make Sure You Understand the General Instructions

    6.4   Make sure you *write your name clearly on the answer sheet.* (*p. 46*)

8 If You Think of Something, Write It Down

    8.1   *As you survey the questions on an essay test, jot down any ideas that occur to you beside each question.* Expand this list of points as you work through the test. (*p. 57*)

    8.2   *If you can't decide which option on an essay test to answer, generate a complete list of points for each option* and then decide. (*p. 57*)

12 Attack Each Question Systematically

    12.4   When you think you have enough information, *organize your essay stating your main point briefly, and numbering your points and ideas* in the order in which you will use them. (*p. 58*)

13 Draft Your Answers So You Can More Easily Find and Correct Mistakes

    13.1   *After drafting an essay, leave it alone* for a little while to work on other parts of the exam. (*p. 59*)

15 Write Something Down for Every Question

    15.2   *If pressed for time on an essay test, write an expanded outline* rather than trying to complete a full answer. (*p. 60*)

Chapter 10
Problem tests

Math and science tests tie a lot of perfectly competent people in absolute knots. Most often this is because the students simply have not yet learned to solve problems quickly, under pressure, even though they may have little or no difficulty working in non-pressure situations. What's involved here is figuring out what the steps are in systematic problem-solving and then learning to do the efficient things deliberately. The last part of this chapter covers the tactics that seem to fall in this class — what works when, and how to do it.

Often the people who have difficulty in taking math and science tests also have trouble *learning* math and sciences in the first place. Usually this is because they have acquired some completely wrong-headed notions about learning in general, and math-science learning more specifically. These "myths" are widely taught and widely believed, but that doesn't mean that they're any more correct. A mistake is a mistake, whether one person believes it or one million people.

The First Myth: There's Only One Right Way To Do a Math Problem

Think back to your experience in junior high or elementary school. What were the subjects in which the teacher would call people to the board to work something out — in the spotlight, right there in front of everyone? Math and Sciences, right? (Sometimes English Comp., too.) And what would happen if you made a mistake? (You were almost sure to make a mistake because you were so nervous.) Most of us can recall the humiliation, the embarrassment, the silent and not-so-silent criticism from the teacher. Almost as bad was getting the right answer, because this would get you instantly labelled as a show-off or a "brain". And the "right" answer did not mean just the right conclusion. It also meant using exactly the procedure that the teacher preferred.

So what do students conclude from this kind of experience?

1. There is only one right answer and only one right way to get the answer.
2. There is only one way to *learn* math and sciences.
3. The teacher knows these ways.
4. If you can't learn using the teacher-approved method, and if you can't get right answers the right way, consistently and without effort, you must be dumb.

All of these beliefs are absolute rubbish!

The year after you graduated from high school, they changed the curriculum and teaching methods. Now there is a new "right" way to learn math. And they'll change it after they get through with another batch of kids. Did you know that in some school systems they are now teaching youngsters to do multiplication and division *on their fingers*! Clearly there is no general agreement on what the "right" way is.

If you need any more convincing, I want you to do a little exercise. Multiply 45 by 9. Go ahead, do it right now. And don't read any further until you've done it.

Okay, now what most of you will have done is something like the following:

$$\begin{array}{r} {}^{4}45 \\ \times\ \ 9 \\ \hline 405 \end{array}$$

But consider that there are at least four other ways to reach the answer. Now who is to say which is the "correct" way?

1. $45 \times 9 =$

$$
\begin{array}{cc}
40 & +\ 5 \\
\underline{9} & \underline{9} \\
360 & 45
\end{array}
= 405
$$

2. $45 \times 9 = (45 \times 10) - 45$
   $= 450 - 45$
   $= 405$

3. $45 \times 9 = (5 \times 9) \times 9$
   $= 5 \times (9 \times 9)$
   $= 5 \times 81$
   $= 405$

4. $45 \times 9 = 45 \times 3 \times 3$
   $= 135 \times 3$
   $= 405$

Now you may think this is trivial. Mostly what I've done is to factor 45 and 9 and recombine (multiply) the factors in different combinations. But really, when you think about it, when you were sent to the board you knew there was only one right way, only one procedure that would be accepted. Teachers would even say things like, "Well, you have the right answer, but you didn't use the 'right' method."

And finally, it has to be noted that what very often counts in whether a particular approach is "right" or not is *not* whether the procedure leads to a correct solution—since there may be many ways of reaching the correct answer—but rather whether the solution is "elegant".

Now this particular criterion has got nothing to do with correctness of reasoning. It has everything to do with the neatness, precision, clarity, and directness of the solution. It is, at base, an "artistic" judgment about the solution; it's a judgment about style. So not only is the student expected to learn correct reasoning, but he is expected to show an early and easy acquisition of precision and "elegance" in his performances.

The Second Myth: Speed Counts

Answer immediately. Beat the buzzer. Quick.

Don't take time to think. You're not allowed to work things out in rough first. Who's got the answer?

All through school there is this constant pressure to learn and to answer fast. (After all, we have to "cover the curriculum".) It's almost as if teaching methods were copied from TV quiz shows.

No reward for diligence, for perseverance, for carrying on in spite of initial difficulty. (Which is probably a more valuable skill in the long run.) You either get it or you don't, and then we're on to something new. The problem being, of course, that if you don't get it, you won't get what happens next either.

Now look, speed, like "elegance", is something that *follows* mastery of an idea. We generally don't expect speed from people who are just learning. When you've learned to solve a particular kind of puzzle, and have practiced that puzzle several times, then we can expect you to solve similar puzzles quickly—but not before. It's nice if you can do it, but it's not essential.

So I always tell people to take the time they need to go back and learn what they need. If you need to go back to Grade IV to relearn complex fractions, get a book and a tutor and do it. If you need practice in multiplying, take it; if algebra is a mystery, take the necessary courses. But don't feel like an idiot just because you didn't learn the stuff the first time around; and don't demand of yourself that you now learn the stuff quickly either. If it takes you two years to get ready for Calculus, it's better to do that and feel confident when you get there than to sign up for Calculus when you're supposed to, take the course, and flunk the final.

And, of course, it helps to keep in mind the fact that we *all* forget technical details very quickly—unless we continue to use them. If a particular piece of information is not used repeatedly, and you haven't used it in the recent past, it's practically guaranteed that you will forget it. So don't feel stupid about this. The information will probably be a lot easier to relearn now than it was to learn the first time you encountered it.

The Third Myth: It's Important To Do It in Your Head

Along with the insistence that there's only one right way to learn and only one right way to do math/science problems, and along with the assumption that if you don't learn to do it fast you must be stupid, goes the assumption that you ought to be able to perform calculations in your head.

If you can do this, that's wonderful. You have a

tremendous gift. Like being able to think on your feet and speak extempore on any topic. But it is a gift. And there is nothing wrong with you if you aren't so gifted.

But you see this myth operating all the time. In restaurants you see parties of people getting all sweaty trying to figure out who owes what, when it would be so much easier if somebody went and got a menu and systematically did the sums on a napkin. You see people stalled in the aisles of the grocery store trying to figure out whether they have enough cash for their purchases, when a few seconds of paper-and-pencil work would tell them irrefutably. On math tests you see people trying to do it in their heads, and making mistake after mistake after mistake, and getting all confused and frustrated.

Face it. If you cannot perform calculations in your head, don't try. Do it the easy way. Take the few seconds that are needed to write out the calculation neatly, rather than trying to work faster than you can.

My grandmother used to say, "How come you never have time to do it right in the first place, but you always have time to do it over?" And that is just about that. Why don't you take the time that is necessary to get it right, rather than putting yourself through the agony of having to do it over?

So,

> 13.2 *Don't try to do mental math on tests.* Take the time to work out the problems using paper and pencil. If you are using a calculator, be sure to write down each step.

Summing It Up

In conclusion, if maths/sciences are a bit of a problem for you, and if you have a history of difficulty with these subjects, it would probably help if you did the following:

1. Recognize that there are many ways to learn. If one way isn't working you can always try something different—and this doesn't mean that you're stupid.

2. Recognize that the "right" answer and the "correct" procedure are stylistic judgments, and that it may take some time before you can either understand or produce these highly polished demonstrations. Speed and elegance are goals, not something to insist on when you're first learning.

3. Acknowledge that you probably missed a lot of what happened in school and that there's nothing wrong in learning that stuff now. (It sure beats never learning it, and hoping against hope that you won't be asked a question that involves this material.)

4. Don't try to do it in your head, if you know that this will lead to problems. Don't try to work fast if you have to work methodically. (Three correct answers arrived at slowly and methodically are better than ten wrong answers arrived at quickly.)

Okay. Enough of this. I mention these ideas only because they seem to make a practical difference for people who have trouble with maths/sciences. Now let's take a look at what to do when you get a test in one of these courses.

Stop!

If you haven't read Chapter 7, "The General Test-Writing Strategies", do it now. Do not proceed in this chapter until you are familiar with the important principles discussed there, since they will not all be repeated in the following discussion.

Taking the Test

The first thing you do in a problem test is, of course, to record the hard-to-remember formulas, decision rules, definitions, etc., that you were carrying around in the minor cram.

> 8.3 *Record items from your minor cram as soon as you have paper on which to write* in the test.

It is so much easier to do this than it is to go through the agony of trying to remember this stuff during the test and inevitably forgetting it. When material is stored in your short-term memory, it can very easily be displaced and lost. Get it on paper and you don't have to remember it any more.

You've surveyed the test, noted the general instructions, noted how the test is put together, and seen what kind of questions there are and how many points are assigned to each question or question group; you have budgeted your time, and now you are ready to start on what looks like the easiest, most familiar question.

Reading the Question

In accordance with Strategy 6 you are going to read the question carefully, underlining key words and deciding what it is that you are expected to do.

We just know that this is where you blow points away, right? How many times have you made serious blunders because you failed to note an important word, or misread a number or the units accompanying a number? How many times have you answered another question and not the one you were asked?

> 11.1 When reading a question on a problem test, be sure to *underline each item of data, the units that accompany the numbers, and the specific instruction* that tells you what you have to do, as well as important modifiers.

Take a crack at underlining the key words in these questions:

> 1. In 1979, International Tom-Tom produced $^4/_5$ of the world's total production of digital hyperextension underdrive units. Its nearest rival, Mifuni Microfas, produced $^2/_3$ of the remainder. If total world production in that year was 75 million units, how many digital hyperextension underdrive units did Mifuni produce?
>
> 2. Two piece-workers are plucking a load of 1000 chickens. Worker A can pluck 14 chickens in five minutes. Worker B plucks 12 chickens in 10 minutes. How long will it take them to pluck all the chickens, and what will be their respective earnings if Worker A earns 7.5¢ per chicken, and Worker B earns 5¢?
>
> 3. A dice is tossed two times. What is the probability that the sum of the numbers observed will be greater than 7? Equal 7?

All right, your questions should now look something like those in Figure 10.1. Did you underline all the key terms? If you didn't, the chances are increased that you will make a mistake on the questions.

> 1. In 1979, International Tom-Tom produced $^4/_5$ of the world's <u>total production</u> of digital hyperextension underdrive units. Its nearest rival, Mifuni Microfas, produced $\underline{^2/_3}$ <u>of the remainder</u>. If total world production in that year was ⟨75 million⟩ units, <u>how many</u> digital hyperextension underdrive units <u>did Mifuni produce?</u>
>
> 2. Two piece-workers are plucking a load of <u>1000 chickens</u>. <u>Worker A</u> can pluck <u>14 chickens in ⟨five⟩ minutes</u>. <u>Worker B</u> plucks <u>12 chickens in ⟨10⟩ minutes</u>. <u>How long</u> will it ① take them to pluck all the chickens, and ② <u>what</u> will be their respective earnings if <u>Worker A earns 7.5¢ per chicken</u>, and <u>Worker B earns 5¢?</u>
>
> 3. A dice is tossed <u>two times</u>. What is the probability that the ⟨sum⟩ of the numbers observed will be <u>greater than 7</u>? ① <u>Equal 7</u>? ②

FIGURE 10.1

Predict the Final Answer

I guess nobody who is reading this book has ever made the mistake of working out a problem on a test, writing down the answer, and then discovering when the test was returned that the answer should have been taken one step further, that you used the wrong units in the answer, or that you were out by a factor of 2 or 10. Nobody has ever made that silly mistake.

Well of course you have. And the reason you did it was because you failed to follow this simple rule:

> 11.2 Before you begin working on a question on a problem test, *try to predict what the final answer will look like*. Write this down in the margin of the test paper.

What will be the *shape* of the final answer? Its magnitude? (How big?) What units will accompany the answer? What *statement* will accompany the answer? Guess if you have to, but write something down!

This is the only way to stop yourself from making the mistake of ending up somewhere other than where you wanted to be.

Now your test will look like this:

1. In 1979, International Tom-Tom produced $\frac{4}{5}$ of the world's total production of digital hyperextension underdrive units. Its nearest rival, Mifuni Microfas, produced $\frac{2}{3}$ of the remainder. If total world production in that year was 75 million units, how many digital hyperextension underdrive units did Mifuni produce? $\frac{2}{3} \times \frac{1}{5} \times 75$ mill units

2. Two piece-workers are plucking a load of 1000 chickens. Worker A can pluck 14 chickens in five minutes. Worker B plucks 12 chickens in 10 minutes. How long will it take them to pluck all the chickens, working together mins. and what will be their respective earnings if Worker A earns 7.5¢ per chicken, and Worker B earns 5¢? A earns $ ___ B earns $ ___

3. A dice is tossed two times. What is the probability that the sum of the numbers observed will be greater than 7? Equal 7? ① about 50% ② < 50%

FIGURE 10.2

If a problem is easy (that is, if it has no more than two numbers and only one instruction), you can skip the next steps. But if there is any chance at all that you are going to be confused, be careful. Be systematic. Take it easy. Take the time to do the next step, rather than having to take extra time later to correct your errors.

12.5   Before beginning work on a problem on a test, *list the data neatly in a table*.

This is just another way of giving your brain a chance to do its job by recycling the information in a slightly different way. You know how that goes: sometimes you can't understand a problem until somebody reads it to you, or until you write it out in a different form. Just rearranging the information will very often be enough to get you started on your way to the solution. Completing a table often helps you see relationships in the data you could not see before, and may show you ways of simplifying the problem or determining what steps are necessary in order to begin working on the question. In addition,

12.6   Before beginning a question on a problem test, *draw a picture, diagram,*

or chart that shows the data and illustrates the problem.

This is not always necessary, but if a problem is giving you any difficulty at all, it is well worth the effort and extra time. Here are some examples of what you could do for the sample questions given above.

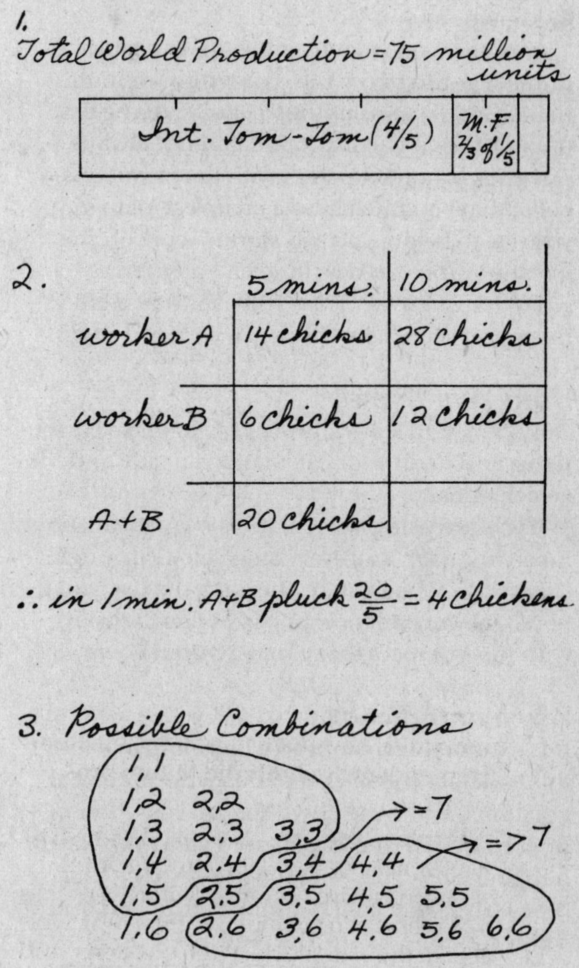

1. Total World Production = 75 million units

Int. Tom-Tom (4/5)	M.F. 2/3 of 1/5

2.

	5 mins.	10 mins.
worker A	14 chicks	28 chicks
worker B	6 chicks	12 chicks
A+B	20 chicks	

∴ in 1 min. A+B pluck $\frac{20}{5} = 4$ chickens.

3. Possible Combinations

1,1
1,2 2,2
1,3 2,3 3,3   = 7
1,4 2,4 3,4 4,4   = >7
1,5 2,5 3,5 4,5 5,5
1,6 2,6 3,6 4,6 5,6 6,6

FIGURE 10.3

The next thing is:

12.7   *In working a problem, identify what it is that you have to find* and *give it a name*. There may be several of these "unknowns" to identify and name.

The usual procedure is to write a statement like "Let Mifuni's share of the market = M," and "Let the number of units Mifuni produced = N," but this particular format isn't dreadfully important. As long as you are clear about what you are solving for, things will be all right.

It is not important that you identify and name *all* the unknowns before you start the problem. You won't discover some of them until you're midway into the solution anyway, so don't paralyze yourself. Start where you can and label the unknowns as you go.

And now you want to come up with a procedure for getting from the data to the solution. Usually this means trying to figure out the first unknown that you identified. But not always. The trick is not to operate with the erroneous belief that you must have a *complete* plan in your head before you can start to work on the question. You can do a little bit and then see what that suggests. Then you can work a bit more and see where that leads you, and so on.

Draft Your Answer
Don't forget to leave lots of space to make corrections, and to do your calculations neatly and systematically.

If you are using a calculator, be fanatical about recording each and every step you go through. Otherwise, when you're checking the test you'll be asking yourself how in blazes you came up with the numbers that you've written down.

When in Difficulty
It is extremely rare to read a question on a test, immediately know what to do, perform the calculations, and write down the final solution in a direct, straight-ahead fashion. That *is* the way it happens on "drills"—practice questions that repeat the same kind of problem over and over. But real problems are different.

The usual course of events in normal problem-solving includes lots of little side-trips, doublings back, detours, and temporary hold-ups. Many students find this alarming after a steady diet of drill-type questions in high school, and they immediately go into shock when they encounter questions that are not of the drill variety.

Here are some things you can do if you find yourself getting stuck on a question:

1. First of all, if you can solve part of the problem, do it. Don't wait for everything to become clear—don't wait for the complete master plan to crystallize. Most often this won't happen until you have done some preliminary work.

2. You can try the problem with smaller numbers. (Don't use 0 or 1, since they have unique computational characteristics that can lead you astray!) Sometimes if the quantities you are working with are huge and complex, this will immediately resolve your difficulties and give you a pattern to follow when you go back to the question itself. The same is true if you have a problem that has *no* numbers (for example, a problem in geometry). Assigning small values to each of the dimensions of a figure can help you see the relationships more clearly.

3. If you have seen a similar problem before, spend a little time outlining how you solved that problem. Often this will help you detect exactly where you are running into trouble and what you can do about it.

4. Maybe you can get some clues by tackling the problem or part of the problem *backwards*. That is, instead of getting hung up on the data and information given to you, take a look at what you predicted for the shape of the final answer. What do you need to know (or find) in order to get the answer? And what do you need to know in order to find those pieces of information, and so on?

5. If you don't know what else to do, take a sheet of rough paper and *play* with the numbers. Put down whatever you can think of. Can you factor the numbers? Does one divide evenly into some of the others? What would happen if you arranged the numbers in order from greatest to smallest? This may seem useless at first, but you will be surprised at how productive it can be in helping you come up with useful ideas.

An example is in order. A while ago I was working with a group of returning adult students who had been away from school for eons and who were terrified of having to take college-level math courses. Nobody could see what I meant when I suggested playing with numbers, so I offered this example:

"Okay, try this question: What is the least common multiple of 12 and 7?"
(Blank stares.)

"C'mon, you guys, play with the numbers."
(Blank stares.)

"Right. You don't know what 'least common multiple' means, right?"
(Nods of agreement.)

"So, play with the numbers!"

At this point, one soul screwed up his courage to ask, very tentatively, "You mean...how about if we just...how about if we just made a list of what numbers you could get by...um...multiplying the numbers by...er...1 and 2 and 3 and so on?"

"Sure," says I. "Let's see what happens." So in a few minutes we generated two lists, reproduced below:

12	7
24	14
36	21
48	28
60	35
72	42
84	49
96	56
108	63
120	70
etc.	77
	84
	etc.

At which point, one student virtually shouted, "Hey, 84 is in both lists! That must be the answer!"

After a bit of discussion, in which the students agreed (remembered, really) that "least" meant "smallest", and "common" just meant "shared", the students all came to the conclusion that 84 was the answer. And they were right, of course.

Now, you're not going to have a group to discuss the questions with when you're taking a test. But really, if you are completely stuck and can't think of anything, it is guaranteed that you're not going to get any credit for the question. However, if you play with the numbers and write down your best guess, there is at least a *chance* that you'll get something. Right?

And When You're Really Stuck

Leave the question alone for a while, and work on something else. Something might jiggle loose. But don't just spin your wheels going over and over the same information and performing the same calculations. If you're not getting new ideas and new information, you need to have a little break from the question.

So Now You Have the Final Answer

Unless you are behind schedule, take a few moments to check your answer.

> 14.2 In problem tests, check your answer
> a) to see if it *matches your prediction*,
> b) to see if it is *reasonable*,
> c) to make sure it *meets all the requirements of the problem*, and
> d) to make sure there are no *computational errors*.

Check your answer against your prediction, to ensure that you have taken the solution through all the necessary steps. If it doesn't match, either you predicted wrong, or you have to do something else to complete the question.

Check for reasonableness. Ask, is this the type of answer I'd expect to find in the real world? (If you have a horse travelling at the speed of light, or a racing-car peaking out at 5 km/hr, something is probably amiss.) A fast way to check the reasonableness factor, and also to roughly check your computation, is to round off the numbers in your calculations (i.e., if you had to multiply $293 \times 37 \times 61$ in the problem, you can quickly check for reasonableness by multiplying $300 \times 40 \times 60$). Obviously this will be just a ballpark estimate, but it will tell you if a closer check is required.

In checking your computation, try to remember the kinds of mistakes you usually make. Are decimal places correct in each step? Have you squared where you were supposed to and correctly found roots when this was appropriate? Do the signs mutate in correct sequence? Are all the numbers accounted for, or have some mysteriously disappeared? Check through each line of your calculations to see if each step makes sense.

And finally, make sure you have produced an answer that meets all the conditions of the problem. Have you used all the data? Does your answer comply with all the restrictions and modifying circumstances presented in the problem? A warning: Don't just check back to the original equation you wrote down. What if you used the wrong equation? Check back to the problem itself and read it one more time to make sure you haven't missed something.

If you decide that the answer is correct, great. Just go on to the next question.

If the answer is incorrect, and you can see what you have to do to correct it (or where you went astray) and *you are on schedule*, then take the time to quickly rework the question.

But if you are behind schedule, you must go ahead to other problems. Put a big "?" in the margin beside the question, leave adequate space on your answer sheet to revise it, and carry on with the test. You should have time to return to the question if you keep yourself on schedule.

Before You Leave

Having attempted all the problems you can, complete a routine check of the whole paper, using the criteria discussed above. Then you can take the remaining time to rework problems that have given you trouble.

Finally, put something down for the questions you have not yet attempted. It doesn't matter what. If you can't think of anything else to do, construct a table for the data and attempt a diagram—you may get a couple of clues that would allow you to quickly complete a step or two in the procedure, or to outline the whole problem. This may get you partial credit. What have you got to lose by doing this? Absolutely nothing. But if you write down nothing, your score on the question is guaranteed to be a big fat zip.

And Naturally

Check that you have written your name on the answer sheet (Tactic 9.2).

And once you have done that, sit there until you are told to turn in your paper (Strategy 11). Deliberately daydream about something else. Perhaps a new idea will come to you, perhaps not. Then read over your test one more time. Perhaps you will think of something to write down, or notice a correction that you can make. But do not leave the exam room until they throw you out.

And When You Get Your Test Back

Take the time to review the test to see what it would have been necessary for you to do in order to have earned a better mark. Be an adult about this. Confront your errors and find out how to fix them and avoid them in the future.

This applies to final exams in courses, as well —if you can get the papers back. You do not know when you will be called upon to use the skills and abilities you were supposed to learn in the course. You can't predict for sure that you will never use these again. So it's worth while to get corrective feedback, even at the end of a course.

Problem Tests

8 If You Think of Something, Write It Down

    8.3 *Record items from your minor cram as soon as you have paper on which to write* in the test. (*p. 63*)

11 Read Questions Carefully, Underlining Key Terms. Decide What You Are Expected To Do.

    11.1 When reading a question on a problem test, be sure to *underline each item of data, the units that accompany the numbers, and the specific instruction* that tells you what you have to do, as well as important modifiers. (*p. 64*)

    11.2 Before you begin working on a question on a problem test, *try to predict what the final answer will look like.* Write this down in the margin of the test paper. (*p. 64*)

12 Attack Each Question Systematically

    12.5 Before beginning work on a problem on a test, *list the data neatly in a table.* (*p. 65*)

    12.6 Before beginning a question on a problem test, *draw a picture, diagram, or chart* that shows the data and illustrates the problem. (*p. 65*)

    12.7 *In working a problem, identify what it is that you have to find* and *give it a name.* There may be several of these "unknowns" to identify and name. (*p. 65*)

13 Draft Your Answers So You Can More Easily Find and Correct Mistakes

    13.2 *Don't try to do mental math on tests.* Take the time to work out the problems using paper and pencil. If you are using a calculator, be sure to write down each step. (*p. 63*)

14 Review and Correct Your Exam Before Handing It In

    14.2 In problem tests, check your answer
        a) to see if it *matches your prediction,*
        b) to see if it is *reasonable,*
        c) to make sure it *meets all the requirements of the problem,* and
        d) to make sure there are no *computational errors.* (*p. 67*)

Chapter 11

Aptitude and intelligence tests

"Attempting to predict future performance on the basis of test scores is much like trying to guess the ultimate size and shape of an oak tree by measuring a sapling in pitch darkness with a rubber band for a ruler, and without taking into account the condition of the soil, the amount of rainfall, or the woodsman's axe. The amazing thing is that sometimes we get the right answer."

— David A. Goslin, *The Search for Ability: Standardized Testing in Social Perspective*, Russell Sage Foundation, New York, 1963, p. 156.

Intelligence or I.Q.

Most people think of intelligence as a single lump of something that you get from your parents when you are conceived, a physical characteristic like blue eyes or a tendency to be short of stature. Actually, there is a wealth of evidence that the ability to solve problems (which is what intelligence is) is the result of many factors, including the social and educational environment of the family, specific instruction in schools, the person's self-esteem, attitudes towards problems, and so on. Heredity is important, for sure, but it isn't all there is to the matter.

Nor is it true that intelligence is a "single lump of something". Intelligence tests, which measure your ability to solve problems and compare your results with averages for your age group (resulting in an I.Q. score), typically only measure problem-solving skills that are considered to be important in school performance. Most people do not score uniformly throughout the test — they don't get all the answers consistently wrong or consistently right. In other words, they appear to be better at some types of problems than at others. In any case, since I.Q. tests really measure a pretty narrow range of human activity (i.e., abilities believed to relate to doing well in

school), this means that there is an enormous range of skills and abilities that I.Q. tests don't measure. It means that it is quite possible to score high on an I.Q. test (and be considered "highly intelligent") and to be a perfect boob at a lot of things.

The folklore recognizes this in the stereotype of "the absentminded professor". He may be a genius at school-related problems, but his abilities in general living skills and social relations are so poor that he needs careful tending if he is not to expire from starvation or from neglecting some important element of the environment — such as whether a traffic light is green or red.

So remember two things: Intelligence is not a single, unitary quality that you either have or don't have — rather, intelligence is your total ability to solve problems, not just academic problems. And second, intelligence isn't fixed at birth. Many things can change your intelligence, since you can *learn* to solve problems, and lots of things will help you do this.

Finally, I.Q. tests are *attempts* to measure intelligence (using "the rubber band on the sapling"). A low test score does not inevitably mean that you are some kind of dummy. Tests measure your ability to do well on tests. Any guesses based on your test performance are just as likely to be false as true. So think twice before you accept the verdict of an I.Q. test as absolutely true.

What About Aptitude Tests?

An aptitude is exactly the same thing as a "gift" for a particular thing, or a "talent".

In other words, an aptitude is an ability to acquire a particular kind of skill, and to learn that skill quickly and easily.

Again, the same thing is true of aptitude tests as is true of I.Q. tests: they usually measure the kinds of abilities that school authorities think are important, and they leave out a huge range of skills and abilities that have little to do with school. So, to repeat, scoring poorly on an aptitude test doesn't mean that you're doomed.

In the first place, the test measures largely how well you do on tests. In the second place, it only compares your performance with that of others in school-related activities.

For example, I don't know of any paper-and-pencil test that could possibly measure whether or not you have a "gift" for working with children, or are athletically "inclined". And I know lots of people who do terribly on tests who have magnificent talents. I know an auto mechanic who is just an absolute whiz, but who has consistently failed to get his papers—because he can't pass tests. A while ago I read of a severely retarded boy in Japan who has established an international reputation as an artist.

And Achievement Tests?

All tests are achievement tests because they all measure what you have learned (including how well you have learned to take tests). But there is a specialized group of tests that focusses on measuring learning in particular areas, and these tests are the ones that are usually called "Achievement Tests".

The SAT (Scholastic Aptitude Test), the GRE, the LSAT, and the Miller Analogies Test are all achievement tests. They all attempt to measure your previous learning in particular areas. But, for that matter, so does the exam you had to complete to get your driver's licence.

There is no magic in any of these tests. In fact, they are all pretty blunt and unwieldy instruments. It is amazing that they are right as often as they are. And it's obvious, isn't it, that since all tests measure your learning, you can do better on these tests by learning more. In particular, you can do better on these tests *if you learn how to take the test*.

Raising Your Test Scores

"Many intelligent people score poorly on I.Q. and similar tests, not because they're stupid, but because *they don't use the intelligence they have*. The evidence is mounting that scoring well on such tests is a skill that can be taught and learned."

—A. Whimbey, "Getting Ready for the Tester: You Can Learn To Raise Your I.Q. Score", *Psychology Today*, Jan. 1976, p. 27.

Whimbey, and other researchers whom he cites in this article, have discovered that people who do poorly on tests usually have two bad habits. (Incidentally, if *you* have problems with these tests I'd really recommend that you find this article. Most big libraries will have back issues of the magazine and the librarian will help you find it.)

Anyway, the two most common mistakes that people make when taking these tests are

1. to use "one-shot thinking", that is, to leap or guess at an answer, and
2. to fail to pay attention to the questions and to use *all* the information they are given in the problems.

"One-shot thinking", more than anything else, is probably due to a defeatist attitude towards the test. The student just feels that these tests are incomprehensible and that he can't do them, and so he just makes a stab in the dark—without going through the systematic business of puzzling it out that high-achievers go through. But look, my friends, if you have learned in your life to solve *any* kinds of problems at all (including things like how to change a tire on a car, how to change a recipe to feed an extra person, how to stop a baby from crying), you *can* learn to solve the kinds of problems that appear on tests. Because *exactly* the same kinds of skills are involved in solving the problems on the I.Q. test as are involved in solving those everyday problems.

To solve any problem, you have to learn to pay attention to detail. (What exactly is the problem here, Junior—how come you're crying?) You have to learn to take things one step at a time and to do things in a particular sequence. (You can't undo the lug nuts on the wheel until you take off the hub cap, and you probably can't do that until you get the tire iron out of the trunk and jack up the car.) And you have to learn to use all the information that is given to you. (If you double the flour in a recipe, you also have to double the other ingredients, including the baking powder.)

So look, just as most people in the world have the ability to learn how to change a tire, quiet a crying baby, and double a recipe, *if they will get past their impatience and their belief that the task is impossible*, they can learn how to score better on I.Q., aptitude, and other achievement tests.

And the keys are, as I've indicated, *patient* work, getting past the belief that you can't do it, and learning to pay attention to the question and to significant details. And again, starting early. If you've got a test in two weeks, you just aren't going to learn as much as if you started several months in advance.

3.14   In preparation for intelligence, aptitude, or other achievement tests, *set aside time to practice, on a regular basis, the kinds of problems that will appear on the test.*

It helps, of course, if you can get as much information about the test as possible, but often such information is carefully guarded. (After all, if people found out what was on the test, why they'd just go ahead and *learn* it, for crying out loud, and then where would we be?) If you can, try to find a description of the test in the most recent edition of *Tests in Print* or the *Mental Measurements Yearbook* (both by O. K. Buros, The Gryphon Press, Highland Park, New Jersey). Any university with a significant psychology department will have these books. But this may be a slim chance if you don't have ready access to a nearby university.

I'd recommend that you spend some time going through the sample problems on the following pages, and you might find it helpful to work through puzzle books that you can find in bookstores.

Now look, if these kinds of things give you a headache, *take it slow*, maybe do only one question a day, and do not allow yourself to be overwhelmed by the large number of questions. Take them one at a time, see if you can figure out the one problem, check your answer with the answers and explanations provided at the end of each set of practice questions, try to practice the correct solution, and don't get frustrated. These things are as easy as fixing a tire, baking a cake, or changing a baby's diaper. (That is, they're enormously difficult until you learn how to do them.) So, slow and steady wins the race.

Things Not Covered by the Practice Questions

I've left out some areas of knowledge because there just isn't room to include them in this book. I haven't included questions about vocabulary, English grammar, mechanical reasoning (basic physics of the inclined plane, levers, pulleys, screws, etc.), or (except for the number-series problems) computation and mathematics. If you've got problems in these areas, I'm afraid I have to leave it up to you to design your own program of review. Check Chapter 6 for some ideas about how to do this.

Verbal Reasoning: Analogies

Each question in Part A of the practice questions that follow consists of two words that are related in some way. Below them are four additional pairs of words, lettered A, B, C, and D. You are to select the lettered pair that has the same kind of relationship as the first pair and indicate your choice in the appropriate space to the right of the page.

EXAMPLE:

1. deer : forest : _____ .
   A. game : arena
   B. meat : table
   C. fish : sea
   D. fish : market

The space under C is blacked in in the answer blank because "fish live in the sea" as "deer live in the forest". All the other lettered pairs have a different kind of relationship (i.e., games *take place* in an arena, meat *is placed* on a table, fish *is sold* in a market).

Part B consists of sentences with the first and last words missing. You are to select the lettered pair to fill in the blanks to make a true and sensible sentence. Indicate your answer as before.

EXAMPLE:

2. _____ is to bread as batter is to _____ .
   A. dough...cookies
   B. sugar...candy
   C. icing...cake
   D. croutons...fish

The space under A is blacked out to complete the sentence "dough is to bread as batter is to cookies"—which means that dough *is baked to make* bread as batter *is baked to make* cookies. None of the other pairs will complete the sentence to make a true and sensible statement.

Analogies: Practice Questions

PART A: Select the lettered pair that completes the analogy and expresses a true and sensible relationship. Indicate your answer by marking the appropriate space to the right.

1. England : Europe : : _____   A B C D
   A. Italy : Germany
   B. North America : Canada
   C. Brazil : South America
   D. New Zealand : Australia

2. brown : cow : : _____   A B C D
   A. long : time
   B. lazy : dog
   C. fish : cold
   D. dog : show

3. eggs : omelet : : _____   A B C D
   A. bacon : eggs
   B. eggs : milk
   C. scrambled : eggs
   D. flour : bread

4. sail : drive : : _____   A B C D
   A. boat : car
   B. ocean : traffic
   C. wind : wheels
   D. sailor : pedestrian

5. hut : hovel : : _____   A B C D
   A. cabin : home
   B. ranch-house : White House
   C. mansion : palace
   D. bungalow : dormitory

6. tall : short : : _____   A B C D
   A. fat : thin
   B. short : fat
   C. tall : thin
   D. wide : heavy

7. eagle : lizard : : _____   A B C D
   A. reptile : bird
   B. cold-blooded : warm-blooded
   C. bird : reptile
   D. animal : bird

PART B: Select the pair from the lettered options that completes the relationship and makes a sensible statement. Indicate your answer as before.

8. ___ are to onions as peas are to ___ .   A B C D
   A. radishes—beans
   B. parsnips—lettuce
   C. radishes—potatoes
   D. corn—squash

9. _____ is to San as Gogh is to _____ .   A B C D
   A. Francisco—Van
   B. Bernardino—Clemente
   C. Van—Angeles
   D. Angeles—Los

10. _____ is to fat as clap is to _____ .   A B C D
    A. mad—thin
    B. crazy—happy
    C. mad—pad
    D. tall—happy

11. ___ is to gone as singing is to ___ .   A B C D
    A. going—sung
    B. singing—sung
    C. going—went
    D. going—sang

12. _____ is to nub as leg is to _____ .   A B C D
    A. bump—tail
    B. hub—walk
    C. bun—gel
    D. bun—peg

13. _____ is to thin as lean is to _____ .   A B C D
    A. spare—extra
    B. spare—tall
    C. brown—brunette
    D. spare—skinny

14. _____ is to sow as buck is to _____ .   A B C D
    A. plant—bill
    B. bull—mare
    C. hen—chicken
    D. boar—doe

15. ___ is to triangle as cube is to ___ .   A B C D
    A. square—sphere
    B. cone—solid
    C. cone—square
    D. rhombus—rectangle

Answers and Discussion—Analogies

1. C—England is part of Europe as Brazil is part of South America.

2. B—Brown is an adjective that applies to some cows; lazy is an adjective that applies to some dogs.

   In these two examples, you should be aware that in the correct solutions the relationships are *parallel*.

   e.g. England—is part of → Europe:

   Brazil—is part of → South America

   and

   brown—cow: lazy—dog

   but not

   England—is part of → Europe:

   North America ← is part of—Canada

   or

   brown—cow: fish—cold

3. D—Eggs are used to make an omelet, and flour is used to make bread.

4. A—You sail a boat and drive a car.

   Another kind of parallel relationship.

   sail: drive : boat: car

5. C—A hut and a hovel are both poor dwelling-places; a mansion and a palace are both expensive and fine.

   hut = hovel: mansion = palace

6. A—Tall and short are opposite in meaning, as are fat and thin.

7. C—An eagle is a bird; a lizard is a reptile.

   The same sort of relationship as in question 4.

   eagle: lizard : bird: reptile

   not

   eagle: lizard : cold-blooded: warm-blooded

8. A—Radishes and onions are both root vegetables; peas and beans are both vegetables with edible seeds.

9. A—Francisco is to San as Gogh is to Van.

10. C—All these words have the same sound for the letter "a". The meanings of the words are irrelevant.

11. A—I *am going* : I *have gone* and I *am singing* : I *have sung*.

12. C—Bun is nub spelled backwards; leg is gel spelled backwards.

13. D—Spare, thin, lean, and skinny all mean the same.

14. D—A boar is a male pig, a sow is a female; a buck is a male deer, a doe is a female.

15. C—A cone is a solid figure based on the geometry of a triangle; a cube is a solid figure based on the geometry of a square.

To handle these kinds of problems besides using all of the strategies and tactics that apply to objective tests (see Chapter 8), what you have to do is

> 12.8 In verbal-analogies problems, be sure to *look for answers* where the relationships are *parallel and specific, and use all of the information in the problem*.

In learning to answer these questions (and in doing them on tests), it really does help if you talk to yourself. (I should have stated this as a tactic quite a while ago.)

> 11.3 In reading a problem and working out the answer, *read the problem aloud*, in a voice that will not disturb those next to you.

You see, reading the problem *sotto voce*, actually forming the words with your lips, forces you to pay attention to every single word. Similarly, *reasoning* aloud can help you attend to details.

Saying the problem aloud practically forces you to pay attention to all the information in the problem and to examine each of the alternatives in turn. It's a good way to avoid "one-shot thinking" and to make sure that you take the time to pay attention to all the details.

In particular it can help you avoid the trap of falling for an answer in which only *half* of the relationship is complete. For example, in question 12, "_____ is to nub as leg is to _____", you might be tempted to pick the answer "hub —walk", because legs and walking go together. But what's the relationship of "nub" and "hub", and what do either of them have to do with "leg"?

Numerical Ability: Number Series

Besides the common problem formats discussed in Chapter 10, you can expect to encounter a special form of question in the "number-series" problem.

What is required here is that you examine the list of numbers and try to figure out how you can get from one number to the number that follows, and then from that number to the next, and so on. And, of course, there are some interesting little wrinkles thrown at you along the way.

The questions that follow illustrate some of the commonest ways in which these problems are presented.

Each question consists of a series of numbers or letters. From the letter options (A, B, C, or D) select the option that would fill in the blank to correctly complete the series.

EXAMPLE:

1. 1, 2, 3, 4, ___ .   A B C D
   A. 6   C. 5
   B. 3   D. 2

In this example, each number in the series is formed by adding 1 to the number preceding it in the series. Therefore, the space under C has been blackened in the answer space.

2. a, c, ___, g, i.   A B C D
   A. d   C. b
   B. h   D. e

In this example, the blank is filled by D.—e, and the series is formed by counting forward in the alphabet two letters.

(If you have to do number-series problems that use the alphabet, the best thing to do is to quickly write out the alphabet and the

corresponding numbers, as illustrated below:

```
1 2 3 4 5...24 25 26
A B C D E...X Y Z
```

Take the time to do this neatly. Now you can easily locate the numerical values of the letters in the problems.)

Number Series: Practice Questions

1. 1, 3, 5, 7, ___ .   A B C D
   A. 6   C. 9
   B. 8   D. 11

2. 14, 17, 20, 23, ___ .   A B C D
   A. 21   C. 26
   B. 24   D. 27

3. 25, 20, 15, 10, ___ .   A B C D
   A. 4   C. 6
   B. 30   D. 5

4. .7, 1/5, .49, 1/25, .2401, ___ .   A B C D
   A. 1/125   C. 1/500
   B. .5765   D. 1/625

5. a, j, c, h, e, f, g, ___ .   A B C D
   A. d   C. i
   B. k   D. c

6. 2, 3, 8, ___, 3968.   A B C D
   A. 1595   C. 197
   B. 69   D. 63

7. n, n, m, ___, h, d   A B C D
   A. m   C. h
   B. l   D. k

8. 16, 18, 21, 25, 27, 30, ___ .   A B C D
   A. 31   C. 29
   B. 33   D. 34

9. 6, 24, 12, 48, 24, 96, ___ .   A B C D
   A. 42   C. 48
   B. 124   D. 54

10. 14, 24, 13, 19, 12, ___ .   A B C D
    A. 19   C. 17
    B. 14   D. 15

Answers and Discussion — Number Series

1. C.—9. Add 2 to the preceding number.

2. C.—26. Add three to obtain the next number in the series.

3. D.—5. Subtract 5 from the preceding number.

4. D.—1/625. This is actually two series:
.7, .49, .2401 and 1/5, 1/25, 1/625. The rule in both series is the same: square the preceding number to find the next.

5. A.—d. This series translates into 1, 10, 3, 8, 5, 6, 7, ___, which breaks down into two series, 1, 3, 5, 7 and 10, 8, 6, ___ .

6. D.—63. The series is formed by squaring each number (multiplying it by itself) and then subtracting 1. So $2 \times 2 = 4, 4 - 1 = 3$; $3 \times 3 = 9, 9 - 1 = 8, 8 \times 8 = 64, 64 - 1 = 63$, $63 \times 63 = 3969, 3969 - 1 = 3968$. So it's important to recognize that *more than one math operation* may be involved between each number in the series.

7. D.—k. Changing this series to numbers, we get

$$14, \quad 14, \quad 13, \quad \underline{\quad} \quad 8, \quad 4.$$
$$\pm 0 \quad -1 \quad ?? \quad ?? \quad -4$$

This missing number is $13 - 2 = 11$, and $11 - 3 = 8$ confirms the correct answer.

8. D.—34. The series is formed as follows:

$$16 \quad 18 \quad 21 \quad 25 \quad 27 \quad 30 \quad 34$$
$$(+2) \quad (+3) \quad (+4) \quad (+2) \quad (+3) \quad (+4)$$

9. C.—48. The rule in this series is:

$$6 \quad 24 \quad 12 \quad 48 \quad 24 \quad 96 \quad 48$$
$$(\times 4) \quad (\div 2) \quad (\times 4) \quad (\div 2) \quad (\times 4) \quad (\div 2)$$

10. B.—14. This series is the trickiest of all. First of all, let's compute the differences between the numbers in the series.

$$14 \quad 24 \quad 13 \quad 19 \quad 12 \quad \underline{\quad}$$
$$+10 \quad -11 \quad +6 \quad -7 \quad ??$$

This doesn't look like much help. But look at the differences between the differences. Doing this we get three unknowns, as follows:

$$14 \quad 24 \quad 13 \quad 19 \quad 12 \quad ?? \quad \text{(a)}$$
$$+10 \quad -11 \quad +6 \quad -7 \quad ?? \quad \text{(b)}$$
$$-1 \quad -5 \quad -1 \quad ?? \quad \text{(c)}$$

If we enter -5 in space (c), then the answer for space (b) is

$$-7 + (b) = -5$$
$$-7 + (b) + 7 = -5 + 7$$
$$(b) = +2$$

Then we can compute $12 + 2 = 14$ to find the final answer. We can call this a "second-order" series, because you have to solve *two* related series problems to find the answer.

Rules for Working Out Number-Series Problems

The first thing to do in a number-series problem is to try to discover how each number is derived from the one just before it.

EXAMPLE:

$$14, \quad 13, \quad 12, \quad 11, \quad \underline{\quad}$$
$$-1 \quad -1 \quad -1 \quad ?$$

and

$$14, \quad 14, \quad 13, \quad 11, \quad 8, \quad \underline{\quad}$$
$$\pm 0 \quad -1 \quad -2 \quad -3 \quad ?$$

But be sure that you investigate *all* the possible relationships between the members in a series. If one rule doesn't work for the whole series, look for another relationship. If adding doesn't work, try subtracting. If that doesn't work, try multiplying, and so on.

If none of these processes work (and you will know fairly quickly if they don't), then look for two different series.

EXAMPLE:

.7, 1/5, .49, 1/25, .2401, ___ .

and 15, 13, 12, 17, 11, 10, 19, ___ .

And if this fails to produce results, you can look for a "second-order" series.

So,

12.9 To solve number-series problems: *first, look for a simple rule* that says how each number is related to the ones before and after it; *second, see if the problem can be broken down into two separate series; third, look for a "second-order" series.*

This sounds complicated, but really it is the kind of thing that people do all the time. If you have a squalling infant in your arms and he doesn't hush up if you rock him, first you look for a simple problem (maybe his diaper is wet), then you go to more complex procedures (when did he eat last?), and finally you look for even more complicated solutions (maybe he's got colic, which means you have to figure out when was he fed? did he burp? has he eaten anything out of the ordinary or that has given him gas before? does he usually do this at the same time of day? is he pulling his legs up?). And you get into trouble if you don't go through the steps.

A *warning* about number-series problems. Unless you are quite clever at math and have a good head for figures,

> 13.2 *Don't try to do mental math on tests*. Take the time to work out the problems using paper and pencil. If you are using a calculator, be sure to write down each step.

A Final Wrinkle

There is one other way in which number and letter series are presented and this is in the form of a chart, typically pie-shaped but sometimes with other configurations.

EXAMPLE:

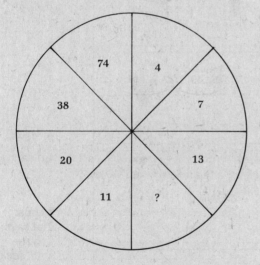

FIGURE 11.1

This breaks down into two series. The first one moves clockwise from 4, and the rule is, double the number and subtract 1. So $(4 \times 2) - 1 = 7$, $(7 \times 2) - 1 = 13$. Could the missing number be $(13 \times 2) - 1 = 25$?

But what about the other side of the circle?

How is this series formed? Well, we can see that a similar rule applies to this side. Moving clockwise, double the number and subtract 2: $(11 \times 2) - 2 = 20$, $(20 \times 2) - 2 = 38$, and so on, but this doesn't help us to find the missing number. How about looking at the relationships between the numbers in both sides?

Aha! Now we can see that the numbers on the left side are derived from the numbers *directly opposite* according to the rule multiply by 3 and subtract 1. This means that 74 equals 3 times the missing number minus 1. Or to put it in numbers: $(? \times 3) - 1 = 74$, which equals $(? \times 3) = 74 + 1$, which equals $? \times 3 = 75$. So the missing number *is* 25.

The same kinds of variations can occur on these circle puzzles as in straightforward number-series problems. Work them the same way but pay particular attention to the numbers opposite each other. Part of the trick is to find out where the series begins—but you can usually figure this out after checking *all* the relationships.

For the Completely Baffled

If you just don't get these problems, an exercise you might try for the next few days is to write some series problems of your own. Write five or so a day for a couple of weeks. You start by picking a number out of the air. Write that number down. Then do something to it—add something, multiply it by another number, multiply it by itself. Then do something to that number. And carry on in a regular fashion, using the kinds of patterns shown in the problems above. With some sustained hard work for a short period of time (and brushing up on basic math and computational rules) I think you'll find that you have a much better understanding of how these problems work.

Space Relations

No, Space Relations does not have anything to do with our communications with visitors from other galaxies. What it has to do with is your ability to imagine things in three dimensions, to be able to look at a plan of a house, for example, and form a mental image of what the house will actually look like. Or to conjure up a vivid visual image of a thing that somebody is describing to you. Again, some people are more skilled at this than other people, but training seems to help.

This ability is vital to people who work with three-dimensional (and four-dimensional) objects, plans, drawings, and pictorial representations of any kind—architects, draftspersons, tailors, designers, carpenters, air-traffic controllers, sheet-metal workers, and many other scientists, managers, and tradespeople.

The usual test involves looking at a drawing or pattern, being able to successfully predict what the pattern will look like when it is folded up, and then correctly selecting a drawing that accurately shows what the object looks like from one angle. Let's look at an example.

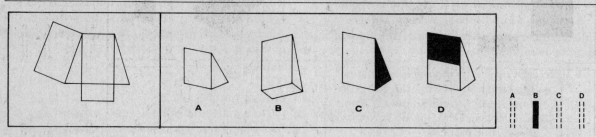

FIGURE 11.2

In this example, A is too short to be correct, and alternatives C and D are also incorrect because they are shaded while the original pattern is all white. B is the correct answer and the space under B has been blackened on the answer space.

Space Relations: Practice Questions

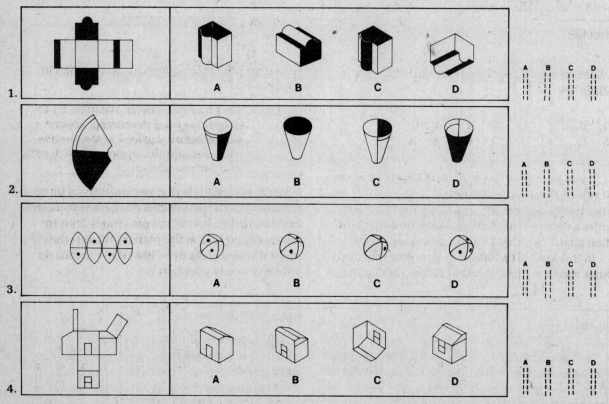

FIGURE 11.3

Go on to the next page.

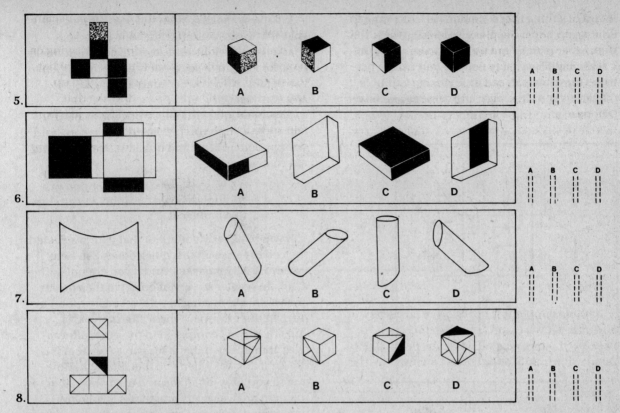

FIGURE 11.4

Answers and Discussion — Space Relations

1. B   2. A   3. B   4. C
5. C   6. C   7. D   8. A

If you got any of these incorrect, go back to see if you can analyze your mistake. Did you incorrectly predict the general shape? Did you miss a detail in the drawing? Did you leap at the first alternative that looked halfway correct?

In this kind of test it is very important that you stick rigidly to the suggested tactics for dealing with multiple-choice questions, as outlined in Chapter 8.

> 12.2 *On a multiple-choice question, try to determine what the correct answer will be before you look at the options. Then look for this option in the list of alternatives provided.*

What this means is that you must try to imagine what the shape will look like *before* you start examining the alternatives presented. Start by taking a good look at the pattern. What is the general shape going to be like? What details do you have to pay attention to?

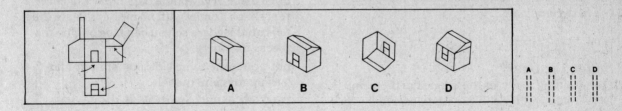

FIGURE 11.5

You're going to have trouble with this example unless you pay particular attention to the features noted above. You need to be able to follow the details as you mentally fold up the pattern. One thing you can do if you have trouble doing this is to label the various sides and edges. Like this:

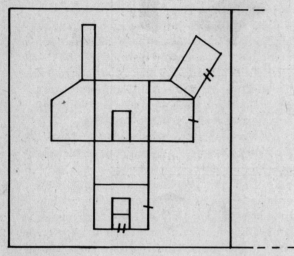

FIGURE 11.6

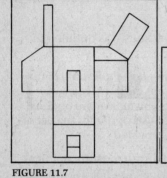

FIGURE 11.7

What this means, when the box is folded up, is that the edges marked with / join, the edges marked with // join, and so on. This should make it easier for you to see what is going to happen to the details. Now you can start looking at the alternatives.

First of all, quickly look through to see if you can spot the one you predicted. If you can, hold your pencil under it and quickly check the other alternatives.

> 12.3 *Make sure you read each option* in a multiple-choice question *and attempt to eliminate it*.

If you're already confident that you've selected the correct answer, this quick check can help you avoid silly mistakes. And if you are not sure at all, then you can very often get to the correct answer by attempting to rule out each option in turn. In our example, where alternative C is "upside down" compared to the other alternatives, it might be difficult for you to see that it is the right answer when you first look at it. However, if you *look for all the wrong answers*, then the right answer is the one that is left. Below I've noted the details that are wrong in the incorrect solutions. Choice C is the only one left, so it must be correct.

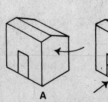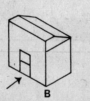

And of course, if you can't decide even at this point, follow tactic 10.1 (p. 48) and leave the question alone for a while while you work ahead on other questions. Then come back and make the best guess you can, *based on the items that you have eliminated*.

Still in the Dark?

Okay. Getting ready for these kinds of problems is a variation on the constant theme: practice the skills you're going to have to demonstrate. It is useful if you start with fairly *concrete* problems

and work progressively towards more abstract ones. For example:

—pick a fairly simple shape in your house, a small box, for example, and see if you can cut out a piece of wrapping paper that will cover that shape exactly with no overlaps (leave little tabs on the edges so you can tape or glue the pieces together).

—buy and make some kids' cut-'em-out-fold-'em-up toys and models.

—copy one of the patterns from the practice questions onto a piece of paper, cut it out, and see what it looks like when it's assembled.

—finally, you might try drawing a pattern and then drawing what the folded-up shape would look like from various angles. Cut out and assemble your pattern, to see if you were successful in predicting what the folded-up shapes would be.

And look, the whole point of this exercise is not to make three-dimensional figures. What you want is practice in *seeing* the relationships between the patterns and the three-dimensional objects—not in producing pretty objects. Working with concrete, physical models may help you develop this ability.

So don't hassle yourself if your shapes are a bit lumpy or if the tape or glue you're using looks messy—that doesn't matter at all. But do keep at it and don't let your frustration with handling the bits of paper slow you down.

Visual Reasoning

This is the ability to see relationships among non-verbal and non-numerical patterns or objects, to perform fine discriminations, and to notice changes in the appearances of things. The tests come in various formats, of which two of the most common kinds are illustrated in the Practice Questions.

At first glance, these problems may look quite similar to the Space Relations questions you have just completed. There are some differences, though. The Space Relations questions assess how quick you are thinking in three dimensions (i.e., working in your imagination with drawings of *solid* objects). The tests that follow have to do with how well you can notice things in two dimensions (i.e., with *flat* patterns). However, there is some spill-over between these two different kinds of abilities—these skills are not completely separate and distinct.

Visual Reasoning ability is important in things like mechanics, drafting, and laboratory work. Naturally, these skills are important for many scientists as well as tradespeople.

Each of the Practice Questions consists of two kinds of problems. You remember verbal-analogies problems? "Cow is to bull as doe is to buck"? The first problem form is just like this, only it is a visual, rather than a verbal, analogy. In the diagram below, figures 1 and 2 are related in some kind of way. You are to look at figure 3 and then find the option that has the same relationship to 3. That is, you are to find the figure that completes the analogy.

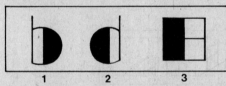 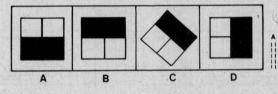

FIGURE 11.8

In this example, figure 2 is the mirror image of figure 1—the problem just flipped over once, from left to right. Nothing else about the pattern changes between figures 1 and 2. So what we want to find in the options is a pattern that is the mirror image of pattern 3. And it is option D.

The second kind of problem you get is like a number-series problem. You are presented with a series of patterns that change in some regular

way, and your task is to identify the next member of the series.

In this example, try imagining that the circle is the face of a clock, and the mark tells you what time it is. In the first diagram, the mark is at 12 o'clock, in the next one it is at the 3 o'clock position, then at 6 o'clock, then at 9 o'clock. So the rule is: move the mark three hours forward. Okay, the next position should be 12 o'clock

 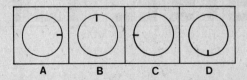

FIGURE 11.9

again. Sure enough, option B gives us the correct response. None of the other options follow the same rule.

Get the picture?

PART A: Visual Analogies. Figures 1 and 2 are related in some way. Find the figure (A, B, C, or D) that completes the analogy 1 is to 2 as 3 is to ___?___ .

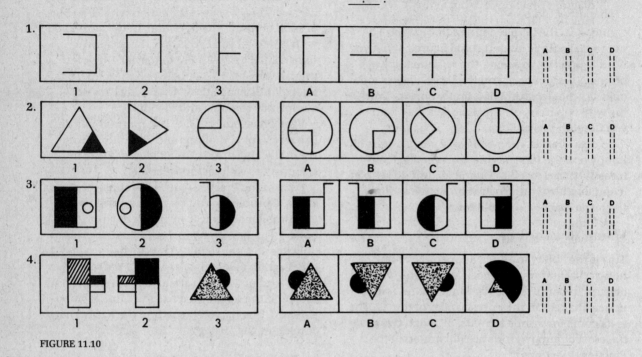

FIGURE 11.10

PART B: Visual Series. Find the next figure in the series.

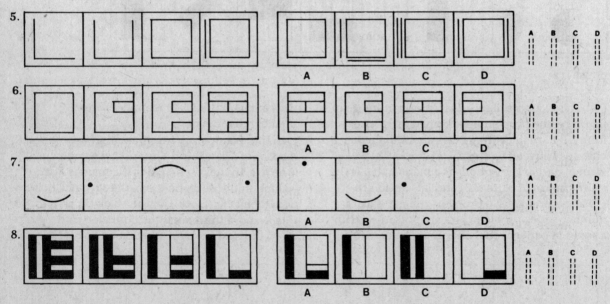

FIGURE 11.11

Answers and Discussion — Visual Reasoning

1. **B**—Figure 1 rotates (turns) 90° counterclockwise to become figure 2. What we want is a diagram that shows what figure 3 would look like if it were turned in the same way. A is no good because there's nothing in the problem that has to do with lines slipping up and down. C is no good because the figure is rotated clockwise. And D won't do because the pattern turns too far.

2. **D**—Figure 1 rotates clockwise 90° to become figure 2.

3. **A**—What happens in figures 1 and 2 is that the shape changes from a square to a circle, the shading moves from the left to the right of the figure, and the little "bubble" switches from the right to the left of the drawing. In 3 we have what looks like the letter b, with the right side of the body of the letter shaded in. Glancing at the options we notice that three of the figures have square bodies and one looks like the letter d. It's going to be one of the square figures. Because the shading was on the right in figure 3, we want the shading on the left in our answer, which narrows the choice to figures A and B. And we want the stem of the "letter" to remain on the opposite side of the figure from the shading, so A's our baby.

4. **D**—At first glance this looks like a mirror image problem, but guess again. The *outline* of figure 2 is a mirror image of figure 1, but the shading doesn't change position (i.e., the light shading is still on the left and the black is on the right. What to do? Well, we can't predict what the answer will look like, so let's scan the options. Alternative A looks attractive, but it is an exact mirror image. B and C are far-out—there's nothing here that looks remotely like what happened in figures 1 and 2. D looks weird—the half-circle has grown and the triangle has shrunk—but looking at 1 and 2 again, this is exactly what has happened.

5. **B**—The rule is add a line to the figure in a counterclockwise sequence. In A a line has not been added. In C a line has been added all right but not in sequence. And in D the sequence has again been ignored. This is a good example of how testers seem to prefer concrete, specific, straightforward solutions. An argument could be made for any of the figures, but only in B is exactly the same progression preserved.

6. **A**—Another additive series.

7. **B**—This is two series in one, with each series following the same rule.

8. **D**—The rule is first you lose a horizontal bar, then a vertical one, and so on.

To do well in these kinds of visual tests you have to follow two basic rules:

1. Notice every detail in the original drawings.

2. Trace what happens to every detail and use *all* the information in the drawings.

For example, if you see that in question 4 the outlines of figures 1 and 2 are mirror images, you might incorrectly conclude that A is the solution.

In order to avoid this mistake, you have to pay attention to what happens to the shading of the figures. What change occurs here? When you notice that the lightly shaded area shrinks, but stays on the left side of the figure, while the dark, left-hand portion grows large—you are on your way to the correct solution.

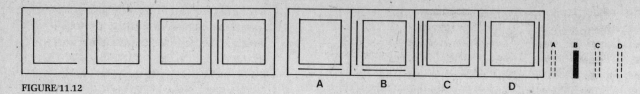

FIGURE 11.12

So the key is watch the details and use all the details. Use every piece of information that is given to you. Part of what this means, of course, is that various parts of elements in the figures can be doing different things at the same time. A very complicated sequence is possible as more elements are added to the drawing.

And, of course, part of the trick, particularly in the sequence questions, is to look for a solution that continues the same sequence as in the orig-inal drawings. Don't pick patterns that represent a change in the rules.

Which is why all the options except B are incorrect in Figure 11.12. All of them make sense, except that they require you to drop part of the rules that form the sequence. The rule is to add a line each time in a counter-clockwise sequence. If you don't add a line, or don't follow the coun-ter-clockwise sequence, the answer is wrong. But you've got to watch it!

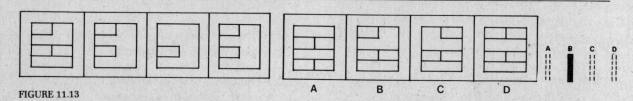

FIGURE 11.13

In Figure 11.13, the sequence starts one way and then begins to reverse. The answer you want will continue the reversal. The answer is option B.

Improving Visual Reasoning

I'm pretty sure that it would be helpful to you to practice and improve your skill in this area by using the same kind of approach I suggested for dealing with number-series problems. And that was, if you remember, to practice building your own problems. Start by copying the diagrams that were used here and see if you can construct some new problems of your own; then you can branch out to more complicated figures. You might use logos or designs from magazines as the basis of more problems.

The key seems to be to learn to pay close attention to detail and to become familiar with the standard "moves"—rotation, inversion, mir-ror-imaging, and so on.

It may take a while to get on to these things. But a little work should make a difference.

Clerical Accuracy—Details, Details

Clerical ability is largely the capacity to quickly and accurately detect differences in written words and numbers, and to transcribe and record correctly. It is an important skill for peo-ple in all the word- and data-processing occupa-tions—from typists to accountants to systems analysts to computer programmers. In these occupations people have to deal with enormous volumes of written material in which minor errors can cause enormous difficulty.

The questions given here illustrate three dif-ferent tasks you may be asked to do on tests of clerical accuracy.

The first group of questions consists of seven four-digit numbers. These numbers are repro-duced on the answer sheet, but in a different order. One number in each question is under-lined. You are to find this number on the sheet and blacken the space beneath it.

For example,

1	5798	<u>5978</u>	9785	3578	4985	7895	5987
2	2430	3420	0432	2403	3420	<u>0423</u>	3240

ANSWERS

1	3578	5987	9785	5978	4985	7895	5798
	( )	( )	( )	(■)	( )	( )	( )
2	3420	2403	0423	3240	0432	3420	2430
	( )	( )	(■)	( )	( )	( )	( )

FIGURE 11.14

In the second task, you are presented with two columns of names. If the names beside each other are the same, you blacken A on the answer sheet. If they are different, blacken the space under B.

| 1 | Stormont Investors Inc. | Stormont Investors, Inc. |
| 2 | Lelani Floral Imports | Lelani Floral Imports |

ANSWERS

	A	B
1	( )	(■)
2	(■)	( )

FIGURE 11.15

And, finally, you are asked to indicate which in a series of numbers is the largest. Mark the space on the answer sheet which indicates the column in which the largest number appears.

	A	B	C	D	E	F	G
1	9876	9978	9493	6949	9499	9987	9899
2	1021	2094	3299	1039	3398	3298	2099

ANSWERS

	A	B	C	D	E	F	G
1	( )	( )	( )	( )	( )	(■)	( )
2	( )	( )	( )	( )	(■)	( )	( )

FIGURE 11.16

Now look, most people can get these things right if they take long enough. The trick is, of course, to perform the task accurately *under* *time pressure*. So what you want to do is to gradually increase the speed and accuracy with which you do questions.

Clerical Speed and Accuracy—Practice Questions

PART A: Each question consists of a line of seven four-digit numbers, one of which is underlined. Find this number on the corresponding line of the answer sheet, and blacken the space beneath it.

1	6291	7191	<u>6541</u>	6519	7161	6519	6915
2	7580	8435	2848	8427	<u>3458</u>	8914	8521
3	8849	<u>6028</u>	8212	7638	8019	0850	8510
4	7638	6873	7362	7889	6975	7987	<u>7377</u>
5	<u>3880</u>	7087	3630	9380	3889	3380	3630
6	2519	0370	<u>2215</u>	2656	2189	2485	2585
7	4258	0434	0950	<u>4795</u>	4385	9155	4255
8	3878	3218	3834	3675	5378	<u>3825</u>	3975
9	6739	2689	6451	6511	<u>5895</u>	9780	6750
10	9533	5339	9567	5455	<u>9543</u>	9567	5895
11	<u>3241</u>	3354	8486	3878	0896	8332	8283
12	7674	7649	7469	7272	7967	<u>4745</u>	4674
13	1137	<u>1158</u>	1124	1401	1058	7418	1137
14	6190	0351	<u>6193</u>	6147	6498	4609	6413
15	5824	5915	9534	5951	5943	<u>5369</u>	5854
16	<u>7171</u>	7117	8775	8796	7817	8709	8177
17	5945	5071	0675	<u>6275</u>	5575	5945	5745
18	3101	0110	3011	3116	3110	<u>0101</u>	3111
19	9807	<u>8897</u>	9103	0879	8097	9887	8079
20	1648	8464	4184	7421	<u>0148</u>	6146	4621
21	3923	4374	2730	4361	3643	3934	<u>3748</u>
22	<u>8765</u>	0835	8421	7923	7365	7765	8756
23	1254	5441	4451	1254	1741	5441	<u>1245</u>
24	4691	4795	9671	4081	<u>4451</u>	9761	5441
25	9519	<u>9359</u>	9639	5939	9159	9539	9889

ANSWERS

1	7161 ( )	6519 ( )	6915 ( )	6541 ( )	6519 ( )	6291 ( )	7191 ( )
2	7580 ( )	8435 ( )	2848 ( )	8427 ( )	8914 ( )	8521 ( )	3458 ( )
3	8510 ( )	8212 ( )	7638 ( )	8849 ( )	6028 ( )	8019 ( )	0850 ( )
4	6873 ( )	7362 ( )	7987 ( )	7889 ( )	6975 ( )	7638 ( )	7377 ( )
5	3889 ( )	3380 ( )	3630 ( )	3880 ( )	7087 ( )	3630 ( )	9380 ( )
6	2215 ( )	2189 ( )	2485 ( )	2519 ( )	0370 ( )	2585 ( )	2656 ( )
7	4795 ( )	0434 ( )	0950 ( )	4255 ( )	4258 ( )	4385 ( )	9155 ( )
8	3834 ( )	3675 ( )	5378 ( )	3825 ( )	3975 ( )	3878 ( )	3218 ( )
9	6739 ( )	6451 ( )	5895 ( )	6750 ( )	9780 ( )	6511 ( )	2689 ( )
10	9567 ( )	9533 ( )	9543 ( )	5895 ( )	9567 ( )	5455 ( )	5339 ( )
11	8283 ( )	0896 ( )	3354 ( )	3241 ( )	8486 ( )	3878 ( )	8332 ( )
12	7469 ( )	7272 ( )	7649 ( )	7674 ( )	4745 ( )	4674 ( )	7967 ( )
13	1124 ( )	1401 ( )	1137 ( )	1058 ( )	7418 ( )	1137 ( )	1158 ( )
14	4609 ( )	6413 ( )	6190 ( )	0351 ( )	6193 ( )	6147 ( )	6498 ( )
15	5943 ( )	5369 ( )	5854 ( )	5824 ( )	5915 ( )	9534 ( )	5951 ( )
16	8709 ( )	8177 ( )	7117 ( )	8775 ( )	8796 ( )	7817 ( )	7171 ( )
17	5071 ( )	0675 ( )	5945 ( )	5745 ( )	6275 ( )	5575 ( )	5945 ( )
18	3101 ( )	0110 ( )	0101 ( )	3111 ( )	3011 ( )	3116 ( )	3110 ( )
19	0879 ( )	8097 ( )	9887 ( )	8079 ( )	9807 ( )	8897 ( )	9103 ( )
20	7421 ( )	0148 ( )	6146 ( )	4621 ( )	1648 ( )	8464 ( )	4184 ( )
21	3643 ( )	3748 ( )	3934 ( )	2730 ( )	4361 ( )	3923 ( )	4374 ( )
22	8421 ( )	8765 ( )	7765 ( )	8756 ( )	7923 ( )	7365 ( )	0835 ( )
23	5441 ( )	1245 ( )	1254 ( )	1741 ( )	1254 ( )	5441 ( )	4451 ( )
24	4795 ( )	9671 ( )	9761 ( )	5441 ( )	4081 ( )	4451 ( )	4691 ( )
25	9639 ( )	9159 ( )	9889 ( )	9539 ( )	5939 ( )	9519 ( )	9359 ( )

FIGURE 11.17

PART B: Look at the name on the left. If the name on the right is exactly the *same*, blacken the space under A. If it is *different*, blacken the space under B.

1	Hindeman & Beal Resources	Hindemann & Beal Resources
2	Lillyman Bros.	Lillyman Bros.
3	Brentwood Investors Inc.	Bentwood Investors Inc.
4	Stearns-Barnes Company	Stearns-Barnes Company
5	Frank R. Bailey	Frank R. Bailey
6	Stagecraft Cosmetic Co.	Stagecraft Cosmetics Co.
7	Evelyn's Hairdressing	Evelyns Hairdressing
8	Fry, Blackburn, Gant and Murphy	Fry, Blackburn, Gant & Murphy
9	Churchland Home Industries, Inc.	Churchland Home Industries, Inc.
10	Gideon Lyczewski	Gideon Lyzcewski
11	Leroy Mavis	Leroy Maves
12	A1 Furniture Rentals, Company Inc.	A-1 Furniture Rentals, Company Inc.
13	Joyce Eng	Joyce Eng
14	Dr. R.F. Adam	Dr R F Adam
15	Torrington Estates	Torrington Estates
16	Parrish and Miller, Grn dlrs	Parrish and Miller, Grn dlrs
17	Alwest Motors	Allwest Motors
18	Walter B. Sondale Co.	Walter B. Sondale Co.
19	Gronigan's Tavern & Grill	Gronigan's Bar & Grill
20	Flanders	Flanders
21	Winston Kimbaugh, Dentist	Wilson Kunbaugh, Dentist
22	Hildegard Stearn	Hildegard Stearn
23	Allan-Michelson Holdings Corp.	Alan-Michelson Holdings Corp.
24	Branwyn Junior College	Branwyn Junior Colege
25	S.L. Sloane	S.L. Sloane

ANSWERS — A   B

1 ( ) ( )
2 ( ) ( )
3 ( ) ( )
4 ( ) ( )
5 ( ) ( )
6 ( ) ( )
7 ( ) ( )
8 ( ) ( )
9 ( ) ( )
10 ( ) ( )
11 ( ) ( )
12 ( ) ( )
13 ( ) ( )
14 ( ) ( )
15 ( ) ( )
16 ( ) ( )
17 ( ) ( )
18 ( ) ( )
19 ( ) ( )
20 ( ) ( )
21 ( ) ( )
22 ( ) ( )
23 ( ) ( )
24 ( ) ( )
25 ( ) ( )

FIGURE 11.18

ANSWERS

PART A:

PART B:

PART C:

PART C: In each row of numbers *find the number that is the largest*. Then blacken the space on the answer sheet which indicates *the column* in which the largest number appears.

	A	B	C	D	E	F	G
1	7161	6519	6541	6915	7191	6291	6519
2	8935	2848	8427	8521	7580	3458	8914
3	7638	8019	0850	8510	8849	6028	8212
4	7889	6975	7987	7377	7638	6873	7362
5	3889	3380	3630	3630	3880	7087	9380
6	2189	2485	2585	0370	2519	2215	2656
7	0950	9155	4255	4285	0434	4795	4385
8	3675	3825	3975	3218	3834	3878	5378
9	6511	9780	6750	2689	6451	6739	5895
10	5455	9567	5895	9543	9560	9533	5339
11	3878	8486	8283	0896	8332	3241	3354
12	7975	7469	4745	4674	7967	7674	7649
13	1401	1124	7418	1137	1058	1137	1158
14	6147	6498	6193	4609	6413	6190	0351
15	5369	5824	5915	9534	5951	5854	5943
16	8709	7171	8796	8177	7117	8775	7817
17	5945	5945	5071	0675	5745	6275	5575
18	3110	0101	3011	3116	3111	3101	0110
19	0879	8897	9807	9103	8079	8097	9887
20	7421	0148	6146	1648	4621	8464	4184
21	3643	3934	2730	3923	3748	4374	4361
22	7965	7765	8421	8765	8756	0835	7923
23	1741	5441	1245	1254	5444	4451	1254
24	4795	4451	9761	5441	4691	9671	4081
25	9359	9159	9539	9889	9519	9639	5939

ANSWERS

	A	B	C	D	E	F	G
1	( )	( )	( )	( )	( )	( )	( )
2	( )	( )	( )	( )	( )	( )	( )
3	( )	( )	( )	( )	( )	( )	( )
4	( )	( )	( )	( )	( )	( )	( )
5	( )	( )	( )	( )	( )	( )	( )
6	( )	( )	( )	( )	( )	( )	( )
7	( )	( )	( )	( )	( )	( )	( )
8	( )	( )	( )	( )	( )	( )	( )
9	( )	( )	( )	( )	( )	( )	( )
10	( )	( )	( )	( )	( )	( )	( )
11	( )	( )	( )	( )	( )	( )	( )
12	( )	( )	( )	( )	( )	( )	( )
13	( )	( )	( )	( )	( )	( )	( )
14	( )	( )	( )	( )	( )	( )	( )
15	( )	( )	( )	( )	( )	( )	( )
16	( )	( )	( )	( )	( )	( )	( )
17	( )	( )	( )	( )	( )	( )	( )
18	( )	( )	( )	( )	( )	( )	( )
19	( )	( )	( )	( )	( )	( )	( )
20	( )	( )	( )	( )	( )	( )	( )
21	( )	( )	( )	( )	( )	( )	( )
22	( )	( )	( )	( )	( )	( )	( )
23	( )	( )	( )	( )	( )	( )	( )
24	( )	( )	( )	( )	( )	( )	( )
25	( )	( )	( )	( )	( )	( )	( )

FIGURE 11.19

Being Fast, Neat, and Accurate

The key to this whole thing is to learn to be ultra-systematic about the way you tackle the tasks. In other words, you must learn to do the things that really good clerks do.

> 11.4   In taking tests, *minimize visual and other distractions* while doing the problems, and use *physical aids to help you focus on details*.

This is the whole point behind learning to underline key words in the test questions: it helps you focus on those important details and stops you from losing track of them. But it's even more important to carry out this approach in tests that involve clerical accuracy.

Some of the the things that you can do:

1. Use a straight-edge or ruler to keep your place in the questions.

2. Use your finger to point to and hold the detail you are looking at on the test.

3. Say the numbers or words to yourself as you first read them and then as you look for them on the answer sheet.

4. Try to develop a rhythm as you work.

5. Use your pencil to hold the right spot on the answer sheet while you check the rest of the options.

What the test-maker is trying to do, of course, is to get you confused by submerging the answer in a mass of details that are visually distracting. You combat his evil intentions by trying to reduce visual clutter and confusion.

And to practice for these kinds of tests, learn to use these same procedures while you engage in day-to-day clerical activities. You can use them while you balance your checkbook or work on your family budget—or in checking an essay for spelling mistakes and typographical errors. Or sometimes, just for practice, you might try to see if you can find the largest or smallest numbers in a list—say, in the stock-market quotations.

Again, practice helps. If you practice being sloppy the rest of the time, and then try to be careful on the test, it gets to be a bit tricky. But if you try to develop the habit of clerical accuracy over a longer period, then the test is not anything special.

If you persist in having incredible difficulty with clerical problems—even after you've made valiant efforts to improve your skill in this area—then it might be useful to check out whether you might have a perceptual or learning disorder. Finding a resource to do it might be a bit tricky, but for starters you could try the Psychology department at a university or the main counselling office of a large city school system.

Aptitude and Intelligence Tests

3   Practice the Skills You Will Have To Demonstrate on the Exam

     3.14   In preparation for intelligence, aptitude, or other achievement tests, *set aside time to practice, on a regular basis, the kinds of problems that will appear on the test*. (*p. 72*)

11   Read Questions Carefully, Underlining Key Terms. Decide What You Are Expected To Do.

     11.3   In reading a problem and working out the answer, *read the problem aloud*, in a voice that will not disturb those next to you. (*p. 74*)

     11.4   In taking tests, *minimize visual and other distractions* while doing the problems, and *use physical aids to help you focus on details*. (*p. 88*)

12   Attack Each Question Systematically

     12.8   In verbal-analogies problems, be sure to *look for answers* where the relationships are *parallel and specific, and use all the information in the problem*. (*p. 74*)

     12.9   To solve number-series problems: *first, look for a simple rule* that says how each number is related to the ones before and after it; *second, see if the problem can be broken down into two separate series; third, look for a "second-order" series*. (*p. 76*)

Chapter 12

Open-book exams

An open-book exam, for those of you who have not been exposed to the beast, is a test where you get to bring texts and/or notes to refer to during the examination. Sometimes only a particular text is allowed and in other cases the choice is left wide open. A variation on the theme is the test where the instructor will permit the use of a crib-sheet or a data-sheet—basically one page of notes with anything you want written on it.

When you have been told that you will be given an open-book exam,

> 6.5   *Make sure you know exactly what materials may be brought with you to the test.*

This goes for other exams as well, naturally, but for open-book exams it is critically important. It is extremely discomfiting to arrive at the test to discover that you cannot use a text that you were counting on employing. And, of course, don't try to pull a fast one by bringing in forbidden materials. Profs have been known to become quite irrational when their relatively generous allowances have been violated by students.

Why Have an Open-Book Exam?

At first blush, it would seem that being able to bring your textbooks and notes with you to the exam should make taking the test a whole lot easier, but a lot of the time students really foul these things up. Usually this is because they have failed to understand why an open-book exam would be staged in the first place, and have therefore prepared for the test inappropriately.

There are basically four reasons why a prof would set an open-book exam:

1. Because he wants to spare you the inefficiency of having to memorize masses of technical details.

2. Because the students will have to make use of extensive or detailed tables, charts, and diagrams to answer the questions, and it is simply uneconomical in terms of time and money to reproduce them for every student if they're already in the text.

3. To get around the problem of cheating. This is kind of like legalizing the possession of marijuana. The professor may not think that "looking it up" is necessarily a desirable habit, but he doesn't particularly feel like employing the police-state security measures that would be required to eliminate cheating.

4. Because the prof objects to the standard examination procedures in principle and sees no reason to erect artificial barriers to student performance on tests. Doing the test, say such profs, should be like doing any other assignment, with the time restriction being seen as an unfortunate, but alas inevitable, concession to the policies of the institution.

I'm sure you can see what kinds of difficulties students could run into on open-book exams. Either they tend to get too casual about studying for the test (thinking that they can always look it up if they're not sure of something), or they go bananas about annotating the text, putting little index tabs on every second page (or worse, sticking little bits of paper between the pages—little bits of paper that make quite a pretty display as they flutter to the floor during the test, to the consternation of the student). Either you get too little studying, or you get inappropriate marking up, indexing, and cross-referencing of the text, which probably has little to do with preparing for the kinds of problems that will be on the test.

So actually open-book exams may be harder to take than the usual test. Not only can the prof insist on a precision that he would not require on the standard test, but having the texts available often serves to distract and disorganize students.

Good Test-Taking Strategies Apply

Basically the approach to take in preparing for and taking this kind of test will not be all that different from your preparation for the usual test. You just won't have time to rely on the text to get you through the spots where your learning has been inadequate, so it doesn't make much sense to try it. If you haven't learned the material before the test, you sure aren't going to learn it during the test.

It does make sense, though, to practice using the textbook in the way that you'll have to use it during the exam. You should really know how the book is organized. You should know how to use the table of contents and the index, and you should be familiar with the tables, charts, diagrams, and so on, that you will have to use to answer the questions on the exam.

Again, the fundamental rules apply (as time goes by). Practice the skills you will have to demonstrate on the test.

> 3.15 To prepare for an open-book exam, *as well as completing your regular form of review, practice answering sample problems using the text as a tool* that allows you to be more precise.

And that's all you should use the textbook for on the test—a tool. Just like your calculator or your drafting instruments or a dictionary. You need to know how to use them before the test starts, but they are not going to get you through the exam all by themselves.

But, for heaven's sake, *do* make use of the text during the exam. The prof is letting you bring

the textbook so that you *can* check technical details and be more precise and accurate in the way that you answer. Trying to show off how smart you are by refusing to use the book at all is just about as dumb as trying to rely on the book to cover the holes in your knowledge of the material. People who take pride in not referring to the book usually are pretty cocky about their achievement—until they get their graded examinations back.

Developing and Using a Crib-Sheet

In many ways, the problem with an open-book exam is an embarrassment of riches. There's simply so much information available to use that you don't know what to do with it. This is not the problem with tests where crib-sheets are allowed.

Here the problem seems to be that people want to overload their crib-sheets with every single piece of information that is at all important (forgetting somehow that they do have a certain memory capacity themselves). So they come to the test with a sheet of notes covered with minuscule jottings and squiggles that are so jammed together that it is almost impossible to use the thing during the test. Some of the crib-sheets I have seen are monuments of unintelligibility.

> 3.16 If you are allowed to bring a crib-sheet to the test, make sure you prepare one that is *neat, well-organized, and easy to read, and that contains only essential, hard-to-remember information*.

Again, a tool. A crib-sheet is a tool. It is not used and cannot be used to cover the deficits in your learning of the subject matter. It is usually not possible to summarize the entire course on a single sheet of paper. If you don't know how to attack problems in the course, or if there are vast gaps in your knowledge of the material, a crib-sheet is going to be of no help at all. All a crib-sheet can do for you is to help you recall a very limited amount of technical information that otherwise would be difficult to remember.

Open-Book Exams

3   Practice the Skills You Will Have To Demonstrate on the Exam

3.15   To prepare for an open-book exam, *as well as completing your regular form of review, practice answering sample problems using the text as a tool* that allows you to be more precise. (*p. 91*)

3.16   If you are allowed to bring a crib-sheet to the test, make sure you prepare one that is *neat, well-organized, and easy to read, and that contains only essential, hard-to-remember information.* (*p. 91*)

6   Make Sure You Understand the General Instructions

6.5   *Make sure you know exactly what materials may be brought with you to the test.* (*p. 90*)

Chapter 13

Oral examinations

Oral examinations come in two forms: the oral quiz, and the major oral.

The oral quiz consists of a (usually private) meeting between you and the prof, in which the prof asks you a short list of questions, and sometimes follows up on your responses to these questions with a few others. Except in small classes and seminars, oral quizzes tend to be quite short, from ten to thirty minutes in length, since the prof has to interview everyone in the class. And because they are usually short, they tend also to be considered only a small part of your grade.

Major orals, on the other hand, are a very big deal.

A Charming Custom

When universities were first getting started in medieval Europe, their organization and government were patterned on the trades guilds. In fact, the medieval communities of scholars *were* guilds. And just as the trades guilds were organized around the idea of "grades" of training and competence (apprentice, journeyman, master, etc.), with advancement to the next level controlled by a comprehensive practical examination, so too for the universities.

You'll remember that this happened prior to the invention of the printing press, and before cheap paper, so naturally the exam was oral: one was examined at some length by a group of masters whose major question was, "What makes this young twerp think that we should let him into our club?" Because that's basically what the guild was — a very tightly controlled club that had a larger function than just the regulation of training. Passing the exam meant a new social status and a new group of colleagues, and it gave you a licence to practice your profession. Since one of the functions of the guilds was to limit competition, by restricting the number of licenced practioners, you can bet that the orals were real toughies.

So that's where this charming custom of the major orals comes from, and it explains largely, I think, why there is still a lot of rather excessive anxiety in students' minds about preparing for and sitting these exams.

Major orals occur as a rite of passage at definite stages in a student's career, typically at the end of an honors or master's degree program, prior to the beginning of the doctoral dissertation, and again after the dissertation has been written. Orals can be "comprehensive orals", examining the student's broad competence in the discipline, or they can be focussed on reviewing and evaluating a major piece of research or a major practical project that the student has completed.

True to their medieval origins, major orals tend to be lengthy (two to three hours, sometimes longer), they usually examine the candidate in some depth, and they are conducted by a committee of masters. Also, the exams really count; if you flunk Biology 201, it's usually just a minor inconvenience that involves some make-up work on your part, but if you flunk your orals, you are really in trouble. Usually you get one more crack at a major oral, but failing to pass the exam a second time means that you don't get your degree. Period.

A charming custom.

I think before we go on with this line of discussion, we'll lighten up a bit to talk about the oral quiz.

Intimidation

(This is lightening up?!)

Lots of people are intimidated by oral quizzes and fear that they are going to fall to pieces under examination by the prof. They feel that it's going to be a "cross-examination" with the prof in the role of Prosecutor.

Usually, but not always, such people are also uncomfortable in other situations where their work is being evaluated (they feel it's their worth as human beings that is being questioned).

It doesn't help to tell such people that their fears are usually groundless—that relatively few professors actually chew up undergraduates for lunch and spit them out. It doesn't help to say that most profs are going to go out of their way to avoid comments that could hurt the students' feelings since, of course, there are a few meanies out there who will behave in this way towards students.

I have a few comments to make about this problem of being afraid of profs, but if the situation is really bad, I suggest you sneak ahead to Section III of this book before you continue reading here.

Some Things You Can Do To Overcome Your Fear of Profs

—Meet with the prof before the class even starts. Set up an appointment and begin your discussion with the comment "I am (I'm thinking of) taking your class next term and I wonder if I could get some more information about the course?", and then follow up with the intelligent questions that have undoubtedly occurred to you. (If you're afraid that you'll forget your questions, write them out clearly and take them with you).

—Learn to smile, nod, and say hello to the prof. If you have to, lie in wait outside the classroom so you can practice doing this before the start of every class.

—After class, ask if the prof can suggest some additional reading material on a topic that interests you (and then make sure you read the things he suggests).

—After class, ask the prof a question about the details of an assignment you're working on.

—During class, ask the prof about the assignment.

You see how it goes. It is like (indeed, it is!) building a relationship with the professor that consists of slightly more than occupying space in the same room three times a week.

And I am not talking about apple-polishing. I am talking about the kinds of steps you must take in order to overcome an unreasonable fear of a teacher. And there is nothing phony, fake, artificial, or dishonest about doing that.

> 3.17 *If you are nervous* at the prospect of being given an oral quiz, begin early in the term to *desensitize yourself by having as many short, non-threatening conversations with the teacher as you can manage*.

Now, for sure, if you really cannot see yourself taking the kinds of steps that I've described, or your fear of the oral quiz looks as if it is going to stick around, I do urge you to flip to Section III of this book.

Okay. Let's get back to some other practical matters.

Learning To Use Your Mouth Effectively

We all recognize and can write more words than we can actually say. Our spoken vocabularies tend to be quite small. And since you will be using your mouth on the exam, and trying to utter words that you've probably only seen in print before, it makes sense to

> 3.18 *Learn and practice the correct pronunciation of technical terms and practice making oral responses to questions* prior to taking any oral exam.

A study group can be invaluable here, but if you have to you can do it on your own with a good dictionary or glossary. But it isn't going to come automatically unless you have already made a habit of learning the pronunciation of new terms as you encounter them.

Believe me, nothing will make you feel quite as stupid as having to refer to the "whatsis" or the "you know, *that* thing" because you have failed to learn how to pronounce a specific term.

Do First Impressions Count in Oral Exams?

Does it matter if your lunch is recorded on the front of your sweater—or on your breath?

Does it help you get a better grade if you come in late, spill your book-bag all over the floor, and knock over a stack of papers on the prof's desk?

Will you get a better grade if you wear a tank top and shorts to your admission interview for Med School?

Will it materially affect your score if you smoke in the prof's windowless office?

Do you really need to think about the answers to these silly questions?

Answering Questions in Orals

The first rule of good speaking (anywhere, any time) is good *listening*.

> 11.5 In oral examinations, *look at the examiner while a question is being asked* or a comment is being made.

Often the reason students don't understand what others are saying is that, while their ears may be registering the sound waves created by the other person's voice, the student's mind is in Never-Never Land. Your attention seems to go where your eyes take it. If you want to pay close attention to what somebody is saying, the first step is to look at the person.

Just to make sure you understand the question, and especially if it is phrased vaguely, or you are a bit nervous,

> 11.6 Seek clarification of questions on oral exams, *first by paraphrasing* the question, and *then by asking for additional explanation*, if you need it.

It can be a *serious mistake* to do this in the reverse order. If you say to a grouchy prof, "I'm sorry, could you explain what you mean by that term?" or "Gee, could you please repeat the question? I was thinking about where I put my car keys," the chances are excellent that you will get an impatient and intolerant response—"You should know what the term means. I've used it often enough in the class," or, "Well, will you kindly pay attention. I've been talking to students since the break of dawn."

However, if you *paraphrase* the question you will almost inevitably (1) get a second run on the question, (2) get it delivered in slightly different terms, and (3) get an expanded version of the question.

Paraphrasing simply means to *repeat the question* to the instructor *as you understand it*. "Okay, what you want me to do is to describe the various phases of the octipilation of the octropol and list the characteristics in each phase?" (Notice that you ask this *as a question*.)

The prof may just say, "That's correct," which tells you that you have the question right, anyway. Or he may say something like, "No, you misunderstood. I want the phases of the octipilation of the octropile, and I'm mostly interested in how you would differentiate the phases by the lab analysis of spectral residues."

Now you have first of all clarified an important point (*octropile*, not octropol), and the prof gave you more information the second time around. He practically outlined the answer for you.

Paraphrasing almost always works. The only danger is that you may have a tendency initially to merely *parrot* the question, rather than repeating the question in your own words. When you parrot back a question the prof starts to feel that either you're stupid or you're making fun of him. But a paraphrase—re-asking the question in your own words—is almost invariably interpreted as an intelligent maneuver that indicates that you are being very careful about understanding the question.

What If You Can't Think of the Answer?

> 15.3 If you can't think of the exact answer to an oral question, *begin by giving the information that you do know*.

The reason for doing this is obvious. It's the same reason you write something down for every question on an essay test. You may know more than you think you do and inadvertently give the prof exactly what he wants. And secondly, while you are talking, you may remember information that *is* directly relevant.

And the reaction of your prof in oral exams—in particular the subsequent questions he may ask you—can be a valuable boost in getting going in the right direction.

If you just sit there like a bump on the chair, or mutter, "I dunno," no points for you. So say something, *anything*, you can recall about the general subject.

Of course, when you're taking an oral, as in other tests, you might later think of more to say about a question the prof asked earlier in the exam.

> 8.4 *If you think of information about a previous question* during an oral exam, *make a note of the idea* so that you can mention it later, *or politely interrupt the conversation to return to the previous question*.

It helps if you have at hand a small pad of paper and a pen that works (as long as you don't fiddle with it). And it really is quite okay to say, "Excuse me, I just thought of something about a previous question. Could I just take a second to make a note of it?", then write your idea down and say, "I'm sorry, I interrupted you..."

Sometimes the prof will ask immediately what it is that you remembered, but if he doesn't, return to that question at the very first appropriate opportunity, while the idea is fresh in your memory.

And that, folks, just about wraps it up. Oral exams aren't that much different from, say, essay or problem exams, except that you're using your mouth instead of your pen. The same approaches work for both types of tests.

But Now For the Really Big Oral...

Because important orals are much longer than quizzes, can range over a wider subject area, and go into more depth in the questions, and because the consequences of your behavior on these tests are important, big orals require much more intensive preparation than oral quizzes.

In most schools it is the role of the student's adviser to prepare the student for the oral, and most supervisors take this responsibility seriously, though they may not do a particularly good job of it.

After all, no prof wants to get a reputation for bringing students forward to an oral exam when the students aren't ready. The prof just doesn't care to get feedback from the committee that says, in effect, that the prof and the student have been wasting the committee's time and that the student has got to do a significant amount of improving before he can be passed. So in many ways your adviser's letting you go ahead to the oral is already a good sign, because it suggests pretty strongly that the adviser is expecting a positive outcome.

But, don't be passive about this. Quiz your adviser about what you need to do to get ready for the oral. He should inform you of the regulations and procedures that will be followed. He should help you try to anticipate the kinds of questions that might be asked. He can give you background information about the theoretical and philosophical orientation of the other members of the committee, to help you figure out what kinds of questions they might ask (I would read everything the committee members had published, for the same reason). And he will probably suggest some ways that you can present your arguments and defend your conclusions most effectively. If he doesn't do this on his own, then prod him to do it.

In a lot of good schools there is a very careful preparation of students for their oral exams — primarily using the technique of "practice orals". If these aren't a feature of your institution, try to set them up.

> 3.19 In preparation for a major oral exam, *stage "practice orals"*, with as much realism as you can manage.

This will require a fair amount of work from *all* the people who participate in the practice drill. It's no good if you just get praise and shallow questions. You want probing, searching questions that will help you anticipate and prepare for the most intensive kind of scrutiny.

The harder everybody works at this kind of practice, the better. And of course you have to do a good job whether you are practicing being the examiner or the examinee — not only will you profit directly by learning more about the general subject, but your colleagues will be more inclined to do a good job for you when it is your turn to sit in the hot seat.

But if the competitive climate of your school precludes this kind of co-operation, you're pretty well forced back on your own resources and those of your adviser and of intelligent students you may know outside your immediate discipline. This is a pity, since it means that you have to be that much more clever about anticipating and figuring out how to deal with the possible questions.

Make Yourself Comfortable

If you read Chapter 11, you will remember the suggestion to minimize visual and other distractions.

Well, for a major oral you want to take this one stage further. It might be helpful to locate the room where the exam will be conducted—first, so you know how you can get there the day of the test, but, secondly, so that you can check out the physical characteristics of the room.

For example, you don't want to wear a heavy tweed suit if the room is as hot as Dante's Inferno.

Basically, you want to take all reasonable measures to make sure that you will be physically comfortable during the exam. Don't overdress. Don't wear clothing that is too tight. Do strive to make a good first impression on the committee members.

But take heart. Most of the people I've talked to about their experience with major orals have commented on the consideration that was shown to them by the committee. The committee is usually at pains to allay the student's anxiety, and even though the discussion may be intense, it is seldom harrowing.

Which Raises an Interesting Point

Many students who go through major orals experience a letdown after the exam. A real slump. A feeling of "Is that all there is?" This usually comes as a surprise, because they're expecting to feel tremendous relief and great happiness. To feel apathetic or indifferent about everything is sometimes a bit distressing.

Sometimes this feeling persists for several days, or weeks even. I think partly this is because of the sudden termination of a period of very intense goal-directed activity, after which there is a real void that cries out to be filled. And sometimes students are kind of discombobulated because they realize, in retrospect, that the oral was not nearly as rough as they thought it was going to be. They may even feel disappointed that it wasn't more difficult. It can be quite weird.

I mention this just because it happens, and I don't want you to be disturbed by this reaction. It can make you kind of a drag at your post-oral party, but it won't damage you for life. Later, when you get your statement of grades or after convocation—*then* you'll feel like a party. But probably after the big oral all you'll be good for is a good night's sleep and a couple of quiet days on your own. So don't fight it. Just lie back and relax. You've earned a break.

What About Other Kinds of Interviews?

Usually people who write study-skills manuals include a lot of comments about interviews—especially job interviews. I'm not going to do that because there is a much better resource for you. Absolutely *the* best book ever written about interviews in the job-hunt is Richard N. Bolles, *What Color Is Your Parachute?*. If you can't get it at a bookstore, you can order it directly by writing the publisher, Ten Speed Press, Box 7123, Berkeley, California, 94707.

I don't have a single thing to say about job interviews that Bolles has not already said, so you might as well go directly to him. Incidentally, he concludes, I believe irrefutably, that the way interviews are normally handled by job-hunters is completely mistaken from beginning to end. Do not miss this book!

Oral Examinations

3   **Practice the Skills You Will Have To Demonstrate on the Exam**

    3.17   *If you are nervous* at the prospect of being given an oral quiz, begin early in the term to *desensitize yourself by having as many short, non-threatening conversations with the teacher as you can manage*. (*p. 94*)

    3.18   *Learn and practice the correct pronunciation of technical terms and practice making oral responses to questions* prior to taking any oral exam. (*p. 94*)

    3.19   In preparation for a major oral exam, *stage "practice orals"*, with as much realism as you can manage. (*p. 96*)

8   **If You Think of Something, Write It Down**

    8.4   *If you think of information about a previous question* during an oral exam, *make a note of the idea* so that you can mention it later, *or politely interrupt the conversation to return to the previous question*. (*p. 96*)

11   **Read Questions Carefully, Underlining Key Terms. Decide What You Are Expected To Do.**

    11.5   In oral examinations, *look at the examiner while a question is being asked* or a comment is being made. (*p. 95*)

    11.6   Seek clarification of questions on oral exams, *first by paraphrasing* the question, and *then by asking for additional explanation*, if you need it. (*p. 95*)

15   **Write Something Down for Every Question**

    15.3   *If you can't think of the exact answer* to an oral question, *begin by giving the information that you do know*. (*p. 95*)

Anxiety and tests

Chapter 14

Why you are anxious

"In six years of teaching young children I had learned that what they feel more than anything else in school is fear—of failing, of not pleasing, of looking stupid, of being criticized or mocked or despised or punished —and that this fear makes it all but impossible for them to learn what the teacher is trying to teach, or indeed [to learn] anything at all."

—John Holt, *Never Too Late*: *My Musical Life Story*, Dell, New York, 1980, p. 142.

Being afraid of or anxious about examinations is an extremely serious matter. At worst, such fears can result in a complete immobilization of the person's intellectual and physical resources—a painful emotional paralysis that can only be relieved by flight. How many people leave schools and universities in fear, from "not being able to handle the pressure", is not known, but my guess is that the number must be enormous. A tragic waste of talent, both from the society's point of view and for the individuals concerned! At best, exam anxiety means many hours or days of great distress each year as the student grimly makes his way through school—nights of sleepless worry, hours of disorganized, even frantic, attempts to master material that others find easy to comprehend. It may mean, of course, much lower grades than those desired, though, surprisingly, many anxious students do exceedingly well, but at great emotional and physical cost and without feelings of satisfaction. This is a terrible way to spend one's life, and it makes one's school experiences a misshapen and stunted mockery of the intellectual adventure it can be.

If you are an exam-anxious person, you probably find your fear to be baffling and confusing. Most likely you have no idea why you should be so afraid of things that others appear to manage without much difficulty. You may not even know when you first became afraid—it was just always there, from the moment you started school. A few of you will know, and will be able to trace the onset of your fear to a specific event in your life —changing schools when you were young, an unpleasant teacher, returning to school after many years at home or in the work force, being required to take a subject unfamiliar to you—but usually no one single event stands out. There's nothing, no disaster, no obvious trauma, that you can point to and say, "There, that's why I'm afraid."

And the dimensions of your fear are baffling. Why such excessive fear? Why such intense reactions? Other students may worry about tests, all right, but they don't lie awake three long nights before the exam. They don't completely lose their ability to tolerate food. They don't get these headaches, or this twitch, or these trembling hands...

Understanding Your Fear

I have found that a major source of relief for anxious people is to finally learn how such inexplicable fears can arise in the first place—how they are produced and how they are maintained. Understanding your fear can be the first step in beginning to eliminate it.

That is what this chapter is about: how fears arise, how they develop and persist, and why it is that some people are fearful and some are not.

But First . . .

If you are anxious about tests, you are probably manifesting this fear *right now*. Your muscles may be tense: your hands clenched, clammy, and cold, your jaw tense, your forehead tightly furrowed. You may be finding it incredibly difficult to concentrate on these words—or to even see them.

If that is the case, right now I want you to put this book down for a few moments, close your eyes, take a moderately deep breath, and slowly let it out, trying at the same time to let go of some of the tension you are experiencing. Try to let your muscles go limp and loose, as if you were a rag doll.

And then repeat the moderately deep breath and slowly let it out. (Don't *hold* your breath, and don't do this more than twice.)

Okay? Go ahead and do it. Before you read another word.

You should feel slightly better—not terrific, but a little bit better. Now, please, repeat that little exercise *each and every time* you experience tension or anxiety as you read this chapter and the ones that follow. Each and every time.

This is important. For you to become less fearful of exams you will have to learn to be more comfortable talking, thinking, and reading about tests. Relaxing, even just a tiny bit, can help you do this.

Don't expect that you will *suddenly* experience tremendous relief from your worries about tests. It is just not going to work that way. Getting rid of your fears will be a gradual process, but you can do it. You can get rid of your fears.

Persistence Counts

Have you been avoiding this book? Did you start reading it, get frustrated, and put it aside, thinking that you would come back to it later—and the later has turned out to be *much later*?

Please understand, if you are a fearful person, this kind of escape and avoidance is entirely natural and to be expected. A person who is afraid of something does not normally seek out situations in which he is confronted with the thing that inspires his terror. So don't feel guilty about this.

But do try to get back to the book as soon as you can; if you absolutely *have* to put it down for a while, please come back. James Baldwin, the black American novelist, once wrote, "Not everything that is faced can be changed, but nothing can be changed until it is faced."

In order for you to reduce and eliminate your fear, you will have to face it. You will have to think about it and read about it. And it will not be a whole lot of fun, especially at first. But please try to carry on. For my part I will try to proceed as gently as I can.

Now, let's get back to the discussion of where fears come from.

Baby's First Fears

You may have heard it said that when people are born, they have only three fears: a fear of falling, a fear of bright lights, and a fear of sudden noises.

Actually, this is nonsense. When babies arrive in this world, they have *no* fears. They don't, for example, worry about whether the nurse is going to drop a tray beside the crib. They don't lose sleep thinking about the next time somebody is going to shine a light in their eyes. They don't have nightmares or frightening daydreams about the possibility of falling out of their mothers' arms.

What is meant by this little bit of folk "wisdom" is not that babies are afraid, but that they will be *alarmed or startled* by these sudden, novel, and overwhelming stimuli. As indeed will any person, of *any* age—or for that matter any animal. The alarm reaction is wired into all our nervous systems. And it's a good thing, too, because it helps to protect us from harm.

So babies really have no fears. But they can quickly acquire them.

The evidence is that fears, all fears, are *learned* reactions. The alarm or startle reaction is not learned, it is innate; but true fears *are* learned. How does this happen?

Peter and the Rabbit

Several decades ago, when psychology was transforming itself from a branch of religion and medicine into a semi-science, a group of eager-beaver scientists ensured their place in history by doing something that was quite devious and mean. They managed, with a little thought, to take a perfectly ordinary, happy toddler by the name of Peter and make him afraid of a bunny rabbit. Fortunately for us all, they then managed to reverse the trick.

How they did it, and then undid it, explains a lot about fears in general. Here's the story.

The scientists took Peter into the lab and allowed him to play around in the place until he felt comfortable. Then they introduced him to a standard laboratory rabbit and let the two of them become friends. Then, just when things were going swimmingly for Peter and Bugs, they set off a really loud buzzer.

Peter, of course, was *alarmed* by the buzzer—he started, cried, called for his mommy, and so on. So, out went Bugs and out went Peter. After a while, they brought the two of them together again in the lab, let them get comfy, and then *zap!*—the buzzer sent Peter into tears. Again and again they gave it to Peter, and always when it was least expected—sometimes as soon as Peter saw the rabbit, sometimes after they had been playing for a while.

Soon, very soon, Peter started to show evidence of being afraid of the rabbit. As soon as he saw it he would start to fret, cry and shrink away from it, and try to escape. (No doubt the rabbit was not so keen on seeing Peter either.) Then the experimenters decided to see if Peter would continue to be afraid even if the buzzer no longer went off to startle him out of his wits. Sure enough, Peter's fear was now securely hitched to the presence of the rabbit. Even with no buzzer, he got scared every time he saw the furry little thing. And, what's more, he also started to demonstrate a fear of *all* furry little things, including some of his favorite stuffed toys at home.

Now, how to get Peter back to normal? Well, the experimenters figured that what they had to do was the complete opposite of what they had done before. Instead of zapping Peter with the buzzer (which was obnoxious, sudden, and overwhelming), they figured that it might just work if they gave Peter some kind of goody every time he saw the rabbit.

So, back into the lab. When the rabbit came in and Peter exhibited fear, one of the scientists popped Peter's favorite candy into his mouth and another one whisked Bugs out of sight. They repeated this, over and over, each time leaving them together for a longer period, each time bringing them closer together, each time stuffing Peter with candy.

In next to no time, Peter and Bugs were quite pleased to spend the afternoon together. Peter's fear was gone. It's as if he never had been afraid.

So What Has This Got To Do with Test Anxiety?

Peter acquired or "learned" his fear of the rabbit after many "pairings" of the presence of the rabbit with the sudden loud eruption of the buzzer. His alarm reaction to the buzzer got hooked up to the rabbit, so that Peter would have the alarm reaction in *expectation* that he could soon be frightened. This shift—from being alarmed by the sudden loud noise to *anticipating it* and connecting it with another thing in the environment —is extremely important.

What this means is that we can acquire a fear of something when that something is connected repeatedly over time with another thing that alarms us already. Sudden loud noises, bright lights, a sudden fall, and pain will do the trick. Similarly, pre-existing fears—of personal injury, death, losing approval, getting yelled at, losing things and privileges—can make us afraid of other things.

The Fear of Exams Is Primarily a Fear of Other People's Reactions

It is only because our performance in school has gotten hooked up with, in Holt's words, "fear... of failing, of not pleasing, of looking stupid, of being criticized or mocked or despised or punished" that anybody is afraid of exams.

There is no good reason why Peter should ever be afraid of a rabbit. It is extremely unlikely that the rabbit could harm him.

And there is no good reason why anybody should be afraid of answering a series of questions written on a piece of paper. Exams in themselves pose no threat of injury or harm. The only reason we are afraid of tests (and think that it is something about the test, some quality of the exam itself, that is frightening) is that the exam has been connected for us with our pre-existing fears.

And this connection is made for us, every one of us, very early and very effectively in our childhood homes, on playgrounds, and in schools.

Freedom from Fear

One of the most interesting things about fears is that, even though all of us are subjected to many of the same kinds of experiences when we're growing up, only some of us acquire specific fears. (Practically everyone has *some* irrational fears, but not everybody is afraid of the same things.) How is it that only some of us are afraid of tests, and others of us take tests with a general feeling of confidence and in a state of only somewhat heightened tension?

Well, let's back up a bit.

Fears, as we have seen, consist of the interaction of two main elements:

1. a situation perceived by the person to be threatening (or a potential situation, potentially threatening), along with the thoughts that accompany this perception; and
2. unpleasant physical sensations that the person cannot control, without escaping from or avoiding the situation, that is.

These two elements comprise the *emotion* that we call fear.

A third component of most fears is something that we could call poor coping skills; since fearful people usually misperceive the situation and may carry around many distorted ideas about the things they fear, they are poorly equipped to respond to the situation in adaptive ways. Such people often make matters worse by the way they act.

A person who is afraid of dogs may cry out and try to run away from a strange dog, which only makes the dog come closer, and may encourage it to leap up and bark. A person who is afraid of falling will look at the water under a narrow bridge, instead of watching his footing. This increases the chances that he will become dizzy from watching the motion of the water and stumble because he isn't paying attention to where he's going. A person who is afraid of wasps may wave frantically at the insect, which

only alarms it and makes it fly around faster and more erratically.

A person who is afraid of examinations will concentrate on the things he or she does not know, and will spend inordinate time trying to master trivial details instead of concentrating on such things as problem-solving skills, understanding the content of the course in its generality, and so on.

Now, the reason that some people do not have the specific fears that you do is

—they have learned to perceive the situation as non-threatening, and their thoughts about the situation focus on its manageability,
—they do not experience excessive physical arousal. They can control and moderate their arousal so that it does not adversely affect either their judgment or their behavior, and
—they have developed a set of coping responses that allow them to remain in control of their own behavior and, possibly, to take action that produces more favorable outcomes.

People who are not afraid of dogs can tell the difference between dogs that are friendly and dogs that are dangerous. They do not experience great emotional arousal even around moderately dangerous dogs, their judgment remains unimpaired, and they can control both their feelings and their behavior. And, finally, they have a set of ready-made responses for dealing with a wide variety of dog-related situations: they know how to pal up to a friendly pooch, how to calm a barking dog, how to deal with a strange dog on the street, and even what to do when faced with vicious and truly dangerous dogs.

The Role of Avoidance in Maintaining Fears

What would have happened to Peter's fears of the rabbit if for some reason he had been withdrawn from the experiment in the middle, just when his fear had been fully developed?

You would probably guess that Peter would continue to be afraid of bunnies and other furry things—unless and until his parents or some other adults in his life took definite programmatic action to reduce his fears. This would probably have involved a lot of short encounters with furry objects, in an atmosphere of caring and confidence, with definite steps being taken to both reassure and re-educate Peter.

Or his parents could blow it, by ridiculing, criticizing, or punishing him for fearful behavior (which would only add the fear of loss of approval to his fear of the rabbit).

Or his parents could blow it by giving up after a few frustrating sessions of trying to coax, cajole, or criticize him into non-fearful behavior. They could have removed all of his furry toys and forever after have said to other grown-ups, "I just don't know what to do with Peter. Everything we've tried just doesn't work."

In either of these last two cases, Peter would probably continue to be afraid of rabbits until his dying day.

Paradoxically, staying away from or avoiding the fear-inducing object is one of the best ways to keep a fear going.

And a person who has developed a fear of exams will usually be a past master at avoiding thinking about or learning about exams—not that they can be totally avoided, except by dropping out of school. Exam-anxious people hardly ever start studying early, and hardly ever think about the test (except to remind themselves how afraid they are) until the last possible moment.

And that's the usual story: fearful people avoid learning how to deal with their fear effectively when it can be done. Instead, they wait for the really difficult situation to come along—the Doberman, the wasp in the kitchen, the important final examination—and then try ineffectively to get things under control. Avoidance maintains fears. Fears are unlearned by gradually bringing yourself into closer and closer proximity to the thing that you fear—but in a way that allows you to relearn you reaction.

This means re-evaluating your fear, learning to rethink the situation so that your thoughts themselves are not frightening and so that you can accurately appraise the situation.

It means learning a set of coping responses that allow you to deal effectively with the practical problems that are connected with the thing you fear.

The key to the whole question of being free from fear is that every single element in both the fearful person's responses and in the non-fearful person's handling of the same situation—every single element—is a function of learning.

And a fear can be unlearned. Just as Peter learned to lose his fear of the rabbit, you can come to lose your fear of exams. It is a bit complicated admittedly, since rabbits and exams are quite different things, but you can do it.

How this is done is the subject of the next chapter.

Chapter 15

A step-by-step approach for reducing test anxiety

In order for you to reduce your fear of examinations to more reasonable levels, it is important that you attend to all the elements that work together to produce your anxiety.

> 5.12 If you are *usually anxious* about exams, learn to *confront your fearful thinking* about tests, learn to *reduce and control exam-related tension* and other physical manifestations of your fear, and learn how to *deal with tests more effectively*.

Test-anxious people usually find that no single part of this equation can be neglected. For example, it won't help much if you read a book about studying for tests unless you do something about your fearful thinking. You just won't be able to implement the ideas effectively. And if the physical aspects of your fear are running unchecked, this will surely interfere with any attempt that you make to study wisely and to attack the exam sensibly.

Letting Your Thoughts Run Wild

Fearful people commonly indulge in what is called "catastrophic thinking" about exams. They tend to think about their fears in very dramatic ways and to concentrate on all the bad, terrible, frightening, embarrassing things that might happen.

They may think:

—"If I don't pass this exam, I'll just die!"

—"My mother will kill me if I come home with another lousy report!"

—"I'm just dreading it. It's going to be a complete disaster!"

Or, instead of this kind of upsetting "self-talk" or internal monologue, they may play "disaster movies" inside their heads. When they think about tests, they get vivid images of the unfolding catastrophe:

—an image (in full color and three dimensions, accompanied by sound in Dolby Stereo) of themselves falling to pieces in the exam and having to rush out of the room in hysterics.

—an image of their parents reacting when the bad news about their school performance is discussed at the supper table.

—a picture of their classmates ridiculing those who did poorly on the exam.

Or, instead of internal dialogues or disaster movies, they may just review the physical sensations they imagine that they are going to have:

—they remember "blanking out" on an exam, and re-experience the accompanying feelings of disorganization, dizziness, and desperation.

—they worry about whether or not their nausea will stay under control during the test (which leads to tension, which leads to nausea).

—they remember feeling as if they were going to wet their pants and project this feeling forward into the coming examination.

The important thing about catastrophic thinking is that it *immediately* produces fear and anxiety. Your thinking about exams, your anticipation, are just as much a part of your fear as the sensations that you get at the actual test. And these thoughts are often more frightening than the actual experience.

Learning to change this fearful thinking about exams is vitally important.

Catastrophic Thinking Is a Rehearsal for the Real Thing

If you tell yourself that something is going to be awful, if you picture yourself blanking out and getting very upset, if you anticipate feeling nauseated or dizzy or whatever, you are very effectively rehearsing to do those things. You are practicing the very kind of performance you fear.

In addition, the anxiety that you generate while you are anticipating these possible future events blocks you from taking appropriate action right now to make sure that the event will *not* happen as you fear it might. If you are busy thinking anxious thoughts—or doing reruns of disaster movies—what you are very definitely *not* doing is reading the textbook in front of you, or planning effectively to meet the challenge you face.

There are two things that you can do to combat catastrophic thoughts. First of all, you can interrupt the thoughts whenever they occur. Second, you can rationally argue against them.

Stop the Movie, I Want To Get Off

All of us are capable of controlling our thinking. Most of us already do it to some extent, but since something that we are *aware* of doing, and since we do it only intermittently, we just aren't very skilled at it.

We all say things like: "I can't think about the weekend right now, I've got to make a shopping list for this afternoon". And then we get a pen and paper and proceed to do it. Or, if we turn on the TV and see a scary movie, we quickly change the channel to another program so that we won't become frightened. We have stopped our thoughts by a change in the environment.

Just to prove to you that you can control your thoughts, I want you to do a little experiment. Read all the steps all the way through before you start.

1. I want you to remember a recent experience

where you had some kind of pleasant emotional reaction. It can be an event where you felt happy or excited, or just had a feeling of well-being. Try to recall the event in as much detail as you can.

2. Now, close your eyes and try to remember the situation as vividly as you can.

3. When you've got a really good image, suddenly yell "Stop" and open your eyes.

The image and the memory will stop. Maybe just for a moment. But it does stop. This means that you can interrupt your own disaster movies or catastrophic thoughts whenever you want.

The thoughts can come back, and probably will, but when they do, you can use the same technique to stop them again.

Our thoughts are greatly influenced by what is happening in the external environment, and by our own muscular activity. If you stop your thoughts, and simultaneously focus on what is happening around you (notice who is in the room, count the objects on your table, whatever), or if you get up and go and *do* something, this increases the probability that the thought you're trying to stop will go away for a longer period of time. If you stay where you were sitting or standing—and go on thinking—odds are that the thought will come back relatively quickly.

Each time you stop a fearful thought, it weakens and loses some of its compelling nature. Being able to interrupt the fearful thought means that you will not get sucked into "trains of thought" about exams, trains that get you nowhere. So it is very important that you stop fearful thoughts immediately, just as soon as you are aware of having them.

Now, thought-stopping does not come easily, nor does it work miraculously overnight. You have developed a very strong habit of fearful thinking, and it will take time and considerable practice to break up this habit.

It is important, in addition, that you use thought-stopping *only* to interrupt and weaken irrational ideas and catastrophic thoughts. If you use it to stop thoughts like "I really should read Chapter 6", and you really *should* read Chapter 6 and have time to do it, then you are misusing the technique. Don't use the technique to stop *rea-*

sonable worries and appropriate thinking about what you need to do.

Getting Your Negative Thoughts Under Environmental Control

Another thing that you can do that may seem kind of silly, but actually works very well, is to try to confine your catastrophic thinking to a particular place.

If you are a catastrophic thinker, you probably think this way anywhere and at any time—in class, in the library, in your car, in movies and restaurants, when you're sunbathing on the lawn, when you're trying to go to sleep at night. And this means that the thoughts can interfere with what you are trying to do anywhere, any time—robbing you of sleep, depriving you of pleasure, and reducing your competence and concentration in a wide variety of other ways.

Now, it is probably impossible for you to completely stop worrying all at once. But it is much easier to *restrict* your worrying to specific times and places. Even expert, veteran worriers find that they can do this very quickly.

What you do is:

1. Pick a specific chair in your home and move it to a place that you don't particularly like to spend time in—the basement, the junkroom, a corner of the living-room that you find unpleasant—and designate this chair as your "worry chair".

2. Do the same thing at school, and if you work, pick a place there as well. A bathroom you don't normally use, a lounge you don't like much, a chair in a section of the library that you don't use will serve the purpose. You should not be too comfortable in your chair, the place itself should not be attractive or interesting, and you should be able to have ready access to your worry chair at any time.

3. Once you have designated these worry chairs, begin to practice *delaying* your worrying until you have a chance to go to your worry chair. If you find that you cannot delay any longer, stop what you are doing and immediately go to your worry chair. Sit there and worry until you feel like going back to whatever it was that you were doing. Try not to worry anywhere except in your worry chair.

4. Don't do anything else in your worry chair except worry. Don't read, knit, do your nails, plan tomorrow's activities, do homework—nothing. Just sit and worry.

5. Whatever else you do, make sure that you make at least two appointments to go to your worry chair *every day*. Make sure that you sit and worry for at least twenty minutes when you go to these worry appointments.

It is extremely important that you *do* allow yourself to worry a bit. There's no way that you'll be able to eliminate worrying right away, and to try to do so only invites defeat and discouragement. But getting your worrying under control, so that it only happens where and when you decide, can be a great leap forward.

And don't be too concerned about setbacks—times when you just allow yourself to go ahead and worry outside your designated places. The chances are good that you will have one or two setbacks, probably at times when you are feeling extra-fatigued or are under a lot of additional stress. Don't feel defeated, just return to the "worry-chair" procedure as soon as it is at all possible.

And I mean this. If you're worrying at three o'clock in the morning and you're just desperate to go to sleep—get up and go to your worry chair! You're awake anyway. You may as well be doing something productive, and developing the habit of not worrying in bed is a fantastically useful habit.

Changing the Scenery in Your Disaster Movie

You run the disaster movie that plays inside your head. Your own memory and your vivid imagination write, produce, direct, and choreograph the production. So one of the ways that you can reduce the emotional impact of the movie is simply to rewrite the script. You see, you can use your incredible imagination to get you out of trouble with your emotions, just as you use it now to keep yourself in trouble.

If you have an image of yourself cracking up and running out of the exam room, rewrite the ending of the scene so that you (the hero or heroine) gain control of your impulse to run. Imagine yourself deliberately calming yourself down and resuming work on the exam, and then imagine yourself leaving the exam and saying to a friend in the hallway, "Well, I had a couple of rough moments in there, but I managed to get them under control. And I don't think I did too badly on the test." Then, practice this new movie.

Or if you have a movie where your parents are giving you the treatment after you tell them about your performance in school, imagine that your dad is sitting at the kitchen table in bright orange underwear with green polka dots. Imagine that he is wearing a party hat and a baby's bib. Imagine that he has a tattoo on his chest that says "Niagara Falls". Dress your mother in a cardboard box and incredibly high heels. Wrap a feather boa around her neck. And just when the abuse is at its worst, imagine that you take out a water pistol and zap them both right in the middle of their foreheads. Watch them fall face forward into their spaghetti and meat sauce.

Countering Your Fears With Rational Arguments

This isn't as much fun as using imagery, but it does seem to make more sense to a lot of fearful people.

Basically what you do here is to analyze your catastrophic thoughts and to counter them with rational, reasonable arguments. And I'm not talking about "positive thinking" ("Every day in every way I'm getting better and better"), which is uncritical, unthinking, and relatively meaningless. No, your arguments have to be rational and convincing.

For example:

Catastrophic Thought	Rational Counter-Argument
"I'll just die if I do badly on the test."	Not likely. Failing a test is not a mortal illness. People survive failure all the time. You've done it yourself. You may not like it, but you won't exactly "die".
"My mother'll kill me if…"	If this is true, then you should seek legal advice. What you mean is that she will throw some kind of emotional display that you really don't like. But again, you've survived it before so you can survive it again.
"I'm so nervous, I'm sure I'm going to be a complete wreck by the time of the test."	This could happen if you let your anxiety develop, if you continue to think in terms of catastrophes, instead of trying to control your anxiety more effectively. You could start by saying to yourself, "If I let myself get all sweaty at this point, I'm not going to study very well right now. So I'll worry about this later."
"I'm sure that by the time I get to the test I won't know anything."	What's bugging you is the frustration that comes because you do know a lot, but since you allow your anxiety to get out of control you can't think straight. So when you say, "I'm sure that I won't know anything," this really means, "If I let things go the way I'm letting them go right now…" In any case *not anything* is a pretty tiny amount. The chances are excellent that, even if you're quite anxious, you will remember *something*.

"This is terrible. I should be able to understand this."

Who said you should? Where is it written in letters of gold that you *must* understand this stuff easily and quickly? In any case, it's irrelevant. If you don't understand it, you don't understand it, and it doesn't make any difference whether somebody says you "should" or not. If you *want* to understand it, getting upset isn't going to help.

"I can't possibly learn how to do this in time for the test."

Are you sure? If you worked calmly and efficiently, would you be able to do it? Even if it's true, wouldn't it be better to try to learn as much as you can in the time remaining? (Partial credit on a test is better than no credit at all.)

Maybe when you say "can't", what you really mean is that it will be difficult, or that you don't really want to do it. Difficult is one thing, impossible is quite another.

"It's just no good. I never have been any good at school. You can't teach an old dog new tricks."

Whoever said you can't teach an old dog new tricks just didn't have the patience. While it is true that many people do not change, it is equally true that lots of other people do—no matter what their age. Saying that you're not able to change because you're "too old" just means that you've given up.

"I have never been any good at school" is just an excuse. It is also true to say that you were never any good at playing hopscotch until you learned how to walk. All this means is that it may be difficult for you to learn how to manage school. Saying this means that you have decided to ignore what you can do right now to change things (even if it's to change them just a little).

Countering the Demand for Perfection and for Instant Competence

A lot of people have it in their heads that *making mistakes is terrible* and that it is *incredibly important to be competent in everything* that they do.

These demands for perfection and instant competence are completely illogical.

In the first place, when you are learning *anything* it is highly unlikely that you or *anybody else* could learn to do that thing without ever making a single mistake. In fact, most people are just terrible when they start. All thumbs, can't

hold the note, fall over their feet, lose track of what they're supposed to do, put their feet on the accelerator and the brake at the same time.

A *learner*, by definition, is *somebody who does not know what to do*. An incompetent and ignorant person, a know-nothing. If he knew already, he wouldn't be a learner.

So it makes no sense at all to get down on yourself because you are a learner. The whole point of instruction and teaching, and the whole point of practice and learning, is for you to get past the stage where you're all thumbs all the time to the point where you're all thumbs only part of the time. But don't ever expect that you'll never be all thumbs—and don't expect that you can magically skip the mistakes part and get to instant mastery.

People who demand instant competence from themselves expect to be able to play the cello like Pablo Casals, write like John Updike, paint like Michelangelo, play hockey like Wayne Gretzky, sing like Nana Mouskouri, bake pies like Madame Benoit, etc., without going through the years of agony and apprenticeship that all of these people endured to get to their present level of competence.

And without going through any of the practice, preparation, sketching, mistakes, problems, and difficulties that all these people go through every single time they sit down to prepare for one of their performances. Do you really think that Updike sits down at his typewriter and types out a novel without having to revise it? Do you really think that Leonardo da Vinci just came in one day and painted the *Mona Lisa* before lunch? Do you really think that anything important, significant, and interesting has ever been accomplished by anybody without their making lots of mistakes along the way?

And in any case, expecting competence in *everything* you do is completely unreasonable. Most people are not very good *at anything*. The most that people seem to be able to manage is some middling competence at one or two things. But you insist that you must be perfect in everything? And feel that it is somehow *terrible* if you make mistakes?

It is reasonable to expect that you will make mistakes (and lots of them) when you are learning anything new and difficult. It is inevitable that you will make some mistakes when you are doing something challenging and complex. And it is reasonable to expect that gradually you will make fewer mistakes as you develop more competence, but you're going to continue to make the occasional boo-boo.

How Do You Know That Something Is a Mistake Before You Make It?
Sometimes people get tied up in little knots when they're trying to do something because they are afraid that they won't be able to do it right—when it is simply impossible to tell beforehand whether what they're going to do is a mistake or not.

If you are working on a math problem, you don't know if you've got the "right" procedure until you try it out.

If you're trying to draw a picture, you won't know if a line is "right" until you actually draw it on the paper.

If you're trying to express an idea in an essay, you can't tell if you've expressed the idea well until you have written it down.

If you're trying to find your keys, you won't be able to tell which was the right place to look for them until you look.

Standing still and trying to get the right solution in your head before you actually do anything is a prescription for paralysis. That is exactly what happens to people who "blank out" on tests. It is also what happens to writers when they get "blocked". They're trying to get it perfect before they put it down on the page, and since it's impossible to do this, they never get anything down on the page. If they would just write something, anything, and keep doing it, they would get something that wasn't too bad; then they could edit it, clean it up, and expand it.

Who Says It's a Mistake Anyway?
Often what people feel might be mistakes turn out to be not so bad after all. Sometimes it happens that what one person thinks is a mistake, somebody else thinks is wonderful.

When I was a kid, it was thought to be a terrible mistake to wear green and blue together. I had teachers tell me that it was a mistake to write a sentence fragment, or to end a sentence with a preposition—under *any* circumstances. I had a French teacher who told us in no uncertain terms that we could not use French-Canadian terms and expressions; they were "wrong", and Parisian French was "correct". Our question was "Correct for whom? Correct for where?"

So, besides assailing yourself for being a learner, for being only a human being and not a god, you often get yourself all upset because you might upset somebody whose tastes, preferences, or judgment are different from yours. (Not that *they* have any divine inspiration.)

Dealing with Mistakes on Tests
The only rational way to handle mistakes on a test is to accept that they're inevitable. No matter how good you are, the chances of your doing a

one-hundred-per-cent-perfect job are practically zero — and particularly if you expect to be able to do it without pausing, without changing one or two things that you wrote down, without having trouble finding exactly the "right" words, and so on. Mistakes are inevitable: the only thing that you can do is to accept that as a given, and to try to set up your exam so that it is easier for you to find and correct mistakes as you go.

The first and second sections of this book are largely about how to do that in studying and in actually taking tests.

Fighting the Irrationality Behind Avoidance and Procrastination

The devious, intricate, and complicated routines that people put themselves through in order to delay studying are sometimes truly incredible. (I know. I used to be a champion procrastinator. I once managed to get extensions of a term-paper deadline for *eight months* after the end of the school term.)

Most of these maneuvers are based on a quite idiotic premise:

—getting a short-term gain (e.g., relief from anxiety or avoiding hard work) is better than long-term pain (being very anxious and poorly prepared for the test, or having to work frantically to meet a deadline).

And the rest of the typical convoluted avoidance behaviors are due to a simple not-knowing-how-to-do-it. How do you go about reading twenty novels, doing five term papers, buying Christmas presents, and handling a job? How do you turn this mountain into a succession of manageable molehills?

Ending this nonsense means, first of all, finding out how to get organized (probably the most valuable skill you can develop in school, in terms of payoff in later life). And secondly, it means rationally confronting your thinking about your anxiety.

Putting off studying doesn't really mean relief from negative feelings — you just trade small amounts of anxiety for small amounts of guilt. Then you get to have a large dose of anxiety at the end of the term just to even up the score. If you're going to do a poor job of preparation, you are going to pay an emotional price, so you might as well pay a little bit now and spare yourself some agony at the end of the term.

Small amounts of anxiety are not that dreadful. If you actually start to work *in spite of your moderate anxiety*, the chances are pretty good that you will get interested enough in the material to learn something. Ten minutes spent studying now means ten minutes less at the end of the year when every moment counts.

Unless you spend some time now doing a good job of learning the material you are covering in class, you will have to *relearn* it when you come to cram for the test. People forget at an incredible rate: if you don't start studying until just before the test, you will have forgotten most of what you covered at the beginning of the term.

And I don't want to hear any of you saying, "Yes, but...". *I am* (or was) The Champ! I know how procrastination works!

Now look, if you really don't know how to get organized, and how to spend your study time effectively, then reread the first sections of this book. It contains a distillation of everything I have learned about these matters, and I am willing to bet Swiss francs that the approaches will work for you. But remember, beginning will mean that you have to overcome a little bit of discomfort.

Liking Failure

In a weird kind of way, many of us take a perverse kind of pride in not being able to spell, sing, plan ahead, get assignments done on time, or whatever.

I know what that's like. I used to practically flaunt my procrastination in front of my friends, and in a strange way I took pleasure in their shaking their heads and clucking their tongues when I'd sleep in till 3 p.m. or miss yet another deadline.

It's almost as if you're saying to other people, "Isn't it cute, my foible." And if you can fool somebody into mothering you...hey, that's great. That means it isn't your fault, it's your mother's!

This very successfully protects you from having to take all the risks (and going through the very hard work) of trying to be different from the way you are now.

But, if you really want things to be different,

and if you are honestly dissatisfied with the way you are now, you just have to drop this foolishness. And that is all there is to that.

Picking Nits

People sometimes react to the principle of using rational counter-arguments by saying, "I don't *really* believe it when I say 'I'll die' or whatever. It's just a slang expression. It's just a little exaggeration. Surely it can't be that important."

But it is. These little slips of the tongue have the effect of producing unhelpful emotions and of getting in the way of your effective performance. They are just as much a part of your fear as the feelings that you get when you're actually taking the exam. And just as you have to learn to relax when looking at pictures of Lassie before you're ready to confront the Doberman down the street, you have to learn to confront all these little moments of slight discomfort before you're ready to take on the more difficult assignments. Learning to challenge yourself when you make idiotic statements is a very important step in reducing your fear.

But Can't You Take This Rationality Business Too Far?

Some people are concerned that, if they start to think rationally about tests and start to control their feelings more effectively, they're going to turn into some kind of robot-like rationality machine with no feelings at all, no delightful impulsiveness, no heart, no soul.

Not true. Rational people still enjoy the sunset, feel thrilled at the birth of their children, enjoy making love and going to the opera.

This is a bit like being afraid that if you learn to do pliés, you won't be able to stop yourself, and pretty soon you'll be practicing forty hours a day, selling all you own to buy tutus, and trying to sign up for the local ballet company.

You are completely in charge of your own life. If you find a particular idea compelling and interesting, then you have a choice about whether or not to pursue it—and how far. Getting control of your exam anxiety isn't going to make you any the less a "feeling person"—except that you'll now have more time for worth-

while and positive feelings instead of this awful stuff you've been going through.

But if you think that anxiety and agony are somehow essential to you as a person, then by all means go ahead, just close this book and forget you ever read it. But remember, it is *you* who make that decision.

Learning To Control Your Physical-Anxiety Reactions

Reducing and controlling your exam-related tension (which is a physical state) is an important part of your overcoming anxiety. Some people find it is enough simply to get their thinking in order and then to concentrate on the practical application of good study and exam-taking skills—but most anxious people find it helpful to learn how to deliberately control their tension.

The next section of this chapter consists of instructions for two relaxation techniques that have been found to be useful in this regard. The procedures are relatively straightforward. All that is required is that you practice the exercise with an open mind and that you be willing to invest some time in the procedures.

How much time? Well, in the Exam Skills program we spend about eight hours in relaxation training, so eight hours is probably a reasonable amount of time to expect to devote to learning the procedures that follow.

Fighting the Tendency To Give Up

There have been many really excellent studies done on the question of whether people can learn to do relaxation procedures on their own, or whether it's better to be taught to do the techniques by a therapist or counsellor. And the results of these studies show uniformly that people can learn the procedures quite well on their own, thank you, but that there is a greater tendency for people to "drop out" of self-managed programs, to stop practicing before they've really mastered the techniques.

What we have here is just another example of how difficult it is to develop a new habit.

If you do want to be more relaxed, the chances are excellent that the procedures on the following pages will be helpful. But you aren't going to get miraculous and permanent results overnight, and you will undoubtedly forget to practice, get discouraged, wonder if it's working, and so on. That is, you will undoubtedly have all the feelings and fears you usually get when you are trying to learn anything.

I want to make a deal with you. Or, rather, I want you to make a deal with yourself. *Either* decide to forget the whole thing and shut this book right now, *or* decide to invest eight hours of your time (time that you would waste anyway in being overwrought and inefficient) over the next two or three weeks, learning and practicing the procedures on the next pages.

You can go ahead and read over the exercises if you want, to get an idea of what you're agreeing to—but you won't *really* know what the exercises are about until you do them.

And I mean *do them*—the whole eight hours' worth, not just a little nibble. No half-baked, half-hearted sort of "trying it out".

So there you go. That's the deal. Either you decide to forget it or you decide to do it. And if you decide that it might be worth a shot, I want you to go and get your calendar or datebook right now, and decide exactly where and when you are going to do the exercises.

Relaxation: Phase One

The purpose of the following exercise is for you, first of all, to develop more awareness of your own body tensions, and, secondly, to begin to learn to reduce and control those tensions more effectively.

Begin practicing this exercise twice a day for two or three days. All you need for the practice is a comfortable chair in a room where you will not be disturbed. The exercise will take about twenty minutes each time you practice.

Do not do the exercise immediately after a meal, and don't do it late in the evening. At either of these times, you will tend to fall asleep, which is not the point. Don't do the exercise lying down for the same reason.

Remove very warm clothing, take off your shoes, and loosen your belt. If you have contact lenses, take them out.

If you are concerned that you might fall asleep, you can use an alarm clock or a timer to tell you when twenty minutes is up, but put the alarm in a closet or under a pillow so it doesn't startle you when it goes off. It's a bad idea to arrange for somebody to come and tell you

when twenty minutes is up because this will tend to startle you as well, which will defeat the whole point of the exercise.

Okay. If you're ready, read the instructions below all the way through and then try out the exercise.

Beginning To Relax:

1. Sit back comfortably in your chair with your hands resting loosely in your lap. Don't cross your feet, just let them rest comfortably on the floor.

2. Close your eyes and keep them closed for the whole exercise.

3. Take a couple of moderately deep breaths. Don't strain or overbreathe—this might make you feel woozy. As you let go of each breath, try to let yourself relax just a little bit.

4. Resume breathing normally, and try to count ten breaths. (Breathe out, count "one", breathe out, count "two", and so on.) Don't try to control your breathing as you do this—just count your breaths as they happen. And don't worry if you lose track of what number you're on—that's quite normal. Just start counting again at "one". The point is not to count ten breaths; the point is to empty your head of distracting thoughts by *trying* to calmly count your breaths.

5. After you've counted ten breaths, do it again.

6. *Lower Arms and Hands*: Clench your fists. Again, don't strain, just tighten them enough that you can feel the tension in your hands, wrists, and forearms. Notice whatever effects that has elsewhere in your body.

    After a few moments relax your fists and notice the changes that occur as you relax— possibly feelings of numbness, tingling, warmth.

    Again tighten your fists and study the effects of the tension.

    After a few moments, relax.

7. *Upper Arms*: Now tighten the muscles in your upper arms by "making a muscle". Flex your biceps. Again study that tension for a few moments.

    Now relax.

    Repeat.

8. *Shoulders and Upper Back*: Try to bring your shoulders up to touch your ears. Study that tension. Then roll your shoulders forward, trying to touch them together in front; then roll them back, pushing yourself away from the chair. Study that tension for a few moments.
    Relax.
    Repeat.

9. *Face, Mouth, and Throat*: Simultaneously squint your eyes together as tightly as you can, clench your jaw (watch out for your fillings, though!), purse your lips, and push your tongue against the roof of your mouth. Try to turn your face into a prune. Study that tension for a few moments.
    Relax.
    Repeat.

10. *Feet and Lower Legs*: Point your toes up towards the ceiling. Try to curl them back so they point towards your knees. Then let your feet back onto the floor and try to push your feet into the floor as hard as you can. (If you get a cramp in your foot, immediately reverse the movement.)
    Now relax.
    Repeat.

11. *Upper Legs*: Imagine that you've sat on an egg and that you have to take your weight off it or it will break. Try to lift yourself out of the chair, just using your upper legs. Hold that position for a moment while you notice the effects of tension in this area.
    Relax.
    Repeat.

12. *Stomach*: Imagine that someone is just about to punch you in the stomach. Tighten those muscles to make them as hard as possible. Notice the effects this has on your breathing.
    Relax. Forget everything you've ever heard about posture and let your tummy just schlepp all over.
    Repeat.

13. *Chest*: Take in a moderately deep breath and hold it. Simultaneously try to push your shoulders down as far as you can towards your waist. Roll your shoulders back and forth a little and study the tension in your chest wall. Notice how tension in your chest dramatically affects your whole body.
    Relax, and breathe normally for a few seconds.
    Repeat.

14. Resume breath-counting—trying to count ten breaths. Again, don't try to control your breathing and don't worry if you lose track. Continue till your twenty minutes are up.

15. To end the exercise, slowly count backwards from "five" to "one" until, when you count "one", you open your eyes feeling quite refreshed and relaxed.

16. After a few seconds, get out of your chair and have a stretch. Move around a little bit until you're fully alert.

Some Comments About This Relaxation Procedure

1. Again, you may not experience a great deal of relief the first time you use this procedure. Often several practices are necessary before you notice that you are able to get significantly more relaxed during the exercise.

2. Everybody has problems with daydreams, so don't get upset about this. Just calmly go back to the exercise when you have discovered that you have drifted away on a different train of thought.

3. Sometimes people experience uncomfortable sensations, such as tingling or a funny kind of tension in a particular muscle group. It sometimes helps if you tense these muscles a little bit and then relax again. If this doesn't work, you can try lightly touching the area with your hand—more difficult than it sounds.

4. A few people find the whole exercise makes them acutely uncomfortable and even heightens their anxiety, sometimes because of the place where they are relaxing or because they have trouble "letting go". These people may secretly fear that if they let down their guard or let themselves be led by suggestions, they lose control. Often such people can do the exercise and derive considerable benefit from it if they keep their eyes open. If that doesn't

work, my sincere suggestion is that they read the next chapter.

5. Falling asleep and dreaming can sometimes be a problem, particularly if you have a scary dream. Being abruptly jolted from a deeply relaxed state can be alarming and upsetting, and you may feel acutely uncomfortable for several hours. If this happens, don't resume the relaxation practice until the next day.

   The next time, take steps to ensure that you won't fall asleep. Sit in a less comfortable chair. Open a window to let in some fresh air. Wear light clothing. And don't relax at a time of day when you're likely to fall asleep from fatigue.

6. Sometimes people will have trouble with a particular muscle group; it just won't relax and may even feel worse after exercising. The biggest problem area is the neck—a tremendous number of people have tense necks.

   Two things might help. First of all, do not hold your head in one position throughout the exercise. Sometimes rolling your head slowly in small circles will help, or changing the position that you were in. If you got a headache sitting erect in a chair, try leaning your head against the chair back, or dropping your head forward so that your chin touches your chest. This may feel tight for a while, until your neck muscles relax and stretch a bit more. Keep at it though. The second consideration is that if you are carrying a lot of tension in your neck all the time, you may just notice it more when the rest of you relaxes.

   Usually the more you practice this exercise and those that follow, the less this will be a problem.

7. The other thing that may lead to problems in a particular set of muscles is an injury or disease in the muscles or related joints (pulled ligaments, tendonitis, arthritis, etc.). Usually just flexing the muscles for a moment will do the trick and the uncomfortable sensation will go away. At other times it may be necessary to apply a heating-pad or a hot-water bottle to the area. Be sure not to overstrain recently injured muscles and joints during the relaxation exercise. Go gently.

8. A few people just have no patience with this procedure. They can't sit still for twenty minutes and need to be up and doing things. These are the people who are constantly pacing, going from one thing to another, talking rapidly—people who are...you know... hyper! And it's not that they're especially anxious, like the people mentioned in 4 above, it's just that they can't sit still! Sometimes doing the exercise for a period shorter than twenty minutes will help. And sometimes it would just be better to forget this relaxation procedure completely. Instead, such people seem to benefit from routine *strenuous* exercise, particularly rhythmic exercise like jogging or swimming. That's okay too.

Relaxation: Phase Two

After you have practiced Phase One at least six times, you're ready for the next part of the procedure. Probably you are starting to be more aware of your own body tension when you're walking around, and have found that sometimes you can get rid of this tension.

Before You Start Phase Two:
Spend fifteen or twenty minutes writing a description of a scene that you find particularly relaxing. Describe everything in that scene so that you can imagine it vividly when you close your eyes. The kinds of scenes that people have used here have included the inside of a ski-lodge with a log burning in the fireplace, a nearly deserted ocean beach at sunset, canoeing on a wilderness lake, and fields of grain blowing in the wind. But you don't have to use this kind of image at all: one person I know developed a scene in which she saw herself as a pat of butter ever so slowly melting in the sun; another person developed an image of himself flying over a mountain range; another imagined swimming in a pool filled with warm iridescent oil. Some people find it relaxing to imagine themselves skiing or jogging.

Don't just think of a relaxing scene. Write it down.

If your visual imagination is the pits, find a single word or phrase that evokes for you feelings of calm and relaxation. Some examples: calm, relax, nice and easy, slow, peaceful, the word "one", and so on.

Okay, Now for Phase Two:

1. Continue to practice relaxation as before, twice a day.

2. No longer tense any muscles during the practice. Forget about tension.

3. Begin as before with two moderately deep breaths and breath-counting. Mentally check off each muscle area and try to see (with your eyes closed) that the muscles are relaxing. Just let the tension go. Let it drain away.

4. Then, try to imagine your relaxing scene in as much detail as you can. If your scene changes, that's all right, but try to feel that you are directing a movie—the only things that happen in your scene are things that you introduce and order to appear. Alternatively, silently repeat your relaxing word over and over. Don't try to be rhythmical. Don't try to control your breathing. Just let your breathing happen the way it wants and repeat your word as it wants.

5. If you drift away from your relaxing scene or word, just calmly start imagining it again, or saying your word again.

6. End your relaxation practice as before by counting backwards from 5 to 1.

Sometimes boredom is a problem. If you become bored with your relaxing scene, just write yourself a new one.

Desensitization: Phase Three

For a small number of people, just learning the relaxation techniques is enough to enable them to prepare for and take tests with greatly increased self-confidence and assurance. However, most people still have trouble with panicky thoughts in particular kinds of situations even though they may be able to get nicely relaxed at other times.

The question to ask is: When you close your eyes, do you think that you could now retake the worst exam you have ever experienced without getting excessively nervous? If the answer is no, then on to the next step.

"Action *begins* with fantasy. We are very unlikely to do something new, difficult, and demanding until after we have spent some time imagining or dreaming ourselves doing it."

—John Holt, *op. cit.*, p. 86.

Well, this is just about what we're going to do next. We're going to have you imagine yourself in situations that relate to exams, starting with situations that usually don't cause much trouble and gradually working up to scenes that typically provoke extreme anxiety. You will move to the next situation only when you feel ready for it, so you should never experience a huge jump in the amount of anxiety you feel. The formal name for this procedure is "desensitization".

What you are doing is learning to relax and at the same time rehearsing and practicing your responses to difficult situations that we have all had to face on tests. When you first imagine each scene you will likely experience some anxiety. Just try to reduce this anxiety any way you can—maybe by trying the suggestions I make about things you can say to yourself. As you continue to rehearse and practice this, your anxiety will decrease, until you are able to imagine yourself being in control of the situation. Notice I did not say "completely relaxed"; I said "in control".

You will continue to have a "startle" or "alarm" reaction, but instead of this becoming the signal for escalating anxiety, you will recognize it for what it is and be able to mobilize your resources to meet the challenge.

There is nothing magical or mysterious about this process. As Holt says, we are most unlikely to do something unless we have spent time imagining or dreaming of ourselves doing it. We are unlikely to ask the boss for a raise until we "feel comfortable with the idea". We are unlikely to stand up in front of an audience and tell jokes unless we can "see" ourselves doing it. Our ordinary language recognizes that this "getting used to the idea" or "seeing" yourself doing it is an important first step in all difficult and complicated actions.

Really what you are doing is learning a new way of thinking about tests and the problems people run into to substitute for the self-defeating, anxiety-producing thoughts you already have. You're going to practice these new thoughts several times, until you actually do feel comfortable with the new idea and are able to see yourself behaving competently and rationally.

Instructions for Phase Four

Look at Table 15.1. You will see that there are six sessions (numbered I-VI) in which you will practice fourteen situations, or "critical incidents". Opposite each situation I suggest some "Coping Techniques"—things to say to yourself or things that you can do to deal with the situation more calmly and competently. These are suggestions only, and you should feel free to invent your own coping techniques. Each session should take about twenty minutes to complete.

It helps if you spend a few minutes before the start of each session deciding how you are going to "personalize" the situations to make them vivid and realistic. Try to get an image of the other people who are in the scene with you, of the room where you are sitting, of what is on the desk in front of you, and so on. Try to imagine the scene as if you were actually in it. In other words, try to see the scene through your own eyes and not as if you were watching yourself in a movie.

Also, try to think of what you would probably be saying to yourself if you were actually in the situation, so that you get a full representation of the kind of thing you typically worry about. This will allow you to practice rationally confronting your own worrisome thoughts.

SESSION I

1. Begin the session by relaxing as in Phase Two: moderately deep breaths, breath-counting, relaxing image or words, and so on.
2. When you are quite relaxed, imagine yourself in Situation 1. Do this for a few seconds.
3. Now return to your relaxing image or words and try to get rid of as much tension as you can.
4. Then repeat steps 2 and 3 at least four more times (keep count on your fingers). Each time extend the amount of time that you spend imagining yourself in the situation and trying to become more relaxed. By the fourth time you should be able to imagine yourself in the situation for about a half a minute.

5. When you've done step 4, spend a few minutes just enjoying relaxation. Try to become really relaxed.
6. End the session as before by counting backwards from 5 to 1.

SESSIONS II-VI

1. As in Session I.
2. Imagine yourself in the last situation you rehearsed in the previous session. Spend a few moments consolidating your ability to think about this situation, calmly anticipating how you will handle the difficulties presented.
3. After a few moments, relax, using your relaxing image or word.
4. Follow steps 2 to 4 from Session I with each situation listed in the session you are working on. Rehearse each scene four times before going on to the next situation.
5. Conclude as in steps 5 and 6 in Session I.

Don't worry if you find yourself daydreaming —just come back calmly to imagine either the situation or your relaxing scene. Don't worry if you are not absolutely, completely relaxed as you visualize yourself in the situation, especially in the beginning. The chances are that each successive visualization will be more relaxed.

If one scene is particularly difficult for you, and you can't seem to get it under control, just forget about trying to master it right now and go back to a scene that you *were* able to get under control. Always end your practices on a positive note. Then, when you have completed all the practices, and have rehearsed for all the other situations, go back and try the scene that gave you trouble. Usually you'll be able to handle it this time.

If it's still difficult the second time around, stop rehearsing that scene and end the session on a positive note by reviewing a situation that you *have* mastered—and, of course, by enjoying a few minutes of relaxation.

At this point sit back and analyze the situation to see if you can determine why you are having such difficulty with it. Is it because of something that you are thinking? Is it because of an unpleasant memory evoked by the situation? Is it a particular element in the situation that was absent from the situations you mastered?

If you can spot the difficulty you can probably figure out what to do. One thing you could do to deal with a new element (if *that* is the problem) is to make a list of situations related to the element (following Table 15.1 as a pattern) and then desensitize yourself to each of those situations. But if you're really stuck, I'd suggest consulting a counsellor who is familiar with desensitization. (See Chapter 16.)

Now, don't worry if you don't follow these instructions exactly. The only important part of the instructions is that you spend a fair amount of time thinking about exam-related situations in a calm and rational way, imagining yourself coping with real difficulties that you encounter and imagining yourself reducing and managing your own self-defeating feelings of anxiety, frustration, or whatever.

Don't expect instantaneous results. I usually tell my students not to expect big changes in how they feel about tests until after they have completed at least Session III. Think about this. The first scenes have to do with learning to be relaxed while you are studying and preparing for the test; it's not until you start to deal with the situations that actually have you working on the test itself that you will begin to deal with the really scary aspects of taking the test. So, if you start feeling panicky, it's just because you still haven't dealt with the kind of situation that gives you trouble. It certainly doesn't mean that the process is not working; it just means that you haven't gone far enough yet.

Can It Really Be This Simple?

For most people, yes.

Learning to analyze and control one's thinking, learning to reduce and effectively manage physical tension, learning sensible and systematic ways to prepare for tests and procedures for dealing with problem situations—for most people, that's enough.

And the evidence is clear that most people can learn to do these things on their own after a few suggestions and nudges in the right direction.

However...individual students may have problems with the procedures that prevent them from fully benefiting from the ideas presented here. If this is the case with you, don't blame yourself, blame the book. If you don't feel a great deal more comfortable about tests it will only be because I haven't directly addressed myself to your own individual needs. It's not your fault.

And I would really suggest that you consult with someone who *can* attend to your personal needs—a professional counsellor or psychologist. If you're not sure how to go about this, see Chapter 16.

TABLE 15.1   *Critical Incidents*

SESSION	THE SITUATIONS	COPING TECHNIQUES
I	1. You are talking to someone you know who has a test tomorrow.	—"It won't help my friend if I become upset." —"This situation does not threaten *me*." —"Just relax, there's no point getting upset about this."
II	2. You're in class. The instructor announces a major exam in two weeks.	—Imagine yourself thinking about your schedule and being able to decide where you could find the necessary time to study for the test. —Imagine yourself making a couple of notes about things that you feel deserve a special review. —Imagine yourself listening closely to the lecturer for any suggestions about the exam. —Think: "Well, I'd better get busy. My anxiety is telling me that I have things to do."

	3. You're in your place of study —reading and preparing for the exam which is one week away.	—Employ good reviewing strategies and tactics as outlined in Section I of this manual. —Say: "Easy does it. I'll just handle one thing at a time and keep on schedule. I only have to think about this chapter right now." —Spend a few minutes before each study session doing "Relaxation: Phase Two"—and again in the middle of the session, if you feel the need.
III	4. It's two days before the test. You're reading and studying for the test.	—Concentrate on review. If you must learn new things, go about it calmly and systematically. —Continue to take measures necessary for your sense of well-being (adequate rest, recreation, relaxation, etc.).
	5. It's the night before the exam.	—Use cramming techniques as outlined in Chapter 2. —Do not allow yourself to be harassed by the thought that there is so much more you *could* learn—you could *always* learn more. Instead, concentrate on keeping your cool and avoiding panicky thoughts. —Be sure to allow yourself adequate time to relax and wind down before bed. —Think: "There's no point getting upset now. It's not possible to learn very much in a couple of hours. I'd better concentrate on what I *do* know, at this point."
	6. It's the day of the exam and you're at your place of study.	—As above for Situation 5. —Think: "Look, it's true that I don't know some things. That will always be true. Who knows everything perfectly?"
IV	7. You're walking across campus on the way to the exam.	—Relax as you walk. —Make sure you've allowed adequate time to get to the test without having to hurry. —Pay attention to your surroundings rather than allowing yourself to engage in anxiety-provoking thoughts.
	8. You're waiting outside the exam room ten minutes before the test. You hear some people discussing the test and you think about not being adequately prepared.	—Do a minor cram as per Chapter 2. —Avoid the crowd and avoid anxious persons. —Don't worry about other people's comments about the test; there's no guarantee that their thinking about the test is correct and yours is not. They may know some things that you do not, but the reverse is likely to be true as well. —Do a brief relaxation exercise. —If you hear someone ask a question you can't immediately answer, say to yourself, "Well, if I thought about it for a few minutes, I could probably get the answer. In any case, there's no guarantee that it will be on the test. Worrying about it at this point isn't going to help."

TABLE 15.1 *Critical Incidents (continued)*

SESSION	THE SITUATIONS	COPING TECHNIQUES
IV	9. You're in the exam room, waiting for the test to be handed out.	—Do a short relaxation exercise. —Think: "Well, there's no point in worrying now. What's done is done. Worrying will not help me to remember anything more." —Say: "I've survived this before. I can survive it this time—maybe even in better shape than before."
	If you have not yet read Chapter 7, do so at this point!	
V	10. You're taking an important test. You look at the test and discover that you cannot answer 1 out of 4 questions.	—Say: "Well, I'll just take some time to think about this one. I'll work on the questions I know most about. Probably I'll think of some more as I work on those questions." —Think: "So, I already knew I wasn't going to get 100 percent. If I stay cool, maybe I'll be able to get partial credit for this question."
	11. As in Situation 10, except that you think that you can't answer 3 out of 4 questions.	—Think: "If I find the exam difficult, the chances are excellent that most other people will also find it hard. We're all in the same boat. If it's hard for me, it's probably hard for the competition." —Resist the impulse to give up. Careful reading of the questions and careful exam-taking tactics may make the questions easier than they look at first. —Go for whatever credit you can get. Some credit is better than no credit.
	12. While thinking about an important question on a test, you look up and notice that everybody else is writing rapidly.	—Think: "What they're doing is irrelevant to what I am doing—which is, being careful and thoughtful." —Think: "This is not evidence that they are doing better that I am on the test—only that at this moment they are writing when I am thinking." —Say: "It's important to take time to think on a test."
VI	13. The monitor announces that there are thirty minutes left to finish the test and you have an hour's work to complete.	—Think: "So what, I already knew I wasn't going to get 100 percent. I'll just do the best job I can with the time remaining." —Say: "Everybody's in the same boat. This is probably rough on the competition, too." —Employ good exam-taking strategies (see Chapter 7).
	14. Ten minutes before the end of the exam, you discover a serious error in an important question.	—Take a deep breath and keep your cool. You have a chance to correct the error and get at least partial credit, if you don't allow yourself to become disorganized. —Follow good exam-taking strategies (see Chapter 7).

A Step-by-Step Approach for Reducing Test Anxiety

5   Safeguard Your Physical and Emotional Well-Being

   5.12   If you are *usually anxious* about exams, learn to *confront your fearful thinking* about tests, learn to *reduce and control exam-related tension* and other physical manifestations of your fear, and learn how to *deal with tests more effectively*. (p. 105)

Chapter 16

Getting help

When To Get Help

—If you've been having trouble and do not seem to be making progress.

—If things are going poorly and you can foresee a difficulty or challenge that you do not think that you'll be able to confront.

—If you notice that your dysfunctional behavior is part of a recurring pattern and that you do not seem to be learning from your errors. Instead, you are just repeating the same old mistakes, the same old approaches, with the same old results.

—If difficulties in one area of your life are starting to spill over and cause problems in other areas.

—If your personal difficulties are leading to illness and physical discomfort.

—If home remedies don't work.

—If other people comment that you don't seem to be yourself or that they're worried about you, and you haven't been feeling too well yourself.

—Basically, if you have a problem that won't go away, or if you don't know what the problem is, but you just feel rotten and you can't think of anything to do about it.

—If you've said, "I'll ignore it and perhaps it will go away," and it hasn't gone away.

—If you find that your behavior is out of control and you're doing inexplicable things, like getting angry for no reason or bursting into tears with no provocation.

—If you begin to eat a lot, sleep a lot, booze a lot, or do dope a lot.

—If you start to feel that you need any of these things more than you used to.

—If you start to feel nervous about things that never bothered you before.

—If the price of not changing looks much bigger and scarier than the risks you feel you might take in at least talking to somebody about it.

Then it's time to get help.

In other words,

> 5.1 *If you encounter difficulties* in your social, personal, or physical life that you cannot handle after making reasonable efforts, *get help* — and the sooner the better.

Don't Wait Until...

—You have a perfect understanding of what's wrong. If you haven't been able to figure it out already, then the chances are that you need a second opinion.

—Things are in such a hopeless mess that it would take a minor miracle to get you out of the fix. Problems multiply rapidly if left alone in the dark.

—Things are irrevocable. If your marriage is falling to pieces, it's a little easier to get appropriate help before the divorce is finalized. If you're having problems with a kid, don't wait till he goes on drugs or gets taken away by the child-welfare authorities. If you're having trouble in school, don't wait till you get kicked out.

Macho Man, Poor Soul

Women usually outnumber men in any therapy program. This may be due partly to social values that blame women for their problems (label them as "neurotic", "schizophrenic", or whatever) but make much wider allowances for men. That certainly seems to be the way things are done with most minority and underprivileged groups.

But, partly, the underrepresentation of men in

therapy has to do with the widespread notion that it is legitimate for a woman to admit weakness and vulnerability and to seek assistance; but for a man to do this is...well...unmasculine. Men are just supposed to tough it out, deal with their own problems, stand on their own two feet. And so they do, toughing out heart disease, ulcers, alcoholism, and the consequences of violent behavior—and getting into all sorts of trouble that they might have avoided if they were only open to a few new ideas. This is kind of idiotic, don't you think? The same guy who wouldn't hesitate to take his tax problems to a good accountant, who would seek the advice of an architect before planning an addition to his house, who spends his entire working day seeking (and giving) advice and information and consulting with others—this same guy wouldn't be caught dead seeking help with a purely "private" matter.

It really does seem to help men who are victims of the "macho myth" to suggest to them that counsellors or therapists are just different groups of *consultants*. They help you explore and understand problems, give you information, help you weigh alternatives, give advice, and assist in developing and implementing a plan of action. And, just as with other consultants, you are quite free to accept or to reject any or all of what the counsellor suggests.

So come on, guys, if you can't figure out what is wrong with your Porsche, you try to find a good mechanic. If the basement plumbing still leaks after you've done your handyman's best, your masculinity is not on the line when you call a plumber. So, if you're getting grief from somewhere, what you've tried hasn't worked, and things are getting worse instead of better—then you might try seeking the help of a professional consultant. Just on an experimental basis. Just to see if it makes a difference. If you really don't like it, you can always go back to doing things your way.

A Medical Checkup

There are about six billion medical things that can cause you to feel depressed and/or anxious and that can interfere with your personal functioning without making you obviously sick.

Some of the commonest medical problems we encounter as counsellors are: infectious mononucleosis, anemia, allergies, thyroid problems, incipient diabetes, low-grade infections, poor nutrition (including excessive use of high-calorie, low-nutrient foods, and over-use of coffee and tea). There are many other rarer conditions of a chronic nature that can also do this to you.

So one of the first things to do if things have not been going well for a period of time is to see your doctor; explain that you have been feeling unwell and would like a checkup just to rule out medical problems. Also, clearly state that if there is no medical problem, you would like a referral to an appropriate service to help you figure out what *is* wrong. Do not accept a tranquilizer on your first visit, and do not accept a merely physical examination. Lots of these things require laboratory work to diagnose. So don't accept just a quick onceover.

Good Help Is So Hard To Find These Days

You should be able to walk into any of the public and private helping agencies and get actual help, shouldn't you? You should be able to go to your family doctor or your minister and get sage counsel, right?

Sure. Just like you can take your car into any service station and actually get it fixed. Just like you can go into any major department store and get accurate product information. Just like any contractor can be trusted to build a foundation for your addition that won't fall in during a spring rainstorm.

Alas, the helping professions are composed of just about the same proportion of thieves, charlatans, nice but ineffectual people, and real professionals as any other trade or occupation. And this is largely because you do not have to demonstrate a great deal of competence in *helping* in order to be granted credentials in the profession. True, most of the professions require some kind of supervised clinical experience before the practitioner is turned loose on the general population, but the fundamental requirement for getting credentials in these occupations (and in many others) is that you have to be good at going to school! This can make things incredibly difficult for the consumer.

When your foundation starts to leak you do not take it personally; you know it isn't anything that you did. When the rattle in your car persists, you are hot at the last mechanic, not yourself. But when you don't get better at the hands of an ineffectual therapist, it is quite easy to blame yourself for your lack of progress—and some therapists will even help you blame yourself by pointing to your "resistance", "transference", or whatever.

Now look, you do have some responsibilities in a counselling relationship: primarily to try to keep an open mind, to at least try out the therapist's suggestions, and to let the counsellor know what you are thinking and feeling. (How can he suggest appropriate courses of action if you deprive him of good information? This would be like asking an accountant for advice without showing him your books.) But the responsibility is not all yours, either.

Getting help with a personal problem is not quite the same as getting something in your house fixed. It's primarily a *human* relationship. And any particular therapist, in spite of special training, extensive experience, and personal skill, may not necessarily be a person with whom *you* can form a useful relationship.

Just as you would not expect that you could become intimate friends with anybody picked at random off the street corner, you cannot expect that you can form a helpful relationship with any therapist picked more or less at random out of the phone book.

So the trick is (1) to exercise some care in selecting a counsellor or therapist, (2) to accept the counsellor's assistance on a provisional or trial basis, involving a reasonable length of time, and (3) to stay results- or goal-oriented. If things do not change as a result of your working together, then probably you should seek a referral to someone else.

Where To Find Help

If you already are a student, you should check first of all on campus. Student counselling services exist on most campuses. Check the college catalogue or calendar if you're not sure that such services exist at your school. Most offer an adequate service and many are excellent. If there isn't a student counselling service available to you, or if you don't think it's for you, you could try teaching departments like Psychology, Social Work, and Clinical or Counselling Psychology. These places may have competent, licenced therapists on staff; or if they don't, the people there may know what other resources are available in the community. In addition, places that have graduate training programs in these disciplines often operate clinics, primarily for the purposes of training therapists. Here you would expect to see a graduate student (an intern or practicing student) who would counsel you under the supervision of a senior faculty member.

Such services are usually free for students, but for non-students there may be a charge.

For non-students, it is usually possible to consult with people from colleges and universities on a private, fee-for-service basis as well—if none of the following free or low-cost alternatives are available or attractive.

—Look in the Yellow Pages of your phone book. Look under Marriage and Family Counsellors, Psychologists, Social Workers. You can't tell much from a listing in this section, but you can at least see who is available for starters. Private firms and individuals will, of course, charge a fee. Agencies supported by the United Way or Community Chest usually charge fees as well, but most often on a sliding scale based on ability to pay. Don't assume there is a fee—you may be pleasantly surprised.

—The local YMCA, YWCA, or YMHA may offer a counselling program. A lot of YWCAs are involved in Women Resource Centers that can be valuable sources of information about counselling.

—Your minister may be a good place to start, but watch it. A lot of ministers think of themselves as counsellors, though many fewer have adequate training or skills in these areas. If you're not sure that your minister can handle the situation, ask him to refer you to a competent licenced therapist or counsellor. Some larger churches sponsor counselling services in the major cities, and, again, these people may be able to help you.

—Ditto for your family doctor. It is often assumed that the initials M.D. are a guarantee of sage wisdom and helpful counsel, but the reality is usually quite different. Most M.D.s have very little training in psychology and counselling. Usually your M.D. can offer you little more than a medical checkup (see above) and some reassurance. Many will try to suggest that you take a tranquilizer. This is usually pretty useless — but both the M.D. and the patient tend to feel the doctor should "do something".

A pill may help you "deal with this crisis", but, pray tell, what are you to do with the next crisis? Clearly, if you have a problem in living, what you need to do is to *learn* to deal with it more effectively. Taking pills doesn't *teach* you anything, except to turn to a bottle for chemical relief.

But your M.D. can be a good place to start. If he cannot actually help you himself, he may be able to suggest the names of a couple of competent counsellors or therapists. He may suggest a psychiatrist, too.

If you live in a small town or a rural area, it is probably going to be a problem to locate these sources of help. You could try the city nearest you, checking out the sources of advice I've listed.

Another thing you could do is to write to provincial or state professional associations for the names of persons who practice near you. A branch of the Canadian or American Psychological Association or the Canadian or American Association of Social Workers should be listed in the telephone directory for the provincial or state capital, and often these associations have a toll-free long-distance number.

Lay Healers, Unlicenced Therapists

Some of these people are actually okay. The problem is that there is no guarantee that they have any competence at all. At least with licenced therapists you have the assurance that they have received some training and have been at least minimally screened for competence.

Also, licenced therapists are subject to the discipline of provincial or state licencing authorities or professional associations, which, while it may be cold comfort, at least suggests that there is the possibility of curbing practitioners who

are astonishingly incompetent or unethical. That is seldom true for unlicenced therapists.

But, as I have said, education does not guarantee competence, and lack of training does not immediately mean incompetence either. It is very much a situation of "let the buyer beware" though, which is a bit tricky when you are not at your best and your self-esteem and judgment are a bit rocky.

To Be on the Safe Side

Get the names of two or three people and *interview each of them* before you make a deal with any one of them to sign up for a course of treatment. You will have to pay for the initial session if the person is in private practice, but it will pay off in the long run because you will probably feel much more comfortable with the counsellor you select.

Interviewing Your Therapist

This may be kind of a novel idea, actually, the idea that you should interview and, in effect, decide who to *hire* as your therapist. But it really makes sense to take as much care in hiring your therapist as it would in getting estimates and checking the work of, let us say, a roofing contractor or an auto mechanic.

Needless to say, this is not the way that it is usually done, and you may get a few surprised reactions from some of the people you interview. (I would run, very fast, from someone who appears to resent or be angered by the idea of your having a right to select your therapist.) A second opinion is always valuable, and is your right.

So you set up interviews with two or three people and are prepared to pay for the interview if this is required (having checked out fees by phone when you make the appointment). You're ready for your "blind date" with the counsellor. Now what do you look for in the first interview?

The First Interview
The *first* thing to say after going into the therapist's office is something like:

"All right, then. I have been having some personal problems (problems with my marriage, emotional problems, whatever). I have gotten the names of several counsellors and therapists, and I want to see each of them before I make a decision to take counselling. I am pretty sure that I need some help, but I'm sure you'll understand that I want to be careful about selecting my therapist."

Do this first. Make sure that *you* set the ground rules. If you wait until you are describing the gory details of your troubles, you may run out of time to say this, and since your emotions may be running a bit high you may not be in the best position to exercise your judgment.

The next part of the interview will probably consist of your describing your difficulties as best you can. The therapist should help you figure this out. Towards the end of the interview the counsellor will probably be advancing some tentative ideas about what might be done about your problems.

Qualities To Look for in Your Prospective Counsellor

For sure, before the end of the interview (do not let it go with a commitment to "see you next week"), you want to collect some information about the therapist.

—First of all, do you *like* the therapist? Since therapy is a human relationship, you're not likely to get very far if you actively dislike the counsellor.

—Does the therapist treat you with *respect* as a human being? If he or she treats you like a "case", as a member of a category, or is quick to put a label on you, this is a bad sign. Similarly, if you feel patronized, put down, or belittled by the therapist, look out.

—Does the counsellor inspire a sense of *confidence*? You want somebody who is not frazzled, anxious, tense, or worried himself.

—Does the counsellor *self-disclose*? Do you know anything more about the counsellor when you leave than when you came in? You should have a feeling that the person is giving you honest reactions and not just stage-managed ones.

—Does the counsellor give evidence of a *sense of humor*? You want somebody who can help restore your sense of balance. If the counsellor is completely deadly serious all the time (or a complete cut-up for that matter), this suggests a lack of the very sense of balance you are striving to attain.

—Is the person able to maintain some *objectivity* or does he or she become too involved in your emotions?

—Does the counsellor talk English (or whatever your language is) or does he or she talk jargon? Do the counsellor's explanations make sense to you or are they full of baffling medical or psychological terminology?

—Does the counsellor *try hard* to understand you and to clarify your ideas and feelings? Good counselling needs accurate, specific information. If your counsellor seems to be satisfied with first impressions, this is definitely a bad sign.

—Does the therapist stay *relevant*? The therapist will need some general background information, but the questions asked should seem appropriate to you. If they are not, beware. He or she may be riding some kind of theoretical hobbyhorse.

—Is the counsellor more *focussed in the present and the future* than on the past? You don't want somebody who is going to spend ninety hours doing archaeological research on your childhood; you want somebody who can help you deal with the problems that you face *today*. The idea that you have to dig deep into the past in order to produce change today has definitely not been supported by the research evidence.

—Is the counsellor *results-oriented or goals-oriented*? Does he or she give any indication that what you are after is new learning and new behavior, or is he or she hooked on a therapeutic process that may or may not result in changed behavior for you? Does the counsellor help you decide what you *want* to happen?

—Is the therapist *specific and concrete* about what you two will do together? Can he or she give you some idea of how long it will be before the two of you evaluate your progress? Is he or she clear about fees?

—Does the therapist have *experience* with people who have had similar problems? Even with extensive training, therapists cannot possibly know everything there is to know about

people. Undoubtedly he or she has specialized in some way. And if your problem is too
far outside that area of speciality, this may not
be the therapist for you.

—Does the counsellor help you *feel more confident and hopeful* that something can be done
to assist you? At the very least he or she
should suggest that you may be able to
become more comfortable with the way things
are; but I'd even be a little wary of this. The
very brief history of psychology suggests very
strongly that all kinds of conditions that were
considered incurable are actually open to
change. Before giving up, a good therapist will
offer to check the latest research literature
and consult with colleagues to make certain
that he or she really is aware of everything that
is happening in the field.

—Is the counsellor up-front about personal
limitations and preferences? Unless the counsellor is comfortable working with you, things
are not likely to go well. The counsellor
should be able to freely admit any biases.

—You should also find out what protection
there is for your privacy and confidentiality.
This is especially important if you are a minor
of if you are seeing somebody affiliated with
your school or your workplace.

(A further note about ethics: Sexual relationships between therapists and clients are absolutely forbidden by all professional codes of ethics, are unhelpful to clients, and have no part in
any reputable therapy or theory of counselling.
If, somehow, a therapist and client do become
personally involved, it is the therapist's duty to
terminate the therapeutic relationship by referring the client to another therapist.)

If You're Not Sure How To Get This Information...

If you don't get the answers to these questions in
the course of your discussion, you will want to
ask more directly. Here are some good questions
to get you going:

—Can you tell me how you got to be in this position and what you like and don't like about
your work here?

—Can you tell me what kind of experience
you've had with problems similar to mine?

—Can you tell me what you would do with a
person who just didn't seem to improve in
counselling, or a person with whom you just
didn't seem to get along?

—Can you tell me what you expect me to do
while I am seeing you? Can you tell me what
we will be doing in our next session, if I decide
to continue with you?

(It is fair for the therapist to answer "I don't
know yet" to this last question. Often, a one-
hour interview is not long enough for the
counsellor to get a really good understanding
of your problems.)

What Happens Next?

After interviewing two or three therapists, you'll
probably be ready to make a decision about
which one to employ as your therapist. Contact
the others just to let them know that you have
decided not to continue therapy with them at
this point but that you may wish to see them in
the future. (This is just basic courtesy.) And
make an appointment to see the counsellor you
have chosen.

What happens next can be an incredible variety of things. There is no one therapy system
that is clearly and unquestionably superior to all
others in every single case. Your therapist will
employ the techniques and strategies which he
or she feels offer the most promise for your
improvement.

But remember—the therapist is your
employee. You are in charge. And you have a
right to get results. If you don't get results, you
have a right to seek help elsewhere.

The Last Word

People change all the time. Often they change for
the better.

My personal conviction is that reason and
understanding are the keys to most improve-
ments in people's lives. In this, facts, information, new ideas are the very ground on which we
build our happier lives.

There is not a single new fact or idea in this
book. All that is new is the way that they are put
together and the personal voice in which they're
expressed. They are good ideas, ideas that have
made a great deal of difference for many people,

I sincerely hope that the book is of use to you and that it helps you to make the most of your opportunities to learn.

Now, can I ask a favor of you? The last page in this book is what I'm calling, with great originality, a "Feedback Form". If you have any comments or questions about the book, want to quarrel with my suggestions, have ideas that aren't included, or have had experiences that aren't mentioned, would you please rip this page out, fill it in, and send it to me at the address given. Your ideas and comments will be used to improve possible future editions of the book. I will personally reply to every letter received in this way. Thanks.

Summary

The key strategies and tactics

1 Start Preparing for the Exam Early (*p. 2*)

1.1 As soon as possible after each lecture, *spend five or ten minutes reviewing and editing your notes.* Do the same after reading and making notes on a section of a textbook. (*p. 2*)

2 Review Step by Step (*p. 2*)

2.1 Prepare a *master calendar*, breaking down the term's work into manageable units and allowing time for cumulative review and cramming. Distribute review times throughout the term. (*p. 2*)

2.2 *Make sure you obtain*, or prepare for yourself, *a course outline and reading list* for every course in which you are enrolled. (*p. 6*)

2.3 *Keep your master calendar current.* As you become aware of tests and assignment deadlines, add them to your calendar and indicate the time you will devote to preparation for these events. (*p. 9*)

2.4 *About once a week, plan your activities for the next week.* Plan how you are going to meet requirements for study and review and your other needs. Plan to keep current in all subjects. (*p. 9*)

2.5 *On a daily basis, keep track of the goals you have accomplished*, and transfer forward the tasks you still need to do. (*p. 9*)

2.6 In changing your schedule, *borrow from free time*; don't steal from time you need for work or reviewing purposes. (*p. 11*)

2.7 *Think small*. Plan study, work, and review sessions for short periods. Give yourself small goals to accomplish. (*p. 12*)

2.8 *Attend the last few lectures before the test.* (*p. 13*)

2.9 *Schedule major cramming sessions as close to the exam as possible.* (*p. 13*)

2.10 *For every test, complete a five- or ten-minute minor cram* just before the test begins. (*p. 14*)

2.11 In case-method courses *assign a priority ranking* of 1,2, or 3 to all the cases on your reading list, *determining the amount of effort you will devote to studying and reviewing each case.* (*p. 34*)

3 Practice the Skills You Will Have To Demonstrate on the Exam (*p. 2*)

3.1 As soon as possible in the course, *try to clarify the skills and behaviors you will be expected to demonstrate during the exam.* (*p. 3*)

3.2 If at all possible, *get hold of copies of past examinations in the course*. Collate questions. List the issues discussed. (*p. 3*)

3.3 *Don't review similar subjects one after the other.* (*p. 9*)

3.4 *If you have difficulty with basic operations and ideas* that the instructor thinks everyone has mastered, *identify a source of instruction* and specifically *schedule time to remedy your deficiencies*. (*p. 17*)

3.5 *If you usually make a specific kind of error on tests, learn how not to make these mistakes.* Practice, practice, practice doing it right. (*p. 18*)

3.6 *Identify a resource* which you can use to clarify technical vocabulary and in other ways to supplement your test. (*p. 18*)

3.7 *Early in the course, design a global map* which will allow you to see the logical structure of the information in the course. Build your global map throughout the course. (*p. 19*)

3.8 *Use flash cards to memorize important details* that must be recalled exactly. Generate flash cards a few at a time and review them frequently. (*p. 27*)

3.9 *In case-study courses, read the cases at least once before the lecture.* (*p. 32*)

3.10 *In case-study courses, develop a checklist of headings that the instructor uses to analyze and evaluate the cases.* Add to this list from secondary sources. Check your understanding of these terms. (*p. 32*)

3.11 *After the lecture* on a case, *go back and complete the case description and analysis.* Mark your test, locating important examples, and explain what they are examples of, and why they are important. (*p. 32*)

3.12 *Long before you have to take a standardized test, try to find out as much as you can about the test* — about the exam format and about the content of the test. (*p. 36*)

3.13 In preparation for any standardized test, *review Basic English and Basic Math*, even if you feel confident about these areas. (*p. 37*)

3.14 In preparation for intelligence, aptitude, or other achievement tests, *set aside time to practice, on a regular basis, the kinds of problems that will appear on the test.* (*p. 72*)

3.15 To prepare for an open-book exam, *as well as completing your regular form of review, practice answering sample problems using the text as a tool* that allows you to be more precise. (*p. 91*)

3.16 If you are allowed to bring a crib-sheet to the test, make sure you prepare one that is *neat, well-organized, and easy to read,* and that contains only essential, hard-to-remember information. (*p. 91*)

3.17 *If you are nervous* at the prospect of being given an oral quiz, begin early in the term to *desensitize yourself by having as many short, non-threatening conversations with the teacher as you can manage.* (*p. 94*)

3.18 *Learn and practice the correct pronuncia-*

tion of technical terms and practice making oral responses to questions prior to taking an oral exam. (*p. 94*)

3.19 In preparation for a major oral exam, *stage "practice orals",* with as much realism as you can manage. (*p. 96*)

4 Get Feedback on Your Performance Before the Test (*p. 3*)

4.1 *Whenever you do anything in a course, make sure you get feedback* that would allow you to do that thing better the next time. (*p. 3*)

4.2 *Form a study group* which meets regularly to work on assignments, do readings, and prepare for exams. (*p. 4*)

4.3 *Make special efforts before the test to identify and resolve any difficulties* you have with the course material. Ask questions of the instructor. Check material you are unsure of with your classmates. Use alternative textbooks. (*p. 13*)

4.4 *As you review, quiz yourself on the important information and ideas*, checking on your global map, in your notes, or in the text to confirm your understanding, retention, and ability to apply the material. (*p. 25*)

5 Safeguard Your Physical and Emotional Well-Being (*p. 4*)

5.1 *If you encounter difficulties* in your social, personal, or physical life that you cannot handle after making reasonable efforts, *get help* — and the sooner the better. (*p. 5*)

5.2 *Make sure you allow time for goofing off.* (*p. 11*)

5.3 *Arrange that pleasant events always follow difficult or tedious activities.* (*p. 12*)

5.4 *Allow yourself to be distracted only when you choose to be distracted.* (*p. 12*)

5.5 *Avoid cramming at the expense of physical and intellectual efficiency.* (*p. 13*)

5.6 *Structure your study activities so that you can wind down before you go to bed.* (*p. 14*)

5.7 Just before an exam, *make sure you allow*

time to take care of *important physical needs*, like eating, sleeping, exercise, and so on. (*p. 14*)

5.8 The night before the test, *lay out everything you need for the next day* so that you don't have to rush to get organized in the morning. (*p. 14*)

5.9 *Make sure you can arrive at the exam on time*, with as little rushing as possible. (*p. 14*)

5.10 Just before a test, *concentrate on what you know*, not on what you don't know. (*p. 14*)

5.11 *Just before a test, do not talk to anybody about* what might be on *the test*. (*p. 14*)

5.12 If you are *usually anxious* about exams, learn to *confront your fearful thinking* about tests, learn to *reduce and control exam-related tension* and other physical manifestations of your fear, and learn how to *deal with tests more effectively*. (*p. 105*)

6 Make Sure You Understand the General Instructions (*p. 40*)

6.1 *Underline key words in the instructions* to make sure you focus on and understand these important directions. (*p. 40*)

6.2 *If you do not understand the general instructions*, if you have any questions at all about how to proceed, *ask for clarification* before you start the exam. (*p. 40*)

6.3 *If you are required to answer on a computerized answer form, make sure you know how to do so.* Look at the examples if there are any. Make sure that you know which way the questions are numbered. (*p. 48*)

6.4 Make sure you *write your name clearly on the answer sheet.* (*p. 46*)

6.5 *Make sure you know exactly what materials may be brought with you to the test.* (*p. 90*)

7 Survey the Test Before You Start (*p. 41*)

8 If You Think of Something, Write It Down (*p. 41*)

8.1 *As you survey the questions on an essay test, jot down any ideas that occur to you beside each question.* Expand this list of points as you work through the test. (*p. 57*)

8.2 *If you can't decide which option on an essay test to answer, generate a complete list of points for each option* and then decide. (*p. 57*)

8.3 *Record items from your minor cram as soon as you have paper on which to write* in the test. (*p. 63*)

8.4 *If you think of information about a previous question* during an oral exam, *make a note of the idea* so that you can mention it later, *or politely interrupt the conversation to return to the previous question.* (*p. 96*)

9 Budget Your Time on the Test. Plan How You Are Going To Attack the Test. (*p. 41*)

10 Do the Easier Questions First. Buy Time To Think About More Difficult Questions. (*p. 42*)

10.1 *On an objective test, tackle the questions in the order in which they are given to you.* If you cannot answer a question immediately, leave it and go on to the next question. Be sure to indicate—by leaving a blank on the answer sheet or writing a "?" beside the question—which questions you have not finished. (*p. 48*)

11 Read Questions Carefully, Underlining Key Terms. Decide What You Are Expected To Do. (*p. 42*)

11.1 When reading a question on a problem test, be sure to *underline each item of data, the units that accompany the numbers, and the specific instruction* that tells you what you have to do, as well as important modifiers. (*p. 64*)

11.2 Before you begin working on a question on a problem test, *try to predict what the final answer will look like.* Write this down in the margin of the test paper. (*p. 64*)

11.3 In reading a problem and working out the answer, *read the problem aloud*, in a voice that will not disturb those next to you. (*p. 74*)

11.4 In taking tests, *minimize visual and other distractions* while doing the problems, and *use physical aids to help you focus on details.* (*p. 88*)

11.5 In oral examinations, *look at the examiner while a question is being asked* or a comment is being made. (*p. 95*)

11.6 Seek clarification of questions on oral exams, *first by paraphrasing* the question, and *then by asking for additional explanation*, if you need it. (*p. 95*)

12 Attack Each Question Systematically (*p. 44*)

12.1 *Avoid superstitious or irrational behavior when taking objective tests.* Attack each question separately and logically. (*p. 48*)

12.2 *On a multiple-choice question, try to determine what the correct answer will be before you look at the options.* Then look for this option in the list of alternatives provided. (*p. 49*)

12.3 *Make sure you read each option* in a multiple-choice question *and attempt to eliminate it.* (*p. 49*)

12.4 When you think you have enough information, *organize your essay by stating your main point briefly, and numbering your points and ideas* in the order in which you will use them. (*p. 58*)

12.5 Before beginning work on a problem on a test, *list the data neatly in a table.* (*p. 65*)

12.6 Before beginning a question on a problem test, *draw a picture, diagram, or chart* that shows the data and illustrates the problem. (*p. 65*)

12.7 *In working a problem, identify what it is you have to find* and *give it a name.* There may be several of these "unknowns" to identify and name. (*p. 65*)

12.8 In verbal-analogies problems, be sure to *look for answers* where the relationships are *parallel and specific*, and use all of the information in the problem. (*p. 74*)

12.9 To solve number-series problems: *first, look for a simple rule* that says how each number is related to the ones before and after it; *second, see if the problem can be broken down into two separate series*; *third, look for a "second-order" series.* (*p. 76*)

13 Draft Your Answers So You Can More Easily Find and Correct Mistakes (*p. 45*)

13.1 *After drafting an essay, leave it alone* for a little while to work on other parts of the exam. (*p. 59*)

13.2 *Don't try to do mental math on tests.* Take the time to work out the problems using paper and pencil. If you are using a calculator, be sure to write down each step. (*p. 63*)

14 Review and Correct Your Exam Before Handing It In (*p. 45*)

14.1 *Change answers on objective tests only when you have a good reason for doing so.* (*p. 54*)

14.2 In problem tests, check your answer
   a) to see if it *matches your prediction*,
   b) to see if it is *reasonable*,
   c) to make sure it *meets all the requirements of the problem*, and
   d) to make sure there are no *computational errors*. (*p. 67*)

15 Write Something Down for Every Question (*p. 45*)

15.1 *After you have worked through an objective test once* and have attempted every question, *make the best guess you can* at the questions you have not been able to answer. (*p. 49*)

15.2 *If pressed for time on an essay test, write an expanded outline* rather than trying to complete a full answer. (*p. 60*)

15.3 *If you can't think of the exact answer* to an oral question, *begin by giving the information that you do know.* (*p. 95*)

16: Use All Your Time (*p. 45*)

Appendix A

Taking lecture notes

Lectures are not the best way to transmit information. They're time-consuming, for one thing. It is difficult to maintain an accurate record of them. You have to put up with wide variability in the skill of the lecturer. And so on. However, lectures are good for three things, and these three reasons may be sufficient justification to permit their continued survival as a teaching instrument:

1. They allow the participants to *observe* scholars demonstrating their art and science as they deal with problems in their field.

2. They allow for *discussion*, clarification of ideas, and debate of contentious issues, something that the most sophisticated electronic technologies do not.

3. Since they are visual and oral productions, they process information in a way that makes it much easier for many people to understand and remember. Not all of us are whizzes at processing the printed word, and for many of us an idea does not become real until we hear it spoken, or until we see it demonstrated.

The big problem with lectures, of course, is keeping a record that allows the information to be *stored and retrieved* for study purposes. The main reasons this is a problem are:

1. Many students assume (after a dozen years of being spoonfed in the public schools) that the lecturer will "cover" everything that is important in the course. This is rarely true. The instructor may allude to many of the most important issues, and he may comment on, criticize, and evaluate much of the material in the course, but there is often no way that he could possibly discuss everything that the course is about, even if he wanted to. The correct assumption for the student to make is that he should independently be employing textbooks, assignments, and private study to augment the information transmitted in lectures.

2. Many, if not most, students do not acquire or develop a method for taking and keeping notes. Students either attempt to record everything (as if every single word the lecturer emits is vitally important) or else take completely random notes. Both of these approaches have the fundamental failing of not distinguishing between what's trivial and what's important.

So the mission of the student is to keep a record that clearly identifies important information in a form that is useful for study.

How to do this?

Preparing for the Lecture

Before any lecture spend a few minutes thinking about the lecture. What ideas are likely to be discussed? What do you know about this already? What questions do you have about these ideas? What can you do, briefly, to become more familiar with the ideas and information before the lecture?

Always give the text(s) at least a onceover before the lecture on the related topic. At least skim the relevant chapters, so that you don't go into the lecture "cold", so that you have some idea of what is happening, and so that you have at least a nodding aquaintanceship with the information. Then, when the professor discusses something complex or difficult, you will at least have the barest notion of what it is that he's talking about, while other, less well-prepared students will be completely at sea. This exercise allows you to be an active and discriminating listener—since you will already have a notion of what is important and won't have to try to figure this out as you listen to the lecture.

Finally, take a brief look at the lecture notes you took on the previous day.

This will help you keep track of the sequence and development of ideas, and will remind you of ideas and questions that you need more help on—such as the points you didn't understand on the last day, the issues you feel are outstanding, the questions you have not been able to answer.

Doing a little bit of preparation for the lecture allows you to develop a *purpose* for being there, and almost automatically (unless you can manage to stop yourself from thinking about the material) you will be able to listen *actively*.

Preparing for the lecture implies two other practical matters. First, you want to be ready to listen as soon as the lecture begins, which implies basic politeness and some primitive organization on your part. And secondly, you will want to be ready to take notes, which will require that you have at least an inkling of how to proceed.

What To Write Down and Why

1. *Before the lecture* write your name, the name of the course, and the date on two or three sheets of notepaper. This assures that it will be done, saves you from having to scramble to do it in mid-lecture, and saves you from having to remember to do it later. Also, number every page, including page 1. This is critical: if you don't do this, one day when you are carrying your notes across campus in gale-force winds, a little old lady on a skateboard will bowl you over and (presuming that you're able to retrieve them) you'll never be able to get your notes in order.

2. *The introduction*. When the professor comes in and begins to speak, he'll usually do a little song and dance to attract everyone's attention. Don't bother writing this down.

3. The prof may briefly *review* what was covered in the last lecture. Don't write this down either. Just quickly check in your notes to make sure that you have the information. Sometimes, too, the prof will be confused about where you left off—particularly if he's doing more than one lecture section in the same course, or if he has a tendency to take off on tangents. Checking your notes can help keep the professor on track as well as yourself.

4. There may be a brief statement of *the topic* of the day's lecture—with the most important points briefly summarized. Note this down as the *headline* for the day's lecture.

5. *The body of the lecture*. There are basically three ways in which the body of the lecture can be organized. Your job is to listen closely, and to watch the prof carefully, so that you are aware of the way in which he has organized the material and so that your notes will reflect this organization.

The inductive approach. Beginning with historical or background information, examples, and detailed case-descriptions, the lecturer can lead up to a *main point*. In such a case, your notes will look like Figure A-1.

The deductive approach. Here, the prof begins with the main point—expressed as a law, a formula, a conclusion, or a summary statement—and then proceeds to elaborate and defend this idea with less important, detailed information. See Figure A-2.

And finally, the *geographical or anatomical approach*. In this method, the prof organizes the discussion around a diagram, chart, or map. The body of the lecture consists of a point-by-point consideration of the diagram. In such a case, you should quickly sketch the diagram and follow this by numbered or labelled notes that clearly refer to elements in the diagram. See Figure A-3.

Of course, within a given lecture the lecturer may switch back and forth among these three approaches. It is important that you detect these switches. Otherwise, you will have difficulty deciding what is important and what is trivial when you come to reread your notes.

Some important principles govern your note-taking:

a) *Big ideas* and important points *should stand out like headlines* or traffic signs. Examples, definitions, and so on, should be clearly identifiable.

b) *Take notes in your own words*, using technical language where required for precision, to be sure. Simply doing a transcription of what the prof is saying is not relevant. Remember the learning equation? One of the most important things is that you *understand* the information. Trying to put the information into your own words is an attempt at doing this.

c) *Use abbreviations*, short forms, and shorthand notation. There is no virtue in writing in complete sentences. Leave out all the forms of the verb "to be". Make up your own abbreviations —for example, by leaving out the vowels in words or writing down only the first syllable— and take a look at a standard reference for the subject (a dictionary, glossary, or encyclope-

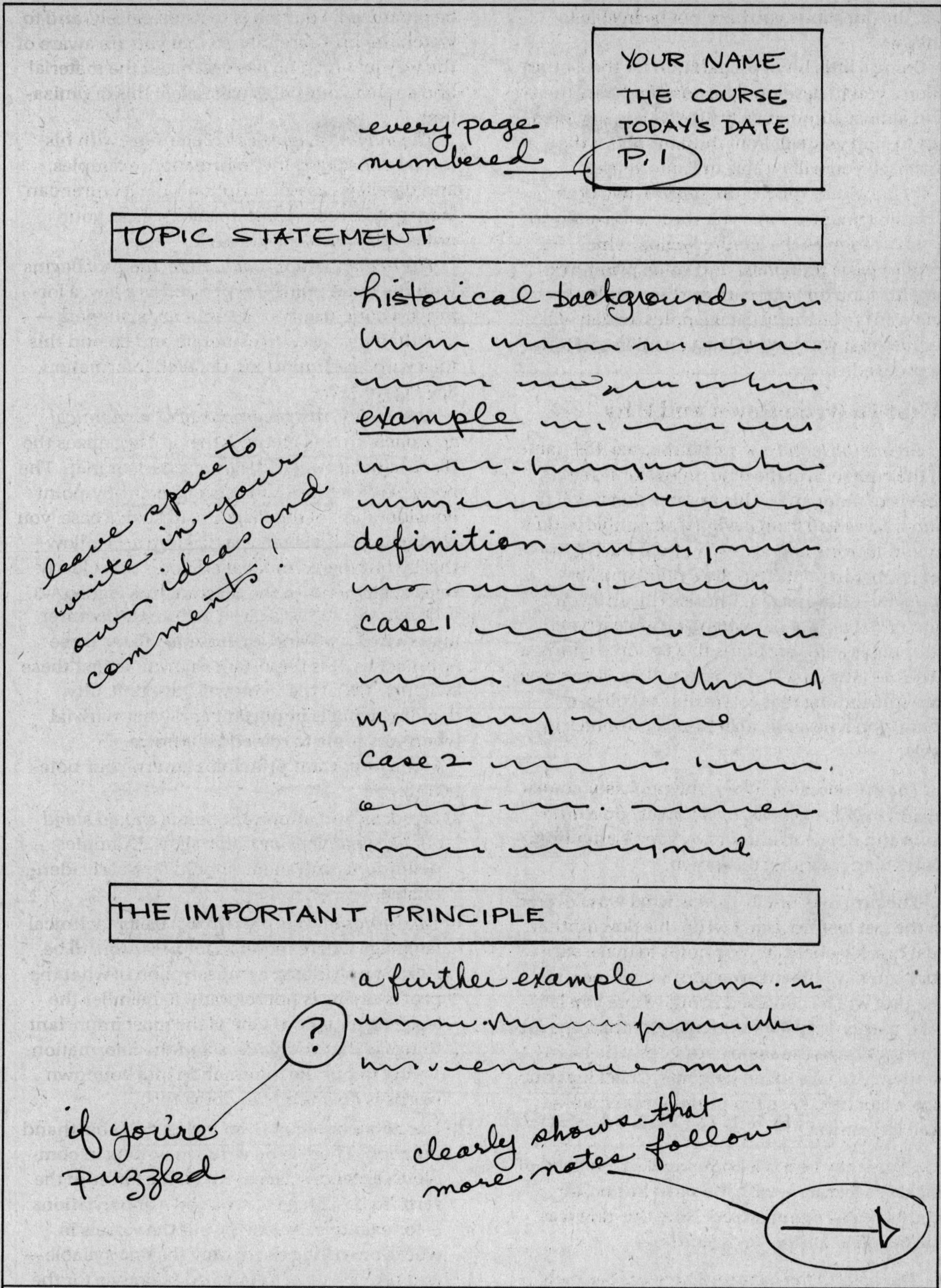

every page
numbered

YOUR NAME
THE COURSE
TODAY'S DATE
P. 1

TOPIC STATEMENT

historical background ~~~
~~~ ~~~ ~~ ~~~
~~~ ~~~ ~~ ~~~
example ~~. ~~~ ~~~
~~~ - ~~~~~~
~~~ ~~~~ ~~~
definition ~~~ ~~~
~~ ~~~ . ~~~
case 1 ~~~~ ~~ ~
~~~ ~~~~ ~~~
~~~~~ ~~~ ~~~
case 2 ~~~~ ~~~ .
~~~~~ ~. ~~~~
~~~ ~~ ~~~~~

leave space to
write in your
own ideas and
comments!

THE IMPORTANT PRINCIPLE

a further example ~~~ . ~
~~~~ ~~~~ ~~~ ~~
~~ . ~~~ ~~~

?

if you're
puzzled

clearly shows that
more notes follow

→

FIGURE A-1   *The Inductive Approach*

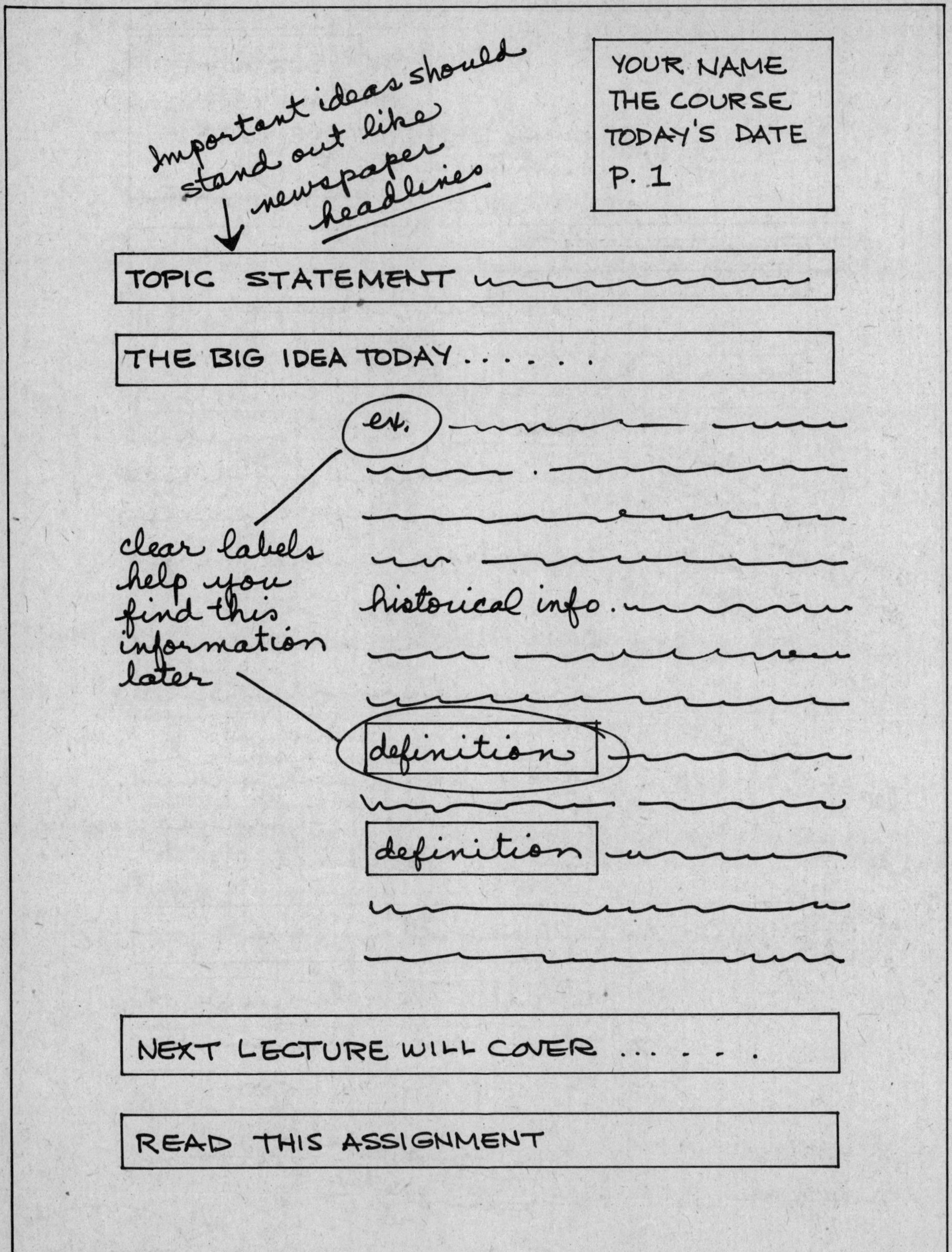

Important ideas should stand out like *newspaper* headlines

YOUR NAME
THE COURSE
TODAY'S DATE
P. 1

TOPIC STATEMENT ~~~~~~~~~

THE BIG IDEA TODAY . . . . . .

ev. ~~~~~~~
~~~~~~
~~~~~~~
~~~~~

clear labels help you find this information later

historical info. ~~~~~~
~~~~~~~~

definition ~~~~~~

definition ~~~~~

~~~~~~~

~~~~~~~~

NEXT LECTURE WILL COVER . . . . . .

READ THIS ASSIGNMENT

FIGURE A-2 *The Deductive Approach*

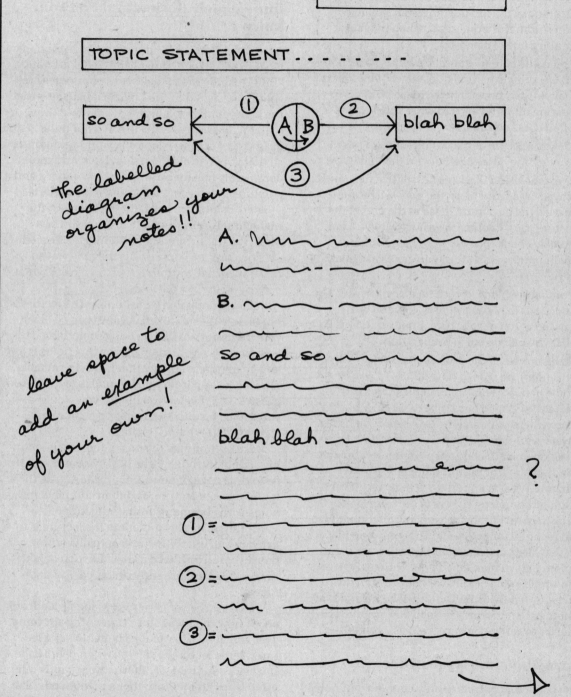

FIGURE A-3   *The Geographical Approach*

dia) and start to use the commonly accepted abbreviations.

d) *Draft your notes.* Leave plenty of space to write in *your own ideas*, comments, and questions, and to make corrections and amendments to the notes. If you lose track of what is being said, simply leave a space in your notes. Begin listening to the lecturer and start making notes from this point rather than playing a frantic game of catch-up.

e) And do be sure to *add your own personal comments*, criticisms, and questions. The only way that you can prevent these ideas from disappearing into thin air is to write them down. Often these comments will be invaluable later.

f) Clearly *indicate* at the bottom of each page *whether the notes continue* on the next page.

g) *The conclusion.* If the professor has time and is well organized he or she may briefly summarize the important ideas at the end of the lecture. Don't bother to write this down, but quickly check that you have recorded the main points, amending your notes as necessary.

h) *Coming soon to a lecture theater near you.* The professor may state what is going to be discussed at the next lecture. Briefly note this so that you can do some preparation.

i) *Assignments.* If the professor assigns work at this point, be sure to note *all* the relevant information. (Think of the questions Who? What? Where? When? Why? and How?) I don't care where you note it—as long as you have a system for doing it! You can write the information down at the bottom of your notes, in a little notebook, or in your datebook. Doesn't matter. What is important is that the information be *complete*, always *in the same place*, and *secure*. For this reason, it isn't a good idea to record your assignments in only one place: if you lose your datebook with all your assignment information for all your courses, you are in a real spot. If you have them written down in your datebook and your master calendar at home, then you only have to flail around a little bit to get the most current assignments.

More About the Issue of Security

I advocate that you carry only your current notes with you. The rest should be neatly filed at home. Then, if your notes get lost or stolen you're not monumentally inconvenienced. In these highly anxious times and in these competitive climes, some benighted wretches will sometimes stoop to larceny in an attempt to gain an advantage over their classmates.

Immediately Review and Edit Your Notes

Aussitôt que possible, immediately if not sooner, as soon as you can, reread and edit your notes. "Edit" just means to make sure your notes are solidly preserved in the English language—that the characters won't blur and shift into Greek with the passage of time. Clarify your notes. Add examples. Fill in the gaps. Fix your handwriting so that you'll be able to read it later. Add more comments, making your notes *your* record and a stimulus to your further study of the material.

Then, before you turn out the lights for the night, briefly quiz yourself, to see if you can recall the important information. This immediate checking and quizzing is the only way to make sure that your notes will do more than occupy space in a file folder.

Do not recopy your notes unless the lecture is hopelessly disorganized. As any typist will tell you, it is quite possible to copy something while your brain is on vacation. Recopying notes is a largely mindless activity that takes up valuable time for no apparent educational reason. It's too passive. You'd be miles ahead if you would use your notes for effective review (see Chapter 3: Figuring Out What to Practice).

Make only one set of notes if the prof is lecturing "out of the book". The best system seems to be to draft a set of notes from the text, take these to the relevant lecture, and then complete these notes with comments from the lecture.

Your most important task in the lecture is to *listen to and watch* the prof. Actually writing notes should only take a small fraction of your time—if you are properly prepared and organized.

Watching the prof gives her valuable feedback about how the ideas she's expressing are going over and allows her to do a better job as a lecturer. If the lecturer can't tell when people are puzzled, confused, or, alternatively, raptly interested, she can't tell whether a point needs clarification or explanation.

Appendix B

Studying textbooks

Most people read textbooks the same way they read everything else—slowly, laboriously, word by word. Students typically read whole chapters at a time, unsystematically, making notes as they go. This is an extremely passive approach—suitable for reading junk fiction for pleasure, but next to useless for studying complex and difficult material.

As in taking lecture notes, students' note-taking from textbooks tends to be either completely random, or else excruciatingly compulsive, with half to three-quarters of the text underlined or copied into a summary. Again the failing is that there is no systematic attempt to decide and record what is important. Such notes tend to be quite useless for study purposes, and students are thrown back on the necessity of having to do extensive rereading of the text when it comes time to review for a test.

The procedures offered here (summarized in Table B-1) are based on the SQ3R method, originally developed by Francis Robinson in 1949 and since published with great regularity by authors of how-to-study manuals. We have found that the SQ3R method has serious deficiencies, and certainly won't do the trick for all types of material and for all types of students. It is a system, though, and for most students any system is better than none at all. Mindlessly applying the system proposed here will probably lead you into difficulties, and you will have to vary the approach somewhat for various kinds of material and for different purposes.

For example, if you are using a text just to check one or two ideas while doing a research paper, the intensive approach summarized in Table B-1 is not required. In such a case, one would complete a textbook survey (Step 1), attempt to locate the relevant passages in the text, and complete Steps 3-8 very quickly, without bothering with the rest of the textbook.

Similarly, for reading and studying many science and math texts, actual reading of the material (Step 4) will probably be downplayed. These texts tend to be almost impossible to read on a sustained basis. You should probably complete a chapter survey, then skip immediately to working sample problems or attempting those problems assigned by the lecturer. If you encounter difficulty, only then would you return to the text and carefully reread sections relevant to the particular problems you are experiencing. One rarely "reads" a math textbook: they're put together as technical "how-to-do-it" manuals, to which you have recourse when in difficulty. (One would no more "read" a math text than one would "read" a manual on how to repair one's Volvo.) It's always wise, too, at some point, to whip through each chapter to make sure that important formulas, definitions, and other significant details have been properly understood and noted. But this is a separate task from checking understanding and mastery of the material by attempting the problems.

A fundamental assumption in this technique, and indeed of all the material presented elsewhere in this book, is that you have some idea of *why* you are doing what you are doing.

Certainly one of the reasons that reading and studying textbooks is often so very harrowing is that you have no purpose in reading the book. It is there, like Mount Everest, so it is read. Hours later, you have nothing to show for your labor except boredom and eyestrain. I'd recommend, really, as a radical departure from the norm, that if you cannot say in one sentence why it is that you are thinking of reading a particular textbook, you don't do it. Spend your time elsewhere. Do something useful (that is, something that *has* a purpose).

So here is our modified SQ3R. Explanatory notes follow the table.

TABLE B-1: *Textbook Study*

Technique	How?	Why?	When? How Long?
1. Survey of textbook	—Quickly read front and back covers (inside and out) —Read and skim Preface —Skim Table of Contents —Read/skim Introduction or first chapter —Locate indexes, references, tables at back of book. Skim for organization, scope, topics —Skim selected chapter in book	—Gives you overview of scope, organization, main ideas of book —Suitable reference? —Topics not covered? —Aids in locating information in book, using book fully —Introductory overview increases your familiarity with book and your ability to use it effectively —Raises questions for your reading	—Before beginning study of book —Before selecting as reference for research —5-10 minutes
2. Survey of chapter	—Read title and introductory paragraph —Read summary or last paragraph —Skim footnotes, questions, references —From beginning of chapter to end, read all type different from main body type (headings, italics, bold-face type, maps, charts, diagrams, etc.) -or- —Skim whole chapter, occasionally reading a sample paragraph	—"Warm-ups" before studying —You know what's coming up, scope, organization, main ideas, many clues as to details —Enables you to organize study of chapter	—Before beginning to read/study chapter —5-10 minutes
3. Question	—Beginning with first section quickly look at section, then form study questions for self —What do you hope to learn from section?	—Enables you to read quickly/actively, looking for answers	—At beginning of each section in chapter —A few seconds
4. Read	—Read quickly, without pausing, to end of section	—For understanding of content —Raises further questions for detailed study, problem-solving, reflection	—5-10 minutes (If section can't be completed in 10 minutes, break into subsections)
5. Reflect/evaluate	—Ask: What do I need to remember from section? —Do you need to study intensively? to work examples or problems? to check meanings of terms?	—Prevents time-wasting, passive reading —Prevents misunderstanding of later sections. —Ensures full grasp of material —Allows you to make useful notes	—A few seconds
6. Intensive study	—Depends on decisions made in Step 5	—Mastery of content	—Varies greatly

7. Record	—Annotate text or —Outline or —Summarize —Do flash cards for important details —Record own examples, comments, reactions, questions	—Creates useful record for study —"Keys" the text —enables you to relocate important passages without extensive re-reading —Helps you remember important ideas	—After reading/reflecting, intensive study —A few minutes
8. Recite	—Without consulting notes, try to recall/restate important ideas, making notes as necessary —Quickly restudy difficult passages	—Checks your understanding —Immediate review consolidates memory	—Before proceeding to next section —A few minutes
9. Repeat Steps 4-9 for each section of chapter.			
10. Review	—Recite each section from beginning to end of chapter	—Helps you understand/see relationships through whole chapter —Further consolidates memory of important ideas	—Immediately after Step 8 —Again for review for tests
11. If studying is interrupted in mid-chapter, survey chapter to point where you left off work and do Step 8 on last section studied. Helps to get you back in the frame of reference you were in before you stopped studying.			

1. *Survey of textbook*. This very brief procedure is designed to ensure, first, that you have selected the right textbook for your purpose, and second, to equip you with a general knowledge of the text so that your subsequent reading and studying can be efficient. I remember reading perfectly boring textbooks for hours before discovering that the particular topic I was interested in wasn't even mentioned in the book! This is the kind of trouble that doing a survey prevents.

2. *Survey of chapter*. Again this just means taking a peek, finding out the lay of the land, before you venture forth. Reading the introduction to the chapter or the first few paragraphs tells you what the author's goals and purposes are. Reading the summary tells you what the author thinks the main ideas are. Reading the questions lets you see some of the practical applications of the material. Checking the footnotes helps you get some idea of the theoretical background of

what's going on. The overview is just a way of reading the road signs, that's all, just taking a look at the route before setting one foot in front of the other.

Now, in reading works of fiction I would skip this step, unless you really are the kind of person who likes to spoil surprises.

3. *Question* simply means to pause before you read the first section and each subsequent section in turn, remember your purpose briefly, and think about what's coming up. From what you know about the chapter and the textbook, what do you think you want from this first section? What are you going to look for?

4. *Read* means to read nonstop to the end of the section. Do not spend a lot of time attempting to puzzle out difficult passages —you will come back to these later. For now, you want to get a grasp of the content of the whole section. Very often your puzzlement will disappear if you sim-

ply continue to read. Read quickly. The page will not self-destruct if you don't get a total understanding. You should aim to finish reading the section in a few minutes. If it takes longer than this, either the section is too long and needs to be broken into subsections, or you are reading too slowly, spending too much time trying to absorb everything. Remember, you can always come back and reread difficult sections.

5. *Reflect/evaluate*. At the end of the section, stop. Decide what you need to do in order to learn the section. Do you need to make notes? What do you need to remember from the section? What do you need to be able to *do* as a result of reading the section? Are there technical details that should be put onto flash cards?

6. *Intensive study*. Do you need to work a problem; go through an example in detail? Do you need to check the meaning of terms? Does a particular passage require analysis? If so, do it here.

7. *Record*. Part of the point of reading and studying a text is to get a set of notes that are briefer than the original text for purposes of reviewing. You don't want to be in the position where you have to reread the whole textbook in depth every time you come to review, so obviously we are after a procedure which will *highlight* the important ideas and enable you to locate ideas and information quickly and accurately.

There are basically three optional methods of taking notes. You can *annotate* —which means marking up the textbook itself. You can *summarize* —make a running list of point-form notes. Or you can *outline* —make a series of notes, emphasizing the organization of the ideas.

When making notes, resist writing whole sentences, and avoid the use of the verb "to be". Keep it short. Keep it simple. Whatever system you use should be consistent. When you are annotating a definition in the text, and you decide to write write "def" in the margin, then always write "def" for this purpose. This abbreviation will act like a stop sign. When you come to restudy the text you want to be able to see where the definitions are without having to search painfully for them.

N.B. Do not make notes before this point. One of the reasons that the underlining in library

books is always in the wrong place is that previous readers have been underlining *as they read*, so their pens hit the page whenever they found something interesting (no matter how important or unimportant it was). It is extremely important to have read the whole section and evaluated/planned what you want to record *before* actually writing notes.

At this point, too, you want to make connections between what the author has written and your own experience. If it is appropriate, list examples (your own) in your notes (thus preparing for the question on the exam, "discuss and give an example of…"). These are just tentative notes. Some of your concerns will be taken care of later. That's okay, but unless you record your ideas they will tend to disappear into the ionosphere.

8. *Recite*. This simply means to close your book and your notes and briefly quiz yourself on the section. If it is appropriate, you can jot down a few rough notes to summarize the ideas or to illustrate a process, or to practice remembering a formula, definition, or whatever. It is important to do this: it is the only way to make sure you *understand* the section before you go into further reading. Don't make this excruciating. You want to stay active, and involved in the material, so taking a long time will tend to dampen your enthusiasm. If there's something you didn't get, just check it in the text and then carry on.

9. After you've done Steps 4-9 on the first section of the text, do it to the next and the next and the next until you have completed the chapter. This may sound boring, but remember that what you do with each section depends on your purposes. Very often you will decide not to record anything, and will just skip down to Step 10. That's quite okay. We aren't talking about memorizing the whole text. That is hardly ever appropriate.

10. *Review*. Once you've given the above treatment to the whole chapter, go back and quickly review the chapter. Do this as soon as possible after finishing it. This will help you consolidate the information in your memory and help you see the relationships of the ideas in the chapter. Feel free to change, add to, or amend your notes as you review. Your notes are not written on

tablets of stone; they should develop over the period of your learning the material.

11. If, for some reason, you have to break off your study of the chapter for a period of time to return to it later, do a mental warm-up to put yourself back in the groove. Just skim the chapter to the point at which you left off and give yourself a little quiz on the last section you read. If you don't do this, you'll be starting cold, and it'll take some time before you're back in a frame of mind that is conducive to good study.

If you just had to go away for a few minutes (or were taking a short break), it will probably be good enough just to quiz yourself on the last section. You no doubt will have maintained enough of a memory of the chapter that you don't have to review the whole thing.

Review for Tests

Reviewing the text in preparation for the test will depend on your diagnosis of what it is that you will have to do on the test. You may want to go back and make sure that you have understood the critical definitions. In such a case you just look through your notes, find the definitions, and make sure you understand them. You may want to practice summarizing important passages or incidents. You might want to work sample problems. Locate them in the text, try them out, and then check your responses.

Or you may just want to skim the text until you come to something that looks difficult, or that you don't remember seeing before, or that strikes you as important, or that you noted gave you problems on your first reading. Then stop and give this passage relevant treatment—reading it in depth or whatever—until you have a handle on that section. Then continue to skim until you find another tricky passage, stop to read it, and so on. Whatever you do, remember the key strategies for reviewing and avoid activities that merely take time without effectively preparing you for the test.

Appendix C

A note about speed-reading

Speed-reading is a highly overrated skill that is intensively marketed by some very aggressive people. In itself, it is not the answer to anybody's prayers. I am both amused and angered by the ads one sees in college papers in which students are quoted making perfectly ridiculous statements like "I read *Moby Dick* in three hours and ten minutes. Thank you, 'Reading Made Easy'. Now I can get through my studying in record time and still have lots of time to get drunk on weekends." Well, if this student read *Moby Dick* in three hours and ten minutes, there is simply *no way* that he has more than a superficial acquaintanceship with the book. It just isn't possible. He may have looked at each page of the book, but he just has not done the analysis that the book requires. He has not studied (even recognized) the symbolism; he has not understood the complexities and the very great depths of meaning in the book—because he has been going at light-speed across the top of the print.

How To Speed-Read

1. Get your telephone book (that's right, your telephone book).
2. Open it to any page.
3. Now, beginning at the top left of the page, run your finger down the column of names and numbers, and then down the next, and the next, and the next, following your finger with your eyes, as if you were actually looking for a particular name.
4. When you get to the end of the page, stop.
5. On a sheet of paper, write down *any* detail you remember from the page—any name, any group of names, anything that particularly struck you.

You should be able to complete a paragraph that begins something like "I was looking at the 'B's', 'Bom' to 'Bow' more specifically. I remember a lot of Italian names beginning with 'Bom'...and three people in the phone book are named 'Bomb'. There is also a 'Boman's Archery Supplies' and..."

See. That's speed-reading. You'll be amazed at the amount and scope of the information you discover in this very brief overview of a random page in the directory.

Other names for this technique are "skimming" or "scanning".

And that is just about all there is to the technique. In the expensive, aggressively marketed classes you may be exposed to a few other procedures, but skimming is the principal procedure taught, by and large.

Now. Do this same technique with a textbook.

1. Pick a fairly simple book to start with, such as a piece of light fiction.
2. Open the book to the beginning of a chapter.
3. Skim the chapter for a few minutes using the same "eyes-following-finger" routine. (If the column of print is wider than the columns in your telephone book, you can move your finger back and forth across the page in a zig-zag movement.) Keep up your speed.
4. After a few minutes, stop.
5. Record your impressions briefly.
6. If you need to, go back to the text to check one or two details.

A little practice in this procedure will convince you of its benefits. It's a remarkably easy and simple technique that pays off handsomely.

But it has its limitations. It is obviously not a substitute for intensive study, or for the word-by-word analysis that is required to understand and master very difficult prose. The main usefulness of the procedure is (1) in giving you a very quick overview of the material, prior to actually studying it, and (2) in reviewing, to quickly remind yourself of the material covered in the text.

You Can Read, Actually Read, Faster (Though at Subsonic Speeds)

What troubles a lot of people, and makes them fair game for speed-reading courses, is the fact that they read everything slowly, slowly, slowly. They read everything the same way—trash novels to physics textbooks—and they get incredibly bored and frustrated. And spend a lot of time thinking about other things as they try to read. And fall asleep. And don't remember what they've read.

Actually, learning to read faster is simple for most people.

Here's how to do it. First of all, tell yourself in a firm, loud voice, "The print will not self-destruct if I do not understand everything perfectly the first time I read it." Repeat this statement three times.

Now open a book—any book, though it would probably be a good idea to pick up something that isn't too heavy and difficult. Put a little mark on the page where you are going to start reading. Now look ahead in the book and put another little mark where you think you can read to in two minutes, going at your normal slow rate of speed. Now go back to the first mark you made in the book. Now *read like crazy*, read as if somebody is going to shoot your head off if you don't get to the second mark in under two minutes. Try to read past the second mark. After two minutes, stop.

Okay, there may be some things you didn't understand, or sort of skipped over. That's all right. Go back and check those bits. The wonder of print is that you can check back if you want to.

Now, if you didn't make it past your second mark, you've got problems. Either you are reading word by word, looking at every single "to", "is", and comma, or you are sub-vocalizing—silently saying the words to yourself—which means that you only allow yourself to read as fast as you talk. Or you are still operating on the belief that just after you read a word it is going to disappear, so you have to drill it into your skull the first time you read it.

If you are reading word by word, you simply need to practice reading groups of words at a time. The easiest way to begin doing this is to take a pencil and put a little dot over every third or fourth word. Don't dot prepositions or conjunctions, just important words. Then read the passage, looking only at the words you dotted. Try this a few times and you will quickly discover that you *can* understand the material, even though you only actually focus on a few words on each line. Then try it without writing in the little dots.

If you are sub-vocalizing, put your hand on your throat so that you can feel yourself talking to yourself as you read. Try to read so that you don't feel anything with your hand. And try to read more quickly, using the approach outlined in the preceding paragraph.

And as for you who still do not believe (you unrepentant, inveterate, die-hard worriers), kindly have a little more faith in the abilities of your brain, which is a wonderful precision instrument, and in the printed word, which was and is a revolution in human history. And forever abolish the notion that remembering has anything to do with how much agony you give yourself when you first read something. Remembering only has to do with trying to remember and with checking your recollection. How did you learn "Mary Had a Little Lamb"? Did you sit down with your Mother Goose, wrinkle up your forehead, and proceed to worry and fret about every word, as if your mother was going to snatch the book away from you and never let you look at it again? No, you looked at it a couple of dozen times and in between practiced remembering.

Now, you don't have to look at your textbooks a couple of dozen times—but you can and will look at them two or three times. Because you're smarter now than when you were three or four, it will be easier for you to invent ways of practicing and using the material.

And if you really don't believe me, do a taste test. Go ahead, take out a textbook and for an hour or so read a chunk of it in your normal useless way. Then continue reading and studying the book *for ten minutes* using the procedures I've outlined. Which was better? Now, really, which was better?

When you read quickly, you always have time to go back and restudy the hard bits. When you read at a snail's pace, you don't have time to do this (indeed you can't even remember what bits were difficult, because you spent so much time thinking about other things as you were reading. So smarten up).

References

Brown, William F., and Holtzman, Wayne H. *A Guide to College Survival*. Prentice-Hall, Englewood Cliffs, N.J., 1972.

Crow, Lester and Alice. *How To Study*. Collier Books, New York, 1963.

Ellis, A., and Harper, R. A. *A Guide to Rational Living*. Prentice-Hall, Englewood Cliffs, N.J., 1961.

Fallows, James. "The Tests and the Brightest: How Fair Are the College Boards?" *The Atlantic*, February 1980.

Goldfried, Martin R., and Merbaum, Michael (eds.). *Behavior Change through Self-Control*. Holt, Rinehart and Winston, New York, 1973.

Holt, John. *Never Too Late: My Musical Life Story*. Dell Publishing Co., New York, 1978.

Jones, G. Brian. "Improving Study Behaviors." In Krumboltz, John D., and Thoresen, Carl E. (eds.). *Behavioral Counselling*. Holt, Rinehart and Winston, New York, 1969.

Lazarus, Arnold A. *Behavior Therapy and Beyond*. McGraw-Hill, New York, 1971.

Millman, Jason, and Pauk, Walter. *How To Take Tests*. McGraw-Hill, New York, 1969.

Morgan, Clifford J., and Deese, James. *How To Study* (second edition). McGraw-Hill, New York, 1969.

North, E. Joan. *Instructor's Guide: The Reading and Study Skills Program*. The University of Calgary, University Counselling Service, unpublished, 1976.

Pivar, William H. *The Whole Earth Textbook: A Survival Manual for Students*. W. B. Saunders, Philadelphia, 1978.

Raygor, Alton L., and Wark, David M. *Systems for Study*. McGraw-Hill, New York, 1970.

Robinson, Francis P. *Effective Study* (revised edition). Harper & Row, New York, 1961.

Schoonmaker, Alan N. *A Students' Survival Manual: or How To Get an Education Despite It All*. Harper & Row, New York, 1971.

Thoresen, Carl E., and Mahoney, Michael J. *Behavioral Self-Control*. Holt, Rinehart and Winston, New York, 1974.

Tobias, Sheila. *Overcoming Math Anxiety*. W. W. Norton, New York, 1978.

Walter, Tim, and Siebert, Al. *Student Success: How To Do Better in College and Still Have Time for Your Friends* (second edition). CBS College Publishing, New York, 1981.

Watson, David L., and Tharp, Roland G. *Self-Directed Behavior: Self-Modification for Personal Adjustment*. Brooks/Cole Publishing Company, Monterey, Ca., 1972.

Whimbey, Arthur. "Getting Ready for the Tester: You Can Learn to Raise Your IQ Score", *Psychology Today*, January 1976.

Wolpe, J. *The Practice of Behavior Therapy*. Pergamon Press, New York, 1969.

Zifferblatt, Steven M. *Improving Study and Homework Behaviors*. Research Press, Champaign, Ill., 1970.

Feedback Form

If you have any questions, comments, or opinions about this book, please write to me at the address below. Your comments will be used to revise the book to make it more useful. I will personally respond to any Feedback Forms I receive.

Patrick Grassick,
The Exam Skills Program,
University Counselling Services,
The University of Calgary,
2500 University Drive, N.W.,
Calgary, Alberta, Canada
T2N 1N4

Your Comments or Questions: _____

_____

_____

_____

_____

_____

_____

_____

_____

_____

_____